IDENTITY POLITICS IN CENTRAL ASIA AND THE MUSLIM WORLD

The Library of International Relations

Series ISBN 1 86064 080 X

Series Editor: Professor Alex Danchev
Department of International Relations, University of Keele

The Library of International Relations (LIR) brings together the work of leading scholars in international relations, politics and history, from the English-speaking world and beyond. It constitutes a forum for original scholarship from the United Kingdom, continental Europe, the USA, the Commonwealth and the Developing World. The books are the fruit of original research and thinking and they contribute to the most advanced debate in both political theory and practice and are exhaustively assessed by the authors' academic peers. The Library consists of a numbered series and provides a unique and authoritative resource for libraries, academics, diplomats, government officials, journalists and students.

1. The Business of Death: Britain's Arms Trade at Home and Abroad
   Neil Cooper 1 85043 953 2
2. The Age of Terrorism and International Political System
   Adrian Guelke Pb 1 86064 338 8
3. Fin de Siècle: The Meaning of the Twentieth Century
   edited by *Alex Danchev* 1 85043 967 2
4. On Liberal Peace: Democracy, War and the International Order
   John MacMillan 1 86064 010 9
5. Organised Anarchy in Europe
   The Role of States and Intergovernmental Organizations
   Jaap de Wilde & Hakan Wiberg 1 86064 062 1
6. Tanker Wars:
   The Assault on Merchant Shipping during the Iraq-Iran Crisis, 1980–1988
   Martin S Navias & ER Hooton 1 86064 032 X
7. The United Nations and International Peacekeeping
   Agostrinho Zacarias 1 86064 065 6
8. The Politics of International Crisis Escalation decision-making under Pressure
   P Stuart Robinson 1 86064 064 8
9. After the Cold War: Security and Democracy in Africa and Asia
   edited by *William Hale & Eberhard Kienle* 1 86064 136 9
10. America and the British Labour Party
    The 'Special Relationship' at Work
    Peter M Jones 1 86064 106 7
11. Hollow Victory: The Cold War and its Aftermath
    Robert H Baker 1 86064 124 5
12. The Nuclear Free and Independent Pacific Movement after Muroroa
    Roy H Smith 1 86064 101 6
13. Identity Politics in Central Asia and the Muslim World
    edited by *Willem van Schendel & Erik J Zurcher* 1 86064 261 6
14. The Struggle for Lebanon
    A Modern History of Lebanese-Egyptian Relations
    Nasser Kalawoun 1 86064 423 6
15. The New Central Asia: The Creation of Nations
    Oliver Roy Hb 1 86064 278 0 Pb 1 86064 279 9
16. Politics of the Black Sea: Dynamics of Cooperation and Conflict
    edited by *Tunç Aybak* 1 86064 454 6
17. Between Past and Future
    Civil-Military Relations in Post-Communist Balkan States
    Håken Wiberg & Biljana Vankouska 1 86064 624 7
18. Diplomacy in the Middle East
    The International Relations of Regional and Outside Powers
    L Carl Brown 1 86064 640 9
19. The Economic Factor in Intemational Relations: A Brief Introduction
    Spyros Economides & Peter Wilson Hb 1 86064 662 X Pb 1 86064 663 8
20. The European Union and Africa: The Restructuring of North-South Relations
    William Brown 1 86064 660 3

IDENTITY POLITICS IN CENTRAL ASIA AND THE MUSLIM WORLD

Nationalism, Ethnicity and Labour in the Twentieth Century

Edited by

WILLEM VAN SCHENDEL

AND

ERIK J. ZÜRCHER

B L O O M S B U R Y

NEW DELHI • LONDON • OXFORD • NEW YORK • SYDNEY

BLOOMSBURY INDIA
Bloomsbury Publishing India Pvt. Ltd
Second Floor, LSC Building No. 4, DDA Complex, Pocket C – 6 & 7,
Vasant Kunj, New Delhi 110070

BLOOMSBURY, Bloomsbury Academic India and the Diana
logo are trademarks of Bloomsbury Publishing Plc

First Published in India 2022
Published in 2001 by I.B.Tauris & Co Ltd

This edition is published with permission from Bloomsbury Publishing Plc.
50 Bedford Square, London WC1B3DP

A catalog record for this book is available from the Library of Congress.
A catalogue record for this book is available from the British Library.

ISBN: 978-93-56400-55-9
For sale in the Indian subcontinent only

Exclusively distributed in the Indian subcontinent by
Manohar Publishers & Distributors
4753/23, Ansari Road
Darya Ganj, New Delhi 110002
Tel.: 23284848, 23289100
Email: sales@manoharbooks.com, manoharbooks@gmail.com

Typeset in 10/12pt Ehrhardt by the Midlands Book Typesetting
Company,Loughborough
Printed and bound in the India

Contents

Acknowledgements

This book is based on contributions to a workshop entitled 'Opting Out of the Nation: Identity Politics in Central, South and West Asia, 1920s–1990s', held in Antalya, Turkey, on 14–16 November 1997. We would like to thank the Asia Committee of the European Science Foundation and the International Institute of Social History, Amsterdam, for supporting the workshop.

Introduction: Opting Out, Opting In, Exclusion and Assimilation: States and Nations in the Twentieth Century

Willem van Schendel and Erik J. Zürcher

There seems to be a consensus among the leading writers on nationalism, people like Eric Hobsbawm, Anthony Smith, Miroslav Hroch and Ernest Gellner, that, while nationalist movements may create states, it is the states themselves which create nations, however much nationalists everywhere may claim that the reverse is true. Most of the writing on nationalism has been based on European case studies, but one could argue that the Middle East and Central Asia offer the most striking early twentieth-century examples of how political structures were created first and a national consciousness underpinning these new political units was constructed afterwards. While this was a development of the interbellum, after World War II the decolonization process in Asia and Africa of course produced many more examples of states which endeavoured to build nations within arbitrary ex-colonial borders.

The contributions to this book explore variations in the relationship between state and nation in societies in the Middle East, Central Asia and South Asia, regions which are rarely compared, although they are each the subject of lively discussions on nationalism and state formation. The book highlights a number of themes. First, it shows the variations in the historical trajectory through which nation-states came into being. In Central Asia and the Middle East states can be said to have created nations. Nationalist movements pre-dated the establishment of the nation, but the nations they envisaged were very different from those which were actually 'built', once the Republic of Turkey, Pahlavi Iran or the Soviet republics in Central Asia and the Caucasus had come into being. In South Asia states emerged out of genuinely popular nationalist movements, but once in existence, these states, too, began to create their own versions of the nation. They never became hegemonic and always had to contend with the nation as imagined before the state existed. That image can be evoked as a critique of centralization and authoritarianism, a lack of civil liberties, and economic exploitation.

A second theme is the exclusionary nature of state-sponsored national projects. Groups which are excluded from the nation on linguistic, religious or territorial grounds, or are included only on condition of speedy assimilation, are likely to respond to this discrimination within the pre-set exclusion–inclusion framework. Hence, their strategies will fluctuate between the polarities of opting out of, and opting into, the nation. Groups which are discriminated against on the basis of their working-class identities, however, position themselves less directly in opposition to the nation but tend to redefine it as a community of interest.

And third, the book draws attention to the fact that, in the late twentieth century, several states (for example, Turkey, Azerbaijan, Afghanistan and Bangladesh) sought to combat cultural pluralism by military rather than political means. This choice may be linked to earlier attempts at homogenizing the population, which in some cases took the form of ethnic cleansing, and in which leaders of the nation were involved. A lack of 'coping with the past' (better known as *Vergangenheitsbewältigung* in the German debate about the Nazi period) may be at the root of both a violent imposition of the nation by the state and a growing appeal of oppositional versions of national imagery.

A clear example of a state creating a nation, or, rather, several nations, is offered by the Soviet Union under Stalin. Bert G. Fragner ('"Soviet Nationalism": An Ideological Legacy to the Independent Republics of Central Asia') argues that the Soviet political leadership, starting with Stalin in his role as commissar for nationalities, developed a model of nationalism which owed little or nothing to Marxist thinking. Not only did the Soviets accept nationalism as a given entity in contemporary history, but they consciously promoted their own brand of nationalism, while at the same time fighting pre-existing or autonomous nationalisms. Soviet nationalism depended on nation-building through territorial demarcation by the centre in Moscow. Soviet manipulative nationalism gave 'national' leaders in the republics a whole range of opportunities to build national subsystems, as long as they remained loyal to the centre. In Fragner's view, this fact explains why the Soviet leaderships in Central Asia and the Caucasus have been able to hang on to power and make such a smooth transition to national leaderships. Structurally, the former Soviet nationalism has continued unchanged. Its main characteristic, as developed by Stalin, is that the nationalities it created are territorial within borders which do not conform to any of the geographical units that have traditionally formed the basis for state-building in Central Asia. However, the older units survive in the mental maps of inhabitants of Central Asia, and the discrepancy between the official nationalism of the post-Soviet states and the ethnic realities as perceived on the ground may yet lead to conflict.

Süha Bölükbaşı's chapter ('Nation-building in Azerbaijan: The Soviet Legacy and the Impact of the Karabakh Conflict') deals with the causes and consequences of nationalism in Azerbaijan in the period of Soviet disintegration. It confirms much of what Fragner says about the handling of nationalities by the Soviet Union, but whereas Fragner looks primarily at Soviet ideology Bölükbaşı focuses on balances of power. He argues that the Soviet regime had created very favourable circumstances for the growth of nationalism itself. It is true that, from Stalin onwards, authentic expressions of separate ethnic identities were suppressed, but at the same time the Soviet regime promoted its own brand of nationalism through the manipulation of history, language and culture and through the strengthening of territorial national identities. The greater leeway granted to local party elites under Khruschev and Brezhnev gave the local leaders the opportunity to forge ties with their own populations through the use of ethnic symbols and patronage.

The relaxation of central control under Gorbachev then enabled the communist leadership of Azerbaijan to keep a tight grip on power, while at the same time encouraging a cautious revival of national culture, until the conflict with Armenia over the possession of the enclave of Nagorno-Karabakh caused nationalist agitation (which had originally been started by the Communist Party itself) to spin out of control in 1988. This ultimately led to the fall of the communist leadership and the election of pan-Turkist nationalists in 1992. The spectacular ineptitude of this new government of 'dissidents' both in its handling of the Nagorno-Karabakh crisis and in internal administration, however, allowed the old party elite to regain power within a couple of years.

At about the same time as Stalin first imposed his nationalities policy in the newly formed Soviet Union, the Republic of Turkey also embarked on an intensive campaign of territorial nation building. The republic was founded in 1923 by the Ottoman–Turkish national resistance movement, which had defeated attempts to partition the core areas of the Ottoman state after World War I and which had been built on Ottoman–Muslim solidarity. The early leaders of the republic, however, based their campaign of nation-building on a common Turkish identity, symbolized by a common language, culture and ideal. In spite of continual reference to the ancient linguistic and social roots of the Turkish nation in Central Asia, the new Turkish nationalism was firmly territorial, in the sense that it sought to unite the inhabitants of the republic within its existing borders, in a common nationality which for many meant forced assimilation to the Turkish majority.

In Iran, Reza Khan (later Reza Shah) managed to gain first power and then the throne in the same period in which Mustafa Kemal Pasha (later Atatürk) consolidated his hold on power in Turkey (1921–26). Inspired in part by the Kemalist example, the new regime in Iran also embarked on a territorially based Iranian nationalism. As in Turkey, this involved homogenizing a linguistically very diverse population, and, as in Turkey, the creation of a strong, centralized state preceded the drive towards a single 'national' identity.

The development of Iranian nationalism is usually associated with the rise of Reza Shah, but Touraj Atabaki ('Recasting Oneself, Rejecting the Other: Pan-Turkism and Iranian Nationalism') demonstrates that Reza did not have to build territorial nationalism from scratch. The long state tradition in Iran, with borders which, since the seventeenth century, had been largely stable (at least in the west), had determined the mental map of the members of Iran's intelligentsia and political elite, even if they did not belong to the dominant Persian-speaking community. Atabaki analyses the conflict between pan-Turkists and Iranian nationalists among the Azeri Turks (the majority population in the south-eastern Caucasus and north-western Iran) in the period of World War I. He is critical of the emphasis usually put on linguistic and ethnic bonds in discussions on nationalism. Instead, he emphasizes the importance of territorial and historical factors.

Pan-Turkism originated among the Turks of tsarist Russia, but from 1908 onwards the Ottoman capital, Istanbul, became the most important centre. When the Ottoman Empire entered World War I on the side of Germany, the political leadership tried to play the pan-Turkist card in order to mobilize the Turkish-speaking population of north-western Iran and the Caucasus. When the Russian army collapsed following the October revolution, pan-Turkist ideas gained a certain popularity in Baku (where a pan-Turkist party managed to gain power for a short while), but in north-western Iran the Ottomans completely failed to win over the intelligentsia or the political elite. The Azeri Turks of the area saw Ottoman policies as a threat to the integrity and continued survival of the Iranian state and opted instead for Iranian territorial nationalism. Quite a number of Azeri-speaking intellectuals actually played leading roles in the development of Iranian nationalism and in the constitutional movement. It was only after Reza Shah's consolidation of power that his repression of Azerbaijan's linguistic and cultural identity created a new conflict of loyalties.

Of course, there are a number of similarities between the situation that resulted from the breakup of the Soviet-Union and the post-war decolonization process in Asia and Africa. In this book an opportunity to compare the two is offered by two chapters on the process of decolonization and the relationship between state formation and nationalism in South Asia.

In South Asia, the mid-twentieth century brought a double shock of state formation. As the huge colony of British India decolonized, it crumbled. The Indian nationalist movement was unable to stay united. Instead, two competing views of nationhood emerged to dominate the political scene in the 1940s. The Indian National Congress, aiming at the conquest of the colonial state, visualized the population of British India as one nation; the Muslim League, aiming at a large share of state power, thought of the population of British India as of two nations: Muslims and others. Although some sort of federated state structure (with Muslim-majority areas and non-Muslim-majority areas co-existing under the umbrella of a coalition government in Delhi) seemed possible almost up to the moment of decolonization, this was not to be. The colony broke into many pieces and when the dust settled, two states could be seen: the republics of India and Pakistan.

These dramatic events underlie two aspects of nationhood which have dogged the guardians of these states ever since: the oppositional, consciously constructed and fiercely contested character of the nation, and the spectre of further breakups. Two contributions to this book explore these as regards Pakistan, a state originally consisting of two large territories (West and East Pakistan), separated by over 1,500 km of Indian soil. Both chapters focus on East Pakistan, which was once the eastern half of the colonial province of Bengal. The western half of Bengal joined India.

The new rulers of Pakistan faced the enormous task of setting up a viable state structure in this divided territory and of encouraging a new sense of nation to keep that structure together. At the workshop which led to this book, Inayatullah Baloch (Heidelberg) argued that Pakistan remains in search of its identity. Ever since 1947, the moot question has been whether Pakistan is a nation-state or a multinational society. This ideological debate, which has taken the lives of millions since the creation of Pakistan, has never been resolved. The state of Pakistan claimed a single Pakistani nation, but the state-fostered nationalism which developed was exclusivist and hierarchical, which was to have far-reaching consequences for the relationship between citizens and the state. Ultimately, it vitiated the survival of the state of Pakistan itself: when the East Pakistani regional elite failed in their attempts to opt into the Pakistani nation on terms acceptable to themselves, they opted out of the state – in 1971 East Pakistan broke away in a bloody war to form the independent state of Bangladesh.

Tazeen M. Murshid ('Nations Imagined and Fragmented: Bengali Ethnicity and the Breakup of Pakistan') shows that, in the mid-twentieth century, the Muslim majority population of Bengal was faced with various options for nationhood. As British India was disintegrating, Muslims in Bengal could imagine themselves to be Indian, Pakistani or Bengali. Twenty-five years later, when Pakistan was falling apart, they were forced to choose again, this time between being Pakistani, Bangladeshi or Bengali. Murshid argues that state formation and nation formation can follow quite different trajectories, that nationalist projects can be recast quite rapidly, and that nations can long remain fragmented. On the basis of an exploration of three nationalist projects (United Bengal (1947), Pakistan (1940s–1971) and Bangladesh (1952–present)), she argues that opting out of an earlier nationalist project (Indian, Pakistani) failed to resolve the problem of the fragmented identity of Bengali Muslims. That identity continues to be fluid and easily manipulated by both the state and oppositional political forces.

Picking up this story from the 1970s, Willem van Schendel ('Who Speaks for the Nation? Nationalist Rhetoric and the Challenge of Cultural Pluralism in Bangladesh') shows that the debate about national identity which lay at the basis of both the Partition of colonial India and the creation of Bangladesh has continued with vigour. While the official ideology of the state has been a strident Bangladeshi nationalism, groups disenchanted with the authoritarianism and lack of effectiveness of successive regimes have formulated alternatives. One of these alternatives is a different interpretation of nationalism, with more attention to democracy and social justice; another is political Islam; a third is that of cultural pluralism.

Pluralists challenge the view of Bangladesh as an exclusively Bengali state and fight cultural homogenization. Pluralists are found primarily among the minority communities in the Chittagong Hill Tracts, who have been excluded from the political process as much in Bangladesh as they were in Pakistan (1947–71). Authors from these communities challenge the two master narratives of which Bangladeshi nationalism is composed: the emancipation of the Muslims from Hindu dominance and the struggle for Bengali nationhood.

Because these authors put their criticism of the political system in Bangladesh into the wider framework of a critique of centralization and lack of civil liberties, their movement may act as a catalyst for democratization in Bangladeshi society at large. Like political Islam, with its universal agenda, cultural pluralism, from a different perspective, is universal in its claim for the recognition of minority rights. In that sense, both these movements challenge the nation-state. They may be better equipped to deal with a globalizing world than Bangladeshi nationalism, which now bears a close resemblance to the intransigent authoritarian nationalism of pre-1971 Pakistan.

Both Murshid and van Schendel illustrate how fear of further breakups prompted the Pakistani and Bangladeshi state elites to adopt a specific style of statecraft. The state being quite restricted in its institutional powers, the Pakistani state elite sought to safeguard the country's future by authoritarian (and militarized) forms of state- and nation-building. This strategy soon backfired. Political exclusion, economic exploitation and West Pakistani cultural hegemonism evoked a fierce reaction in East Pakistan. State attempts at assimilation by repression failed and the further strengthening of the Pakistani state implied the progressive destruction of the Pakistani nation as an 'imagined community'. Having freed themselves from Pakistani overlordship in a bloody war in 1971, the ruling elite of independent Bangladesh repeated the mistakes of their predecessors. Authoritarian, militarized and exclusionary forms of state-building jeopardized the new nation, alienating many citizens and inducing them to look for alternative forms of community.

From the mid-1970s, when the Bangladesh state had to deal with armed resistance by a regional alliance in the Chittagong Hill Tracts, it devised a strategy of 'demographic smothering'. It settled Muslim Bengali peasants among the non-Muslim, non-Bengali local population. Population settlement is, of course, an old strategy of both counter-insurgency and nation-building, but it requires a state apparatus strong enough to enforce assimilation to the state-defined nation and determined enough to go for outright ethnocide of those it excludes from the nation. It remains doubtful if the Bangladesh state is able and willing to go down that path. State terror was the preferred policy in the 1980s and early 1990s, when horrific massacres by the armed forces occurred, but in recent years the Bangladeshi state has sought to contain the resistance by political means.

Bangladesh is witnessing a process which is very similar to the early stages of the process analysed for Afghanistan by Gabriele Rasuly-Paleczek ('The Struggle for the Afghan State: Centralization, Nationalism and their Discontents'). She describes the failure by the rulers of Afghanistan to establish a uniform Afghan nation-state from the late nineteenth century onwards. In Afghanistan, a strong collective identity has not emerged, and efforts at centralization and nation-building have created new cleavages and divisions.

The chapter is based on a case study of one of the largest minority groups, the Uzbeks, and addresses three issues: Afghan state policies to achieve effective state control and national unity, Uzbek strategies to resist this control and unification, and the construction of an Uzbek identity in a Pashtun-dominated society. Afghan state policies used to involve depriving and dividing Uzbeks, and establishing Pashtun settlements in Uzbek territory. In response, Uzbeks sought to keep the state at bay and resist Pashtun 'intruders' by means of regional alliances with other non-Pashtun local ethno-linguistic groups.

This pattern changed in the 1980s and 1990s. Participation in the struggle against the Soviet-backed communist regime and then the civil war brought Uzbeks (and others) onto the national scene and legitimized their claims for equality within Afghan society and politics. A strong Uzbek ethnic consciousness developed: it replaced the inter-ethnic alliances of the earlier period and manifested itself nationally in political movements demanding minority rights within the Afghan state. The Uzbeks now stand for many linguistic and religious groups in Afghanistan demanding the right to opt into the Afghan nation.

Groups that are excluded from the nation on linguistic or territorial grounds are likely to respond to this discrimination in terms of self-inclusion, for example by means of assimilation, or self-exclusion, for example by means of separatist identity politics. But groups without a separate linguistic or territorial identity have different options. Asef Bayat addresses the case of workers. In his chapter 'Does Class Ever Opt Out of the Nation? Nationalist Modernization and Labour in Iran', he points to the differences between ethnic and class identities vis-à-vis national identity. While ethnic identities may lead groups to opt out of nations constructed by state elites, working-class identities do not. Workers' struggles for more power and profit are directed against employers and international capital, rather than against nation-states. Working-class consciousness is articulated in the language of rights and citizenship.

Bayat examines the case of workers in Iran after the Islamic Revolution of 1979. He argues that workers struggled against employers and the government, and tried to provide alternative visions of Islam and national development, but were strongly nationalist. The revolution created a new sense of nationhood couched in the language of rights which, under a regime of heavy-handed labour discipline, in turn contributed to labour militancy. Labour unrest in Iran was an important factor in the disruption of the state's national project and its economic planning. Although workers did not attack the nation, their resistance revealed that they imagined it differently. For them, it excluded exploiters and corrupt people. Bayat suggests that, by asserting their particular identities and imagining the nation in their own ways, working-class groups do not undermine the nation but rather make it a negotiated entity. This involves redrawing the boundaries of the nation to exclude those who are seen as traitors to the working classes and thereby asserting the image of the nation as a community of interest.

In the final chapter ('"Fundamentalism" as an Exclusionary Device in Kemalist Turkish Nationalism'), Erik-Jan Zürcher considers a specific form of exclusion perpetrated by the Turkish ruling elite. Taking the Kemalist nation-building project as his starting point, Zürcher argues that the 'Turkish ideal', which was one of the constituent elements of the Turkish nation (next to 'Turkish culture and language') as defined from 1923 onwards, came to mean support for the Kemalist modernization programme. Advocates of different models of modernization, based on a combination of Western technology and an Islamic value system, have been excluded from legitimate political debate all through the almost eighty-year history of the republic. Instead of engaging them in political or intellectual debate, the Kemalist elite, led by the army and the judiciary, have branded them 'religious reactionaries'. The conflict has often been described (both by the Kemalist elite itself and by students of Turkey) as being one between secularism and fundamentalism. This is not the issue, however. For most of the postwar period, and certainly after 1980, the Kemalist state has propagated its own brand of statist and nationalist Islam, which has also been enshrined in the school curriculum. Rather, the issue is control over religion, and it is those groups which have questioned the primacy of the state in this area, as well as in other areas, which have been branded 'reactionaries' or 'fundamentalists', and thus actively excluded from the true Turkish nation.

With this, we seem to have come full circle in our discussion of the complex relationship between states and nations. We started out with several cases of nation-building on the basis of territorial and political units which were either historic (as in the case of Turkey and Iran), or created for the purpose (as in Soviet Central Asia and the Caucasus). This in every case involved the inclusion, and ultimately the forced assimilation of minorities. We discussed the options of the minority communities: demanding inclusion, seeking cultural pluralism, transcending the majority–minority divide through Islamic solidarity or, finally, 'opting out' of the nation dominated by the majority. We have ended with a discussion on the use of exclusionary devices on the part of the nation-state. In South Asia, states did not create nations to begin with. Pakistan and Bangladesh grew out of genuine popular movements in which people opted for a specific communal identity (Muslim, Pakistani, Bengali), but these states have turned into authoritarian and at times militarist regimes projecting a narrowly defined nationalism which has alienated many of their citizens. Ironically, the intolerant nationalism of these states turned out to be a catalyst for the development of national consciousness among minorities. When the claims to equality and full citizenship of minority groups are disregarded, sections among them may opt out of the nation altogether, as the current cases of the Kurds in Turkey, Tamils in Sri Lanka, Kashmiris in India, or Karen in Burma demonstrate. Whether this is what the future holds for states like Pakistan or Bangladesh is not yet clear. In Afghanistan, the country with the weakest state tradition of those under review here, centrifugal forces for the moment have been controlled by the consolidation of Pashtun power in the form of the Taliban movement, but the loyalty of communities like the Uzbek or the Tajik to the state of Afghanistan (as opposed to the regime of the Taliban) has yet to become clear.

The twentieth-century history of the Middle East and Asia bears the indelible mark of the nation. At the same time, the history of the nation as an idea and as a community can be illuminated by the trajectories described in the following pages. The career of the nation as a powerful concept shaping world history started in late-eighteenth-century Europe and America. The nationalism of the American and French revolutions, which in turn built on the achievements of the Glorious Revolution in Britain, was built around the concept of the rights of citizens. With its spread to Central and Eastern Europe, where state formation rather than citizenship was the priority of German and Slavic nationalists, it lost its democratic and liberating properties. Many recent theoretical contributions on nationalism present anti-colonial nationalism in the various European empires as the next stage in the career of the nation, one in which, once more, nationalism became a liberating and democratic ideology. The cases in this book show, however, that there was an intermediate stage: the early to middle twentieth century was the era of the nation in Turkey, Iran and Soviet Central Asia. In each case, nation-building was a crucial tool in the hands of authoritarian modernizing state elites in their pursuit of national independence through the strengthening of the state, but also of authoritarian control over a well-defined territory and its population. It is an irony that such projects sometimes came to fruition only after their originators had left the scene. Post-Soviet nationalism in Central Asia and the Caucasus is a case in point, as is in another sense the Islamic Republic of Iran.

The origins of the nation in Pakistan and Bangladesh were different. Here the nation is an early representative of the anti-colonial avatars of the nation which came into prominence from the mid-twentieth century. But towards the end of the twentieth century strong 'official nationalism' had developed in these two countries. It had become very difficult to distinguish this brand of nationalism from the inherently authoritarian forms of nationalism in the Middle East and Central Asia. The only lasting difference was, perhaps, the rallying power which the legacy of emancipatory nationalism continued to exert among opposition groups in South Asia. In the Middle East and Central Asia it is hard to ascribe any liberating properties to contemporary nationalism.

1· 'Soviet Nationalism': An Ideological Legacy to the Independent Republics of Central Asia

Berg G. Fragner

Since the breakdown and subsequent dissolution of the Soviet Union, there are uncountable reports, analyses and speculations on what often is called the 'rebirth' of nationalism on the soil of the former Soviet Union. In many cases, the authors express their surprise about the rise of nationalist attitudes and even fanaticism in an area where they had believed that this category of ideological thinking had been weeded in the nowadays extinct motherland of 'Proletarian Internationalism'. In this essay, I aim at presenting post-Soviet nationalism not as a break with Soviet traditions but as a more or less unconscious continuation of Soviet habits towards the 'National Question'. Moreover, there is some sound argument that a specific model of nationalist attitudes may be postulated, which I call 'Soviet nationalism'.

In Western scholarly understanding of Soviet policies towards national and ethnic groups or minorities, Soviet communism and nationalism were usually perceived as contradictory, at least until 1991. A famous example is Hélène Carèrre d'Encausse's *L'Empire eclaté*,[1] in which the breakdown of the Soviet empire was predicted; the cause was given as nationalist riots. Carrère d'Encausse followed in many aspects studies done by Alexandre Bennigsen and his co-writers. Even deeper and much more elaborate analyses of Soviet attitudes to nationalism from the October Revolution until the 1980s, for example Gerhard Simon's *Nationalismus und Nationalitätenpolitik in der Sowjetunion*,[2] present the problem as a rather antagonistic one. The Soviet system was supposed to oppose nationalist attitudes and to aim to melt various nationalities into the model of *sovietskii chelovek* ('homo sovieticus'), in principle, and therefore to be tolerating nationalist habits rather reluctantly, if at all. This attitude in Western scholarly reasoning about Soviet policies toward nationalism and national problems has a long tradition, as a classic study on the subject shows: Richard Pipes' *The Formation of the Soviet Union.*[3] It goes without saying that Soviet history offers much reason for such an evaluation but, one must not forget that Soviet, and even pre-Soviet Bolshevik, policies dealt with the 'national question' very intensely and, in the long run, contradictorily. Therefore I raise the question whether the Soviet system may have contributed to the development of nationalist ideology, not only by refusing the principles of nationalism but also by nourishing specific aspects of nationalist thinking.

This questioning is not at all congruent with tendencies to be found in texts by biased writers who tried to defend Soviet nationality policies, either in total, as Soviet writers or those under the influence of Marxist–Leninist ideology used to do; or in part, as by Western observers (among them a large number of linguists) deeply impressed by the results of Soviet campaigns against illiteracy and the support of standardization of many lesser-known languages of the USSR. Especially as seen by ideologically pro-Soviet writers, dealing with the 'National Question' was understood as the logical result of applying Marxism–Leninism to politics in general, and to nationalities and their problems in particular, or to put it another way, as a straight extension of Soviet ideology.

My intention is to prove the opposite. Under the auspicies of the leading Soviet political class, a specific ideological model of nationalism came into existence, relatively early in Soviet history. But I doubt very much whether this ideological model was really derived from Marxist thinking. It seems to me that this specific ideological model was rather independent from Marxist reasoning, apart from some borrowings which entered this peculiar model of nationalism. One example is the differentiation between oppressed and oppressing nations – clearly a borrowing, and not an application of Marxism, because this model replaces class by nation; another is Lenin's *dva potoka* ('two paths') concept, which differentiates positive and progressive trends from conservative and reactionary elements within a national culture, the latter having to be destroyed, but the former having to be supported and developed. This concept is structurally identical with any type of modernist or emancipatory nationalism, bourgeois or leftist or romantic, as one easily can trace by reading Benedict Anderson's, Ernest Gellner's or Eric Hobsbawm's texts on the subject. Otherwise, the concept of nationalism developed by generations of Soviet politicians seems coherent enough to make it a specific model, 'Soviet nationalism'.

'Soviet Nationalism'

Before going into details, I must make clear my approach to the subject. My scholarly field is not Soviet studies, or Eastern European history. My studies concentrate on the social, political and cultural history of Iran and the neighbouring areas, in pre-modernity and modernity. This approach led me into what was then Soviet Central Asia.[4] Dealing with the regions of what one may call the Eastern Muslim World (excluding the Arab nations), various models of 'forced modernization' can be perceived: the Kemalist and the Royal Iranian patterns but, also the Pakistani and eventually the Islamic Iranian ones, not forgetting the Soviet model. In comparing and contrasting this Soviet model to the other patterns we are used to stressing the importance of class struggle, in the Marxist–Leninist sense, on the Soviet side, while we ascribe to the other patterns nationalist (Kemalism, Pahlavism, and the case of Afghanistan following the Kemalist model, in the 1920s), mixed nationalist–religious (Pakistan), or, apparently, purely religious (Islamic Iran) intentions. This view deserves some revisionism. In the longer run, the Islamic Iranian model, for instance, contains many more nationalist elements than superficial observers in the West may have expected. Moreover, Soviet politics was by no means always hostile to nationalist attitudes among the Soviet peoples. On the contrary, Soviet politicians and politics rendered consciously creative contributions to the abundant diversity of nationalist thinking. I shall offer a rough sketch of this specific ideological complex which I call – hoping it does not sound too provocative – Soviet nationalism. This is exactly what I shall try to prove: the existence of Soviet nationalism, not to be confused with nationalism in the Soviet Union. In this context, I shall mainly refer to the traditionally Muslim regions of Central Asia, though not excluding neighbouring territories.

What was Soviet nationalism? Did ever anything exist that could be called Soviet nationalism? Was there ever anything like nationalism under Soviet auspices, created, supported and fostered by Soviet politics and ideologists? The answer must be Yes. Moreover, this Soviet nationalism was not at all – in the mathematical sense – functional to and derived from the concept of class struggle, but was an autonomous concept in Soviet political ideology.

Ideological Prerequisites of Soviet Nationalism

The political scientist Theodor Hanf did once point out that Karl Renner's and Otto Bauer's Austro-Marxist model of how to solve the 'National Question'[5] was nothing less than an early attempt by Marxist theoreticians to separate nationalist thought and movements from the revolutionary process. In their famous studies, they offered a rather innovative, but also revisionist, model for the solution of problems caused by quarrels and frustrations among ethnic and national groups in Austria–Hungary. According to Hanf, Renner and Bauer understood at the beginning of the twentieth century that the mobilizing capacity of nationalism was too strong and intense to be simply neglected in favour of 'class struggle'. Aiming to foster the idea of the proletarian revolution, they preferred a strategy of separating nationalism from the revolutionary discourse, rather than suppressing it, as Marxists until then had been strongly inclined to do. By serving the requirements of Marxist rhetoric, they developed in fact a model outside Marxist thinking. They developed a model of administrative and political organization within the Habsburg monarchy which refrained from territorializing these groups but offered them individual and political rights of national autonomy and identity. These ideas had a practical reflex even in the structure of the Social Democratic Party (or better: Parties) in Austria–Hungary, which were organized along ethnic and national concepts.

Within the frame of Marxist thinking, the idea of detaching the solution of the 'National Question' from class struggle was clearly reproduced by Stalin in his article 'Marxism and the National Question' (1913), conceived as a refutation of Renner and Bauer, whose hypotheses had gained much attention in the international realm of Marxist thinkers before World War I. This had happened particularly among intellectuals in Russia, where the ethnic, linguistic and national setting was to be compared to Austria–Hungary, to a certain extent, at least. In 1912 Stalin spent a couple of months in Vienna writing his essay, aiming to produce another text on the subject by a 'Marxist' writer. There were obviously some points in Renner's and Bauer's programme which did not at all go with Lenin's concept of 'Democratic Centralism', which was to be applied not only to the structure of the Social Democratic (Bolshevik) Workers' Party of Russia (SDWPR) but also to questions of nationalism. One of the most important contradictions between the 'Austro-Marxist' concept and Lenin's ideas concerned Lenin's efforts at that time to construct a homogeneous, all-Russian revolutionary Party disregarding national or ethnic peculiarities. As early as prior to the Second Party Congress of the SDWPR (1903) Lenin had a harsh controversy with the leaders of another leftist party in Russia – the so-called Bund (German–Yiddish for 'confederation'), the General Jewish Confederation of Workers in Lithuania, Poland and Russia. The Bundists, an otherwise very radical and revolutionary party, insisted on organizing themselves as a Jewish party in all the countries mentioned in their official name.[6] For this reason, they rejected all aspects of territoriality – and were therefore very close to Renner's and Bauer's principles. It was, perhaps, this particular debate between the Leninists and the Bundists that might have become decisive for sending Stalin to Vienna in order to compile arguments against the Austro-Marxist concept.

The result was Stalin's essay referred to above, 'Marksizm i natsional'nyi vopros [Marxism and the National Question]'.[7] Even the title indicates that it was conceived as a polemic reproach to Otto Bauer: 'Marxism and the National Question' versus *The National Question and Social Democracy*. Since Stalin was not a notably gifted philosopher or analyst, it is not surprising that his article was, in many respects, much more flat than Renner's and Bauer's ideas. On some points – such as the problem of territoriality – it contains strong arguments against Bauer and Renner, but in many places Stalin implied Austro-Marxist views on nation and nationality, without specific reference. The charge of revisionism, usually levelled at the Austro-Marxists by Soviet authors, applies to Stalin at least as much as to his Viennese counterparts. He confined himself to four principles that mark a well-developed 'nation': common language, common territory, common economy, and common mentality and psychological attributes (the 'national character'). A dispassionate observer must confess that this was not a very impressive programme, considering all the ideological texts and books that had been produced worldwide before the early twentieth century. And, in particular, he says nothing specifically Marxist at all!

In the following years, Stalin's concept was corroborated and approved by Lenin himself. After the revolution, Stalin became the leading figure in Soviet nationalities' policies. Subsequently Soviet nationalism emerged step by step, referring repeatedly to Stalin's basic ideas, and reaching full development with the invention of 'Soviet patriotism' during World War II.[8] But its foundations had been laid much earlier.

As Theodor Hanf noted in Renner's and Bauer's Austro-Marxist programme, the problems of nation and nationality were, in the case of early Leninism, conceived as being something apart from class struggle. According to him, the intention was to maintain nationalism as an element not directly dependent on the relationship of basis and superstructure, in class analysis. This means that, under given conditions, nationalism could even serve the goals of proletarian revolution. According to Lenin, Stalin and their successors, nationalism was accepted as a given entity in modern history, rather constant than variable. The aim of Soviet policies was not to root out nationalism but, instead, to dominate it and to monopolize the hegemony within nationalist discourses, both within the USSR and throughout the Soviet bloc. Through Moscow-orientated Communist parties, Soviet policy aimed ultimately at full command over nationalist discourses everywhere in the world. Lenin's hypothesis of differentiation between suppressing (reactionary) and self-defending (progressive) nationalisms, fostered by his theory of the 'two currents', the *dva potoka*, turned out to support nationalism heavily. Oversimplified, this concept tells us that in the cultural heritage of each ethnic element, each nation or ethnicly defined people there are two currents to be found: a proto-proletarian tradition (positive, 'the goodies') and an exploiting and oppressive tradition (reactionaries, 'the baddies'). By applying this concept, class struggle would by no means extinguish nationalism as a whole: the goodies would remain, at least as companions and fellow-travellers for forthcoming revolutionary epochs. By interpreting history permanently along these lines, the Soviets never ceased to produce nationalism as a mass-mobilizing instrument or element. They invested much political and economic energy in fertilizing this specific form of nationalism. We have to understand that, in this sense, to Soviet political thinking there was no basic contradiction between the principle of class struggle and nationalism.

In the twentieth century, the worldwide impact of this specific Soviet nationalism was, and still is, very strong. In many parts of the world we witness a curious blending of traditional romantic nationalism with leftist, and for a long time rather pro-Soviet, political attitudes, or, at least, attitudes that were not explicitly anti-Soviet. This was an important achievement of Soviet policies during the Cold War. Basques and Catalans, Irish movements and various post-World War II antifascist nationalisms from Western Europe down to Greece, including phenomena like Austrian nationalism, served as, at least, intermediating elements during the hot phases of the Cold War, mostly rather in favour of Soviet ambitions. In our days, Arab and Palestinian nationalism, and particularly the Kurdish nationalist discourse, are deeply influenced by the traditions of Soviet nationalism. Third-Worldism, in general, was clearly an offshoot of this conception, but somewhat inverted: Third-Worldists do not simply separate nationalism from class struggle but try to replace class struggle by nationalism in a Hegelian synthesis.

Whenever we conceive the Soviets, in retrospective, to have fought nationalism within their realm we have therefore to put this into a more precise wording. They resisted any autonomous nationalism, seeing it as incongruent with their own type of nationalism. Structurally, the most outstanding and typical aspect of Soviet nationalism was the high degree of arbitrary invention and construction invested in this concept. Within the Soviet Union, Soviet nationalism had, above all, one task: to support the national units created by '*Sovyetskiy vlast*'. These units had to be perceived as integral parts of the Soviet political system, but they also had to perceive themselves and to act as functioning nations but deflecting from uncontrolled political power or independence.

Peculiarities of Soviet Nationalism

If these were the basic requirements, we should now look for the consequences. According to the Soviet concept, nations had to have their own specific territories. Territorialism was obligatory according to Stalin's basic theses on the National Question. The Soviet principle of territoriality clearly and outspokenly contradicts the theories of Renner and Bauer, who rejected territorial requirements for national minorities etc. Within the Soviet system, any decisions on the limitation of territory were the exclusive prerogative of the central power in Moscow. Economic considerations and planning were also largely concentrated in central hands. The Soviet power created territories for created nations like planned habitats or biotopes, according to their utopian vision of human and social engineering.

This means that in Soviet nationalism there was no place for direct political leadership towards national independence, and no place for a nation's independent economic growth. But there was an important task for potential national leaders: to support distinct collective identification with the specific nation, that is, its territory, its (regulated, or at least standardized) language, and its internal administration. This set of tasks was to be crowned by the development of a specific and distinct culture within the Soviet frame, not to be confused with others. Therefore, Soviet nationalism was less harmonizing than was widely believed: it accepted inner-Soviet nationalist contradictions and dissent on territories, divergent interpretations of the cultural heritage (such as: Was al-Farabi a Kazakh? Was Ibn Sina – Avicenna – a Tajik or an Uzbek? To whom does al-Biruni belong?).[9] It was up to the central power to solve these kinds of contradiction by arbitrary decisions. This makes clear that Soviet nationalism was embedded into the political structure of what used to be called 'Democratic Centralism'.

The territorial principle was extended to all aspects of national histories, not only in space but also in time: 'Urartu was the oldest manifestation of a state not only on Armenian soil but throughout the whole Union (and, therefore, implicitly the earliest forerunner of the Soviet state)',[10] 'Nezami from Ganja is an Azerbaijani Poet', and so on. The Georgian linguist Nikolai Marr's bizarre, not to say extremist, theoretical rejection of any migrations in world-history[11] was, after some years of disastrous consequences, officially rejected itself, during Stalin's lifetime. In practice, this concept never vanished from the national discourses in the Soviet Union, albeit on a scholarly or on a popular and even folkloristic level. There was a popular joke in the old Soviet Union. A Georgian and an Armenian quarrel about the question whether the first human being belonged to the one or the other nation. The Armenian argues for his own stock, saying that his earliest ancestor's name was 'Oranggutanian' but the Georgian refers to a certain 'Chimpanadze'.

This is a typical joke serving the goals of Soviet Nationalism. It reflects the thousands of books and research articles on the earliest stratum of the inhabitants of any given region, the discussions whether the people of the so-called Ants were early Russians or not, whether early findings point to brachiocephalic skulls or not, in comparison to the racial shaping of the contemporary population of this region, and so on.

Within Soviet nationalism, non-Russian nations were not allowed to produce political heroes serving as landmarks within their national history. There should be no equivalents of Czar Peter the Great or, eventually of Ivan Grozniy among other nations. Bohdan Hmel'nickii was an Ukrainian hero because of his acceptance of Ukraine's unification with Russia. In the late 1960s Academician Ibrohim Muminov, a prominent Uzbek historian, was summarily dismissed from his academic posts when he emphasised the 'progressive' role of Amir Timur in so-called 'Uzbek' history. Muminov maintained that Timur anticipated the modern Uzbek republic by his efforts to unify all the various historical regions of Transoxiana that are now part of Uzbekistan. Most Azerbaijanis celebrate the founder of what the well-respected historian Oqtay Äfändiyev called the '*Azerbaidzhanskoye gosudarstvo Sefevidov*', Shah Ismail Xata'i, primarily as a revolutionary folk poet and a popular leader who somewhat erroneously involved himself into politics for a while but later withdrew from that field and became a great national poet. Contemporary Mongol historians were constantly criticized for their attempts to re-evaluate Chingiz Khan and his place in Mongol history.

In the West, under the influence of Alexandre Bennigsen and his group, there was a clear tendency to understand everything 'nationalist' within the vanished Soviet Union as something basically anti-Soviet and anti-communist. In my view, this is a wrong perception and a biased attitude in research, which deserves criticism. A good deal of intra-Soviet nationalism, often perceived as the main danger to the Soviet 'état eclaté' (Hélène Carrère-d'Encausse), was by no means anti-Soviet, as the reluctant attitudes of many national republican leaders toward the dissolution of the USSR in 1991 prove convincingly. Soviet manipulative nationalism offered a wide range of self-assertion to national leaders below the level of political independence. They may have successfully created subsystems of internal political power jealously dismissed by others from outside as, for example, the 'Uzbek Maffia'. This phenomenon resembled far more closely the proper and adequate understanding of the wide capacities of nationalist action that a Soviet local leader like the Uzbek Sharof Rashidov was offered by Soviet nationalism.

There were other important specific features of Soviet nationalism.

1) Nationalism was supposed to be a very important (perhaps the most important) mass-mobilizing element, based on national (administrative, ethnic, linguistic and 'cultural') self-identification. The Soviet regime did not, obviously, refrain from using this mobilizing tool.
2) Soviet nationalism was perceived as a promising tool in the process of forced modernization, being an integrative part of this process – as are all other kinds of nationalism.
3) Its basic ideas and imagination did not directly emerge from an older stage of deep-rooted and indigenous nationalist or ethnocentric thinking (dating back to times earlier than World War I). They were externally invented and offered to the Soviet peoples as coercive gifts.
4) The absolute value given to territorialism by Soviet nationalism made it compulsory to create national territories for invented and constructed nations with externally standardized languages. In this sense, Soviet nationalism was a central element of the Soviet project of human engineering. As for the ideological value of this kind of 'territorialism', one has to understand that Stalin, in April 1917, was still convinced that 'nine-tenths of the peoples of Russia' would prefer to remain within the borders of revolutionary Russia, but after the October Revolution he declared that any aspirations toward national separation were 'counter-revolutionary'.[12] It was for this reason that, later on, internal territorialization within the Union was perceived as the result of Stalin's 'central position', between unconditional nationalists and Bolshevik hardliners refuting any kind of nationalism. What looks like a somewhat emasculated version of nationalism turns out to be one of the basic preconditions of Soviet Nationalism. In a next step, in 1929 Stalin coined the concept of a 'Socialist Nation', which approached de facto Austro-Marxist ideas (Renner and Bauer) very closely, although their concepts were constantly rejected by Stalin and his successors. In the 1960s and later, the 'Socialist Nation' gained very high theoretical value among Soviet ideologists. The whole concept is a clear indication that Soviet Nationalism was already far from Marxist reasoning in a more narrow and rigid sense.[13]
5) Soviet nationalism was directed against any other competing nationalist concepts, but not against nationalism as a principle. It aimed at dominating and monopolizing the nationalist discourse.
6) For a considerable period, Soviet nationalism was effective even

outside the Soviet bloc and was possibly an important element even in the Western hemisphere in the cultural discourse during the Cold War.

Soviet Nationalism and its Impact On Post-Soviet Societies in Central Asia and Caucasia

There may be many matters of debate on this issue, but let me now turn to some aspects of the present situation in ex-Soviet areas. In the following statements, I rely mainly on observations concerning Uzbekistan, Tajikistan and Azerbaijan.

My root idea is that present-day nationalist governmental politics in ex-Soviet Central Asia and in Caucasia have not yet witnessed substantial changes of paradigms. They continue structurally the former Soviet nationalism.

The territorial principle is a basic heritage taken over from Soviet nationalism. With the exception of the disputed area of Karabakh in the Azerbaijani Republic and the strife within Georgia, the borderlines of the former union republics (the so-called 'SSRs') remained basically unchanged. While Armenia claims Karabakh, which belongs to Azerbaijan, most of the disputes about territories take place within the republics they used to belong to. There is much quarrelling and conflict about the future political destiny of a great number of areas in the CIS, but the territories themselves have remained astonishingly stable, at least until now. Remarkable intentions of revisionism concerning territories and borders are to be observed only in Tajikistan, and even there it is not, so far, an official demand for the incorporation of Samarkand and Bukhara into Tajikistan instead of Uzbekistan, to which they have belonged since the coming into existence of that republic in 1924–5 (and Tajikistan 1926 or 1929, respectively). The creation of Uzbekistan and Tajikistan as territorial nation-states was a particularly irrational decision by the central powers under early Soviet rule. Azerbaijan, as a political territory, came into existence two years earlier than the establishment of Soviet power in Transcaucasia. The territorialization of Azerbaijan was somewhat more logical than the artificial invention of Uzbekistan: Azerbaijan was conceived as that part of Transcaucasia which could be maintained by its Muslim population against Armenian and, to a lesser extent, Georgian aspirations.

In the case of Azerbaijan, there is another irrational assault on sober treatment of history to be witnessed: its denomination. The borders of historical Azerbaijan crossed the Araxes to the north only in the case of the territory of Nakhichevan. Prior to 1918, even Lenkoran and Astara were perceived as belonging not to Azerbaijan proper but to Talysh, an area closely linked to the Caspian territory of Gilan. Since antiquity, Azerbaijan has been considered as the region centred around Tabriz, Ardabil, Maragheh, Orumiyeh and Zanjan in today's (and also in historical) Iran. The homonym republic consists of a number of political areas traditionally called Arran, Shirvan, Sheki, Ganjeh and so on. They never belonged to historical Azerbaijan, which dates back to post-Achaemenid, Alexandrian 'Media Atropatene'. Azerbaijan gained extreme importance under (and after) the Mongol Ilkhanids of the thirteenth and fourteenth centuries, when it was regarded as the heartland of Iran. During the nineteenth century, Azerbaijan and Tabriz still held a particularly honoured position within Iran. Linguistic considerations played no part in the traditional identification of Azerbaijan until the beginning of the twentieth century. Touraj Atabaki has offered some beautiful indications concerning the arbitrary transfer of the ancient toponym Azerbaijan from the south towards the north, in his essay in this volume.

Under Soviet auspices and in accordance with Soviet nationalism, historical Azerbaijan proper was reinterpreted as 'Southern Azerbaijan', with demands for liberation and, eventually, for 're'-unification with Northern (Soviet) Azerbaijan – a breathtaking manipulation. No need to point to concrete Soviet political activities in this direction, as in 1945–46 etc.[14]

The really interesting point is that in the independent former Soviet republics this typically Soviet ideological pattern has long outlasted the Soviet Union. At present, I don't see any potentially successful political grouping in the Republic of Azerbaijan revising this theory. By interpreting Azerbaijan as one of the oldest political entities in Transcaucasia, Azerbaijanis implicitly challenge the Armenian claim, on account of Urartu, to be the most ancient culture on Soviet soil. Marrism is particularly strong in interpreting the continuous development of statehood in Azerbaijan as, *a*, if not *the*, main theme in today's Azerbaijani national history. According to Marr, it is not peoples who change their places but rulers and oppressors. It is the people, the *'khalq'*, who are permanently and tightly bound to their 'eternal' and 'sacred' soil. Their language was present much earlier than written evidence indicates, the sources always having been manipulated and falsified by the ruling oppressors, who saw the *khalq* not only having as class enemies but as foreigners too. This accords as perfectly with former so-called Soviet patriotism as with present-day Azerbaijani (or any other post-Soviet) nationalism. Marr's theories were too bizarre even for Stalin himself, and as a consequence, Marr became, especially in linguistics, somewhat outmoded. But in national history, cultural history, and – most important – in scholarly research, Marrist ideas remain and are highly esteemed, even today, whether in the eyes of ruling nationalists or in those of the opposition. In many cases, these ideas are nowadays deeply rooted in the public mind, so that scarcely anybody attributes them any more to Marr – they have found a value in themselves.

Further evidence of the survival of Soviet nationalism is offered by the Republic of Uzbekistan, or, to be more precise, by the political elites of that state.

Contemporary Uzbek intellectuals are well aware of the flimsy historical background of what was established as 'Uzbekistan', and later also 'Tajikistan', by the Soviets – as an invented territory, an invented titular nation with an invented titular language – in order to create a powerful and arbitrary answer to earlier (Jadidi) conceptions of indigenous nationalism in Turkestan. Historical evidence concerning Uzbekistan's territory shows that nothing like contemporary Uzbekistan was to be found on any imagined maps of medieval or ancient Central Asia. The separation of Tajikistan from Uzbekistan, in the late 1920s, was perhaps even more artificial and arbitrary in terms of territory, titular nation and titular language.

In the pre-modern past, very stable regions of identification and concepts of ethnic consciousness existed in Central Asia, including contemporary Uzbekistan, and there were early concepts of nationalism emerging up to the 1920s. It is worth recalling them.

Regionalism

From antiquity and the early Middle Ages, settlements were concentrated in three regions in Central Asia, following the courses of the Amu Darya and Syr Darya rivers. South to the Aral Sea, and approaching the eastern shores of the Caspian Sea, the region of Khorazm can be traced back in history to Achaemenid times. Khorazm included the Amu Darya deltas (its Aral branch, but also its temporary connection to the Caspian coast) and also bordered the Syr Darya delta. In the south-east, next to Khorazm, ancient Sogdiana was located, along the middle parts of the 'two rivers' and named after the river Zarafshan. Sogdiana much resembled what is known as Transoxiana. The third region of high importance for settled civilization in Central Asia is that along the upper part of the Syr Darya river: the Ferghana valley. In eastern Central Asia, these regions found their equivalents in the areas of Khotan, Kashghar and Turfan.

These three central regions – Khorazm, Sogdiana/Transoxiana and Ferghana – were surrounded by and closely connected to a series of other stable historical regions, also recognized since ancient times: Parthia, Areia and Baktria south to the Amu Darya (unified as 'Khorasan' since Sasanids times), the Üst-Yurt plateau and Semirechiye ('Yettisuv'), and Dzungaria in the north, and the Tarim Basin east of the Tienshan ranges.

It is interesting to observe that throughout history these regions have always served for mapping political entities. There were principalities of long continuity in Khorazm; Sogdian princes held sway in Transoxiana, and the rulers of Akhsikat and Usrushana dominated Ferghana in late antiquity and the early Middle Ages. During the Islamic Middle Ages, we find administrative entities of the 'Eastern Caliphate' conceived in accordance with these three regions. The regions nourished consciousness of territory and identity among their inhabitants as well as through the perspectives of their external neighbours.

'Ulusism' in Central Asia

A marked change in mapping territory and identities in Central Asia happened as a consequence of the Mongol conquest of Eurasia (in the thirteenth century). Among other aspects, the Mongols were highly experienced long-distance conquerers. In this capacity they had developed an intense imagination of space in political thinking, and therefore a deep understanding of territoriality. Under the rule of Chingiz Khan himself, the Mongol Empire became defined as composed of four political territories, the so-called 'uluses' named after the four official sons of the great conquerer. This was a new type of regionalization, combining regional definitions with political ones, or, more precisely, with dynastic principles. Under the ulus system, Khorazm became part of Ulus Juchi. The plateau of Iran belonging to the

Ilkhanids maintained a special relationship to the Tuluids in China and Mongolia proper. Transoxiana, Ferghana and the eastern regions of Central Asia comprised Ulus Chaghatay. Khorasan was claimed by the Irano-Tuluid Ilkhanids (and later, by those who perceived themselves as their legitimate successors on Iranian soil), and by Ulus Chaghatay as well. For the next centuries, the military and political history of Central Asia is to be understood through this Chingizid regional consciousness, for which I have coined the term 'ulusism'. Mental mapping in the case of all political and military Central Asian actors within the 'Middle Period' (the fourteenth to eighteenth centuries) was closely based on ulusism.

In the eighteenth and nineteenth centuries, however, the traditional regions experienced a kind of 'come back'. The three great political entities in western Central Asia were congruent to the three traditional regions, Khorazm (the khanate of Khiva), Transoxiana (the amirate of Bukhara), and Ferghana (the heartland of the khanate of Khuqand). Russian tsarist colonialism and its administration did not destroy this regionalist concept, but continued to rely on it.

It was left to the Soviets to create new territories and new boundaries but, unknown to the new rulers, the regions continued to exist in the minds of their inhabitants, enriched by some additional micro-regions: in Uzbekistan, we find a clear internal delimitation between Khorazmians, those belonging to the Zarafshan valley (Samarkand, Bukhara, etc.), and the Ferghana people. The region of Tashkent does not belong to any of them, but was associated with the khanate of Khuqand, for a while, and is rather part of the colonial heritage of Uzbekistan.

In Turkmenistan, we also find Khorazmian identity in the north-east of the republic, clearly contrasted to the southern, historically Khorasani regions of Marv and Ashgabat. I wonder whether, in Charjui, Transoxanian (Bukharan) identity still survives?

In Tajikistan, for decades fierce rivalries between northern and southern Tajiks were reported. This difference reflects an ephemeral Ferghani (Khujand) and formerly Bukharan identity: in Tajik scholarly publications this part of Tajikistan is consequently referred to as 'former Eastern Bukhara', an explicit indication of Transoxanian identity. The Pamir heights shaped an additional region, not considered in this scheme. Recent competing and hostile attitudes have tended to take place within these regions' border (especially in the south). This is to be perceived as an historically recent phenomenon.

If we understand southern Kazakhstan (the lower Syr Darya area) as historically bound to the khanate of Khuqand, it is easy to indicate surviving remnants of this subordination in current regional thinking in this republic, too. Until the Russian conquest, the Syr Darya region (including Tashkent) was regarded as an extension of the Khuqand khanate; the areas along Chimkent up to Auliya Ata, Aq Masjid (Soviet: Qyzyl Orda) and so on never belonged to one of the great Kazakh 'hordes' (*'juz'*). They still show a non-Kazakh identity, usually described as 'Uzbekized' and traceable back to the Khoqand period in the nineteenth century.

While ulusism fell into oblivion, the three traditional regions have succeeded in surviving in the public mind.

Premodern Ethnicism

I shall refrain from giving detailed facts and figures on tribalism and tribal affiliations in Central Asia. Anyway, in administrative documents of the sixteenth and seventeenth centuries promulgated by Shaybanid and Ashtarkhanid rulers, a traditional parsophone expression for indicating 'the whole population' was noteworthily modified. The expression, 'Turk-u Tajik' ('the majority of inhabitants', the 'people'), was based on a sociological understanding of premodern society in regions eastern to the Ottoman Empire. 'Turk' refers to 'tribally affiliated, transhumant or nomad, militant, Turkic-speaking etc.', and 'Tajik' to 'non-tribal, sedentary, and even urban, non-military, Persian speaking etc.'. In Persian texts from Muslim India, 'Turk-u Tajik' is sometimes modified to 'Turk-u Tajik-u Hindu'. In the documents from Central Asia we find the expression 'Uzbek-u Chaghatay-u Tajik', an amazing indication of ethnic consciousness in our region, because 'Uzbek-u Chaghatay' replaces 'Turk'. This is excellent source evidence for Ingeborg Baldauf's differentiation of ethnic roots of the modern Uzbek 'nation', which she bases on some ethnographic observations by the Soviet researchers Karmysheva and Sukhareva.[15] Tribal groups dating back to the Chaghatay–Timurid rule (and earlier) were 'Chaghatays' (see also Beatrice Manz on this subject). 'Uzbek' indicates the Qypchaq tribal federation that migrated to Transoxiana under Shaybanid leadership. The term 'Tajik' in premodern times refers to the non-tribal, sedentary, non-military element of society; in this respect language was much less crucial than we may assume today. Within a widely bilingual (Persian and Turkish) setting it was not language but social specifications that signified identity – in combination with other elements, like macro- and micro-regionality, confessional affiliation within Islam (Sunni versus Ismaili was similar to Tajik/Uzbek/Chaghatay versus Pamiri) and non-Islamic peoples such as the Jews.

Historically, Soviet nationalism shaped the last stage in this panorama. Because of political conditions from the 1920s onwards, it was the decisive ideology in nation-building in Central Asia, in contrast to the pre-Soviet early modern Jadidi and other modernists' ideas, which used to be popular among enlighted intellectuals at the beginning of the twentieth century, but were eventually suppressed by the Soviets.

Conclusion: Soviet Nationalism as a Non-Marxist Ideology

What are the implications of these macro-historical considerations? As I tried to show in the first part of this essay, in my view Soviet nationalism should be perceived not as an ideology derived from Marxist thinking but as one created parallel to Marxist conceptions. Though it was adapted to Marxist requirements it was itself clearly a non-Marxist concept, albeit serving Marxist goals. Soviet nationalism, although not a Marxian concept, was nevertheless a coherent ideological system. It cannot be appropriately understood if we interpret it in pragmatic terms. Its concepts were less arbitrarily developed but consciously constructed and refined by Marxist thinkers – but it should not be mistaken for a Marxist concept.

Therefore, it fits excellently with the present day tasks of post-Soviet national leaders in the independent CIS republics. Being an autonomous ideological system following its own specific rules, it can be easily continued at a time when Soviet Marxism–Leninism has been officially, and substantially, abolished. Perpetuating the systemic concepts of Soviet nationalism does not affect new conversions to a market economy, to – more or less – open societies, and so on. To contemporary political leaders and elites, Soviet nationalism offers the possibility of continuing to use a familiar ideological tool of public mobilization without maintaining any debt to Marxism–Leninism, to vanished Soviet ethical standards, or to other former holy cows such as the class struggle. Since Soviet nationalism was a very important and widely used connective medium linking Soviet political and ideological standards to 'the masses' it can nowadays recall familiar attitudes among a large part of the peoples of Central Asia, and can therefore be effectively used to transfer from the rulers to the ruled not only former Soviet policies but also post- and even anti-Soviet policies.

By maintaining the structures of Soviet nationalism, its contemporary protagonists have no difficulty in cleansing its content of any Marxist–Leninist and Soviet elements. It has an excellent chance not only to survive but to dominate political ideology, intellectual thinking and even scholarly discourses in the humanities and social sciences, at least in some of the new republics of the CIS.

The newly independent states cannot find a better vindication of their existence than in surviving Soviet nationalism. The new rulers may easily replace obsolete ex-Soviet maxims with better ones. In this sense, the new cult of 'Amir Timur' in Uzbekistan is a bit of a masterpiece. Following up the (typically Soviet) theory that a nation's progress consists mainly of establishing national territory and statehood, it is natural that Timur is now officially perceived as the great forerunner of Uzbekistan, having united in his state the three historical regions of Central Asia for the first time in history. In fact, we should not forget that no other contemporary Central Asian national state includes parts of all three regions (Khorazm, Transoxiana and Ferghana) in its territory. I owe this observation to the French geographer Daniel Balland.

Amir Timur's statue has replaced that of Karl Marx in the centre of Tashkent. His iconography closely follows that of Lenin's monuments. Once, there were roughly four main types of statues of Lenin, and we have, so far, at least three types of Amir Timur: riding a horse (Tashkent), standing upright (Shahrisabz), and sitting on his throne (Samarkand). His physiognomy is modelled on the famous reconstruction of Amir Timur's skull by Mikhail Mikhailovich Gerassimov (1941), thus laying claim to scholarly seriousness.[16] His mausoleum, repaired and restored, can easily serve for ceremonial requirements. The Tashkent Lenin Museum has been closed, but a museum devoted to the Timurids was recently inaugurated. Newly married couples dedicate their bridal bouquets to Amir Timur's monuments wherever they may be. Even former anti-Soviet dissidents' interests are served by the new cult: together with its unconditional independence, the Uzbek nation-state has acquired an eminent political hero in its national history, with a clearly positive message, and in contrast to former Soviet regulations. For further details on this subject, I refer to the interesting studies in progress by Lutz Rzehak (Berlin) on this subject.

There can be no doubt that many new political leaders of CIS republics rely heavily on perpetuated Soviet nationalism. Many of the nationalist dissidents shaping the political opposition today do the same. A prominent Tajik dissident put this aspect into the wording 'To tell the truth, we Tajiks (as a nation) owe a lot to Stalin's policy.' He did not and does not feel any nostalgia for Stalinism, he was well aware that his concept of nationality follows the principles of Soviet nationalism by means of which the Tajiks were retrospectively offered their own tradition of statehood in medieval and ancient history: Stalin himself once declared that the Tajiks had the most ancient ethnos in Central Asia. They celebrated, and still celebrate, the Sogdians and the Samanids (tenth century) as the forerunners of their own Tajik national statehood – with the result that there are still unsolved and controversial double claims to the Zarafshan valley and its splendid old cities of Samarkand and Bukhara. The dissidents are sometimes more insistent in their irredentist demands than are the ruling politicians in Tashkent.

At the same time, in what Robert Musil might have called a 'parallel action', we witness intensifying micro-regional conflicts or, at least, self-demarcations. This goes mainly for Tajikistan. Many political observers therefore define Tajikistan as a 'not yet fully developed nation' in 'search of its own identity'. There can be no doubt that Tajikistan is one of the weakest CIS states. But its perceived lack of identity is rather an external construct. The Tajik nation was successfully created by Soviet nationalism, and it has just as much national identity as the other ex-Soviet nation-states. The troubles of the Tajik state are not necessarily to do with lack of national consciousness or identity.

To sum up, when studying present-day nationalism, national consciousness, ethnic identity and connected fields of inquiry as regards the Central Asian CIS republics, it may be useful to understand Soviet nationalism as a structure and as a consequent ideological system, apart and autonomous from Marxism–Leninism. As a nationalist ideology, it survives strongly in the independent republics in Central Asia (and elsewhere). It is not only the rulers' nationalist discourse that is influenced by this post-Soviet 'Soviet nationalism'; the dissidents' discourses are as well. It should be considered not as a fading or even vanishing phenomenon but as a vital concept influencing various aspects of post-Soviet political thinking. It should not be regarded as contradictory to premodern and more traditional concepts of identity, like regionalism or early modern pre-Soviet nationalism. Being substantially non-Marxist, it can easily be enriched by elements like these.

Eventually, understanding this conception of Soviet nationalism may offer a valuable methodic tool for research concerning the political culture of contemporary Central Asia, and perhaps also of other post-socialist societies of our world. Moreover, it ought to be understood as one of the most successful ideological exports of the former USSR to the West, even, and above all, during the Cold War. Nationalist ideologies based on historicist reflections, mainly but not exclusively in what we are used to calling the 'Third World', follow closely the main lines of Soviet nationalism in their arguments, especially by constructing and even inventing 'progressive' and 'revolutionary' histories, serving the apotheosis of an abstract principle called 'the People', in the name of which everything can be done by the powerful.

Notes

1 Hélène Carrère d'Encausse, *L Empire éclaté: La Révolte des nations en URSS* (Paris, 1978).

2 Gerhard Simon, *Nationalismus and Nationalitätenpolitik in der Sowjetunion: Van der totalitären Diktatur zur nachstalinschen Gesellschaft* (Baden-Baden, 1986; Eng. trans.: *Nationalism and Policy toward the Nationalities in the Soviety Union: Totalitarian Dictatorship to Post-Stalinist Society*, Boulder, CO, San Francisco and Oxford, 1991).

3 Richard Pipes, *The Formation of the Soviet Union: Communism and Nationalism 1917–23* (Cambridge, MA, 1957).

4 Bert G. Fragner, 'Sowjetmacht und Islam: Die Revolution von Buchara' in 'U. Haarmann and P. Bachmann, eds. *Die islamische Welt zwischen Mittelalter und Neuzeit. Festschrift für Hans Robert Roemer* (Beirut, 1979), pp. 146–66; and Fragner, 'The Nationalization of the Uzbeks and Tajiks', in Edward Allworth, Andreas Kappeler, Gerhard Simon and Georg Brunner, eds, *Muslim Communities Reemerge* (Durham & London, 1994), pp. 13–32.

5 Otto Bauer, *Die Nationalitätenfrage und die Sozialdemokratie* (Vienna, 1907); Karl Renner, *Das Selbstbestimmungsrecht der Nationen in besonderer Anwendung auf Österreich* (Leipzig and Wien, 1918).

6 Monika Schäfer, *Nationalitätenpolitik der KPdSU in Geschichte und Gegenwart* (Berlin, 1982), p. 19, quoting Lenin in the German edition, *W. I. Lenin – Werke* (Berlin, 1955–72), vol. 6, p. 329: 'Braucht das jüdische Proletariat eine "selbständige politische Partei"?'.

7 I used a German translation, 'Marxismus und nationale Frage' (Vienna: Stern-Verlag, n.d.).

8 Erwin Oberländer, *Sowjetpatriotismus und Geschichte* (Cologne, 1967).

9 Yuri Bregel, *Notes on the Study of Central Asia* (Bloomington, 1996), p. 11.

10 The official history of the Soviet Union says that Urartu was the oldest state organization on Soviet soil: Michail Heller and Alexander Nekrich, *Geschichte der Sowjetunion*, vol. 1, 1914–1939 (Känigstein/Ts, 1981), p. 2.

11 An interesting description of Marr's ideas and their impact on Soviet historical research can be found in Bregel's polemic book, *Notes on the Study of Central Asia*, p. 13. Bregel gives a moving account of the Soviet (Russian) orientalist and historian Aleksandr Iakubovskiy, who in his research (*K voprosu ob etnogeneze uzbekskogo naroda*) obeyed Marr's concepts although he did not accept them.

12 Simon, *Nationalismus und Nationalitätenpolitik*. p. 35.

13 Ibid, pp. 154–6.

14 Tadeusz Swietochowski, 'Islam and the Growth of National Identity in Azerbaijan', in Edward Allworth, Andreas Kappeler, Gerhard Simon and Georg Brunner, esa, *Muslim Communities Reemerge* (Durham and London, 1994), pp. 46–60, especially p. 56.

15 Ingeborg Baldauf, 'Some Thoughts on the Making of the Uzbek Nation', *Cahiers du monde russe et soviétique*, vol. 32, no. 1 (January–March, 1991), pp. 79–96.

16 Mikhail Mikhailovich Gerassimov, *Ich suchte Gesichter. Schädel erhalten ihr Antlitz zurück – Wissenschaft auf neuen Wegen* (Gütersloh, 1968). For Timur and the Timurids, see pp. 154–87.

2· Nation-building in Azerbaijan: The Soviet Legacy and the Impact of the Karabakh Conflict

Suha Bölükbaşı

Ernest Gellner once said that nationalism was 'natural and probably irresistible'.[1] Writing years later, an observer of the developments in the Soviet Union, Alexander J. Motyl, seconded that opinion by saying that 'nationalism makes sense in a world of nation states. It is rational – which is to say that it suggests an excellent solution, statehood, to a variety of contemporary problems.'[2]

The nationalists not only make a conscious or unconscious commitment to modernization – that is, to development, industrialization, mass education and mass participation – but also promise to deliver the goods, to guarantee and promote life, liberty and the pursuit of happiness.[3] In other words, nationalism is a broad symbol which entails values and goals that make it worthy of notice and acceptance.[4]

In the Soviet Republic of Azerbaijan, during the tumultuous three years from 1988 to 1991, when nationalist feelings were at their highest, the nationalists challenged the local leadership as well as Moscow to attain the 'national goal': preventing the loss of Karabakh; and when this proved unattainable they fought for independence in order to achieve, among several goals, the liberation of Karabakh. Although the tsarist and Soviet rule over Azerbaijan contributed to ethnic consolidation of the Azeri community as a self-conscious

---

Suha Bölükbaşı is Professor of International Relations at the Middle East Technical University, Ankara.

nationality, the turbulent 1988–91 period probably made the Azeris more self-conscious. Hence, the Azerbaijani experience in nation-building leads one to identify nationalism not only as the combination of culture, cultural identity, ethnicity, and ethnic solidarity, but also as the promise of a better future, as heralded by the nationalist Azerbaijan Popular Front (APF). The Azeri experience during these critical years shows that nationalism acquired the characteristic of what Hagopian called a 'broad symbol' that made it worthy of notice and acceptance.[5]

This essay aims to examine the causes and the consequences of nationalism in the Republic of Azerbaijan between 1988 and 1991. This period is significant because it was in 1988 that the Azerbaijani (or Azeri) intellectual elite and the APF militants began vigorously to espouse nationalist goals. The Azeri elite could afford to challenge Moscow's guidelines partly because Gorbachev's policies of *glasnost* and *perestroika* had by late 1988 created conditions in which opposition groups could organize and articulate political demands. Yet it was the demonstrations in Yerevan (Armenia) and in Nagorno Karabakh in February 1988, demanding the unification of the mostly Armenian enclave of Karabakh with Armenia, which provided a greater boost to the appeal of Azeri nationalism.

For many Slavists the nationalist fervour in Azerbaijan came as no surprise. They had for a long time been predicting that sooner or later the nations within the Soviet state would rebel and that they would be unmanageable in the long run. Yet had Gorbachev not set out to establish economic and democratic accountability throughout the USSR it would have been much more difficult for opposition groups in various republics to challenge the pro-Moscow leaders by adopting nationalist programmes. In the Azerbaijani case, the nationalist rhetoric emanating from the 'enemy' – from Yerevan and Stepanakert (capital of Karabakh) – and the state of undeclared war since 1989 between Yerevan and Baku made inevitable the adoption by the elite and the masses of nationalist goals.

Although the Gorbachev reforms and the Nagorno-Karabakh dispute contributed to nationalist fervour, the seventy years of Soviet rule had also created favourable conditions for nation-building. Contrary to the assumptions of many Sovietologues who argued that Moscow tried to stamp out all the remnants of nationalism, the various policies implemented throughout the USSR inadvertently made nations out of 'ethnics', or proto-nations, which had existed prior to 1917.[6] Soviet policies included nativization, or the employment of the native cadre between the 1920s and the early 1930s; the economic and social transformations of the 1930s, which nevertheless preserved 'national education' and 'national cadres'; territorialization, or the creation of ethnolinguistic cultures without political nationalism; imperial centre–periphery relations; traditionalism, or the survival of traditional practices and traditional social structures, localism, or the establishment of ties between the republican leadership and the people, based on favouritism, patronage, limited national pride, and economic freedom; and promotion of 'selective local nationalisms' side by side with patriotism, or loyalty to the USSR, which led to the emergence of secular, conscious and politically mobile nations.[7] By the 1980s the republic had become increasingly homogeneous, and the national elites ruled by persuasion, giving concessions to the native populace, 'delivering the goods' to constituents, allowing greater freedom of nationalist expression, and using mafia-like networks of clans to link political power with the 'second economy'.

The expectation that world revolution was near contributed to the adoption by Lenin of the principle of federalism, which meant granting major nationalities (or ethnie) their own republics. The principle of federalism was implemented (1924) almost simultaneously with the *korenisatsiya* (Nativization) of the republican administrations after 1921. This helped to curb the opposition of the petty-bourgeois elite (called *jadid*s in Azerbaijan and Central Asia) by co-opting them into the government. By the early 1930s, however, Stalin's misgivings about nativization – which he had harboured from the outset – had reached such proportions that he decided to give up cooperation with the competent yet unreliable 'bourgeois' *jadid*s in favour of more reliable Slavs and the less-educated but seemingly more loyal Central Asians and Azerbaijanis, who had working-class backgrounds.[8]

Despite the breakup of the alliance of convenience with the *jadid*s, the policy of nativization (this time using working-class natives) continued, while coercion was used to transform the Turkic communities, with official campaigns against Islam, nationalism (*millatchilik*), the promotion of a uniform socialist culture, and linguistic engineering (Russification of Turkic languages and styles of expression). Nevertheless, no matter how forceful the transformations were, they ironically – yet deliberately – contributed to the creation of national intelligentias, who differed from the pre-Soviet *Jadids* in their apparent commitment to the Soviet ideals. Despite the manipulations (which emphasized the difference between various Turkic dialects) native languages were supported, and the titular ethnicity in the state apparatus – regardless of its decision-making capacity or incapacity – was given prominent status. The establishment of national operas and national academies of sciences also took place during this period and, although they were dismissed by some as symbolic and controlled institutions, they nevertheless contributed to the emergence of nationalist feeling later on.[9]

The economic and social transformations of the early 1930s included the shift to the centralized command economy, anti nationalism campaigns, the liquidation of native communists, forced collectivization, and more emphasis on Russification. At the 17th party congress in 1934, the USSR Communist Party (CP) ceased denouncing 'great power chauvinism' and many more Slavs were promoted in the Turkic states' administration. Yet, owing to the preservation of national education and the limited political control by the native cadres in the republics, the characteristics of nativization were not eliminated.[10]

The principle of territorialization also contributed to the sense of nationhood by identifying nationality with territory. Although this policy eliminated some of the subnational (such as tribal) and supranational (religious, pan-Turkic) loyalties, it created loyalties to the newly constructed titular nations of the republics. In short, ethnolinguistic cultures without political nationalism, or what Tom Nairn calls, 'reservation cultures', were created.[11]

Some scholars have objected to the argument that Moscow helped the nation-building process, on the grounds that Moscow weakened historical identity; confined identity to folk-dancing and handicrafts; manipulated and applied identity; manipulated and applied artificial nomenclature to languages, and vilified national literature; falsified history; and banned oral histories (*dastans*).[12] Although these observations did not contain much exaggeration, they did not preclude the possibility that a national, or proto-national – though differing from the pre-Soviet characteristics of a given community – consciousness might eventually emerge. As discussed below, the Azerbaijani experience attests to this possibility.

Another factor was the existence of imperial centre–periphery relations between Russia and other republics. They were disguised by reference to a supranational ideology and a compelling vision of history sanctioning the rule of the Communist Party. In time, however, the disguise became even thinner. The republics' inability to oppose Moscow's directives (for example, Moscow's emphasis on cotton monoculture in Uzbekistan or on oil production in Azerbaijan) was not lost on their populations. The lack of a real ability to make important political decisions without Moscow's agreement eventually led to popular hostility toward Moscow's omnipotence.

Despite Soviet transformations in economic and social life, traditional cultural practices and social structures – though not in their original form – remained largely intact. Although traditional patterns of leadership were destroyed, religion suppressed, and social environment fundamentally changed, old unities based on kinship, customs, and beliefs largely survived. The so-called 'second economy' flourished mainly due to traditional networks protected by favours, family loyalties and codes of silence.

In the post-Stalin period another trait emerged which could be characterized as localism. Starting in the mid-1950s, Khrushchev and later Brezhnev granted greater – but still limited – independence to republican Communist Parties. This led to the expansion of areas of permitted national expression. By using ethnic symbols, republican leaders forged their own ties with their populations, and the republics were essentially ruled by national cliques which occupied high state and party positions. The republican CPs promoted patronage, favoured titular nationality and economic freedom, and allowed the people to have limited national pride. Nevertheless, the perception of a colonial or quasi-colonial situation persisted in most – including Turkic – republics. This also contributed to the feelings of solidarity between people in a particular republic. As Michael Hechter said, 'where economic disadvantages are superimposed upon objective cultural differences – where a pattern of "internal colonialism" exists – political demands are most likely to be made on a status-group basis.'[13]

During the 1970s while 'official nationalism' provided 'patriotism', or loyalty to the USSR, a selective local nationalism was promoted which included 'ethnic pride' and respect for 'historic achievements'. In such an atmosphere dissidents and even human-rights activists based their demands on ethnic or linguistic issues, which had become tolerable and fashionable. Even within the Helsinki Communities, ethnic and linguistic issues were popular.[14]

By the 1980s, partly owing to politics pursued by republican leaderships, the republics had become demographically more unitary; articulate national political and intellectual elites had emerged and developed a shared national consciousness; and the ruling elite ruled mostly by persuasion, concessions and 'delivering the goods' to their constituents. It was perhaps inevitable that the ruling elites consisted mostly of mafia-like networks of clans linking political power with the 'secondary economy', while allowing limited nationalist expression which Moscow tolerated or was unable to curb.

In the modern era throughout the world, such factors as urbanization, industrialization, mass education, and greater access to print and other media consolidated ethno-linguistic groups into nations. However, the Soviet experience shows that additional and unique factors created secular, conscious and politically mobilizable nationalities.

How Does the Azerbaijani Case Relate to Recent Research on Nationalism?

The findings of recent emphasis on 'invented' or constructed nationalism have had little or no impact on Soviet and post-Soviet studies. Karl Deutsch had earlier stressed the importance of 'new forms of social communication' (urbanization, development of markets, railways, and so on) which accelerate the political integration of a community.[15] Benedict Anderson likewise emphasized the emergence of a standardized usable language, which becomes possible with the arrival of 'print-capitalism', which in turn coincides with a system of production (capitalism) and productive relations (capitalist). The standardized usable language, for its part, makes communities (or nations) imaginable.[16]

Partha Chatterjee objected to Anderson's and others' apparent restriction of the modes of anti-colonial nationalism by suggesting that the most creative results of the nationalist imagination in Asia and Africa are posited not on identity but rather on a difference from the 'modular' forms of the national society propagated by the modern West. He argued that 'anticolonial nationalism creates its own domain of sovereignty within colonial society well before it begins its political battle with the imperial power'.[17] Yet like Anderson and some other theorists, Chatterjee also suggested that this domain of sovereignty concerns the 'spiritual' field, or national culture, and the nationalist elite refuses to allow (openly or in a subtle way) the colonial power to intervene in that domain. As I shall show, the nationalist elite in Azerbaijan also engaged in the post-Stalin era in a gradual and successful process of reclaiming Azerbaijani history and culture.

Unlike those post-World War II theorists who identified state with nation,[18] Ernest Gellner and Eric Hobsbawm also stressed that social and cultural processes cannot be conceived simply as objective forces outside the given nationality. The active work of individuals, parties, newspapers, intellectuals and the state is the key to the creation (or articulation) of national consciousness. Gellner argued that the state ensures common (homogenous) culture by ignoring pre-existing cultures to invent a new 'high' culture.[19] Like Gellner, Hobsbawm also argued that states make nations and nationalisms not the other way round.

In order to survive, a polyethnic empire must adopt a homogenizing and centralizing state structure, which inevitably brings changes. Anthony D. Smith offered three options which intelligentsia of the non-ruling nation within such an empire may adopt in order to survive and cope with the changes: traditionalism (rejecting all modernization); assimilationism (transfer of loyalty to the new, efficient, problem-solver state); reformism (combining the first two options and synthesizing modernization and tradition).[20]

In Azerbaijan, the post-1920 leadership tried to adopt the third option when faced with Moscow, centralizing and homogenizing reforms. Although the liquidations of the 1930s interrupted this process, after Stalin's death the reformist tendency once again characterized the policies of the Azeri leadership.

As in other parts of the world, the Soviet ethno-linguistic groups were consolidated into nations as a result of urbanization, industrialization, mass education and greater access to print and other media. The above-mentioned Soviet institutions and policies, however, created unique and descriptive circumstances.[21]

Miroslav Hroch also emphasized the role of the intellectuals and the political role of the elite. His three-stage evolution of nationalism included an incremental process involving: scholars stressing the culture, language and history of the oppressed nationality; activists diffusing nationalist ideas; and broad masses joining the nationalist movement.[22]

The pre- and post-independence experiences of states which became independent in the aftermath of World War II seem similar to Azerbaijan's experience. Whereas in Europe discoveries, advances in communications and 'print capitalism' led to the emergence of 'imagined communities', in the Third World the colonial states contributed to the rise of nations. They drew artificial boundaries, published maps of the 'country' (delimiting the 'nation'), held censuses (determining the members of the 'nation') and excavated the ruins of the former dynasties (establishing the missing links in the historiography of the 'nation').

Azerbaijan's post-Soviet experience is similar to that of the postwar decolonized states. As in Azerbaijan, independence occurred quickly (in the late 1950s and early 1960s) in those colonies because it was mostly a simple transaction of transfer of government on paper. For France, for instance, 1960 was the year of decolonization in Africa.

Moreover, in both cases state offices have uncertain authority; government is highly ineffective and plagued by corruption; and the political community is segmented ethnically into several 'publics' (such as tribes or regions). Most elites of the newly independent states belong to two publics, the civic and the primordial, and consider themselves part of the primordial. As Peter P. Ekeh argued, 'the unwritten law is that it is legitimate to rob the civic public in order to strengthen the primordial public'.[23]

Government is less an agency to provide political goods such as law, order, security, justice or welfare, and more a foundation of privilege, wealth and power for a small elite who control it. Those who occupy state offices, civilian and military, high and low, are inclined to treat them as possessions rather than positions: to live off their rents and use them to reward persons and cliques who help maintain their power.[24]

Tsarist and Soviet Contributions to Azerbaijani Nation-building

If one looks at the events that took place while the USSR was still intact one discovers that both uniquely Soviet-era factors and factors common to most colonized regions influenced the Azerbaijani experience. Urbanization, industrialization, mass education and greater access to print and other media consolidated the Azeri ethno-linguistic community into an Azeri nation, as was the case in many other parts of the world.

The establishment of tsarist bureaucratic and military rule in Azerbaijan in 1928, and the undermining of the local elites, led to resistance by both the Azeri gentry and the peasantry. Yet in the mid-nineteenth century the more moderate policies of Viceroy Mikhail Vorontsov drew Muslim and Christian warlords into the Russian nobility and employed them as local governors. Thus the initial nationalistic or quasi-nationalistic anger at the imposition of 'infidel' (or Christian) rule subsided. Moreover, the Russian presence was always low, and anti-Russian feelings were therefore moderate.[25]

Until the 1905–6 Armeno-Tatar (the Azeris were called Tatars by Russia) war, localism was the main tenet of cultural identity among Azeri intellectuals. It comprised emphasis on spoken vernacular, local history, and a preoccupation with local problems in such localities as Baku, Ganja, Tblisi, Nakhichevan and Shusha. Pan-Turkic issues, including Azerbaijanism, and solidarity with Turkey and other Turkic or Muslim communities within tsarist Russia, were unpopular.[26]

The 1905–6 Armeno-Tatar War forced the Azeri elite and the population at large to ponder whether localism was a sufficient tool to weather the tsarist and Armenian encroachment. The war was partly due to increasing class differences between the Armenians, who had better jobs and higher wages in the booming oil industry, and the less-educated and less technically adept Azeris, who put up with menial jobs and lower wages. To the class differences should be added the real or perceived bias of tsarist officialdom in favour of the Armenian community. The better-off Azeris, including merchants, oil and textile industrialists and the landed nobility, felt squeezed by their Armenian counterparts and also perceived a pro-Armenian Russian bias.[27] By the time war broke out, wealthy Azeris had begun to subsidize educational, cultural and other communal activities. After the war, they began to look to Turkey and Iran as allies.[28]

Incidentally the 1905–9 Constitutional Revolution in Iran, the Young Turk revolution in 1908, and the reformist thoughts of the Tatar *jadid* Ismail Bey Gaspirali and the modernist/religious Jamal al-Din al-Afghani professionally influenced the thinking of early-twentieth-century Azeri intellectuals.[29] Unlike their Tatar counterparts, who were mostly educated in St Petersburg or Berlin, Azeri intellectuals were educated primarily in Istanbul. Among them were such influential leaders as Mehmet Emin Rasulzadeh, Nariman Narimanov, Ahmad Ağaoğlu, Ali Huseinzadeh, Hashim Vazirov, Uzeyir and Jeyhun Hajibeyli, and Mardan Bey Topchubashi.[30]

The Azeri intellectual elite were strong proponents of secular modernism and constitutionalism, due both to the Young Turk influence, to hostility to the Iranian monarchy – which had lost all real power to Russia, Britain and other European states – and the Shi'i clerical hierarchy. Like their contemporaries in Iran and Turkey, the Azeri *ziyalilar* (intellectuals) were receptive to populist and socialist ideas, and used nationalism interchangeably with socialism because to them anti-imperialism meant mainly anti-Russianism.[31] The Azeri *ziyalilar* remained united until the 1905 Russian Revolution, after which the socialist *Himmat* (Toil) group was born. Somewhat belatedly, the more nationalist but still socialist *Musavat* (Equality) was established in 1911.[32] Until 1917, the two groups cooperated against the tsarist regime and the religious conservatives, and it was perceived as natural that they exchanged members. For instance, Mehmet Emin Rasulzadeh, who became president of the independent Azerbaijan Republic (1918–20), was a Himmat member but joined Musavat in 1913. Nariman Narimanov, who became first secretary of the Azerbaijan Communist Party (AzCP), had earlier been a Musavat member.[33]

Himmat was the Baku branch of the Russian Social Democratic Party, because Lenin had made an exception to the rule by allowing it to represent only Muslim socialists. Yet Himmat's ideology included Muslim solidarity and pan-Turkism, in addition to socialism.[34] Independence, however, was not a pre-1914 goal of either Himmat or Musavat. Narimanov demanded the nationalization of education, with such subjects as language studies, literature and religion to be taught in Azeri. By the time of Azerbaijan's incorporation into Bolshevik Russia (1920), the Azerbaijani socialist and nationalist elites had more or less the same goal, more autonomy in socio-political and cultural spheres,[35] though it is not clear to what extent the Azeri population at large subscribed to this goal. Nevertheless, the establishment of Soviet rule increasingly made any reference to nation and nationalism not only unacceptable but illegal.

During the early 1920s, most former Musavat members and nationalists either escaped to Turkey and other neighbouring countries or were executed. During the late 1920s – as in Central Asia – many native communists and former Himmat members were politically liquidated or executed. Nariman Narimanov was probably spared the ordeal of execution when he mysteriously died in Moscow in 1925 of 'a heart attack'.[36] Yet in 1937 he was denounced posthumously as 'a bourgeois nationalist'. During the late 1930s – parallel to what was happening elsewhere in the Soviet Union – most of the remaining native communists were executed after being charged with Trotskyism or pan-Turkism. What happened during and after the show trials of this period can only be described as a total terror, during which even slight suspicion over one's loyalty to Stalin could send someone to death row or the Gulags. Even national epics (*dastans*) were banned in the atmosphere of total paranoia.[37]

With the German assault on the USSR in 1941, Stalin decided to loosen the reins throughout the USSR, and until the end of the war the union republics enjoyed a spell of fresh air. *Dastans* were rehabilitated, one of the four Muslim spiritual directorates was established in Baku in 1943, and 'loving one's homeland [Azerbaijan]' became acceptable.[38]

After the war, however, the brutal clampdown on 'nationalist' tendencies resumed. Kamran Baghirov, first secretary of the AzCP (1933–53) and a former KGB head in Azerbaijan, dutifully implemented the orders.[39] Ironically, the same AzCP that declared war on nationalism embraced the Iranian Democratic Party of Azerbaijan's (DPA) declaration of independence in the mostly Azeri-populated northern Iran in 1945–6 with the support of the Red Army.

During the Stalin era, Azeri historians were forced to link Azeri history to Persian Medes, whose appearance in Iran and the southern Caucasus dates back to the ninth century BC. In the post-Stalin era, this theory gave way to one which linked the Azeris' origins to the Atropathenes and the Caucasian Albanians.[40] (The Atropathenes were the descendants of the Medes in southern Azerbaijan. Among the early Christians, the Caucasian Albanians emerged in northern Azerbaijan after 500 BC and established various Christian kingdoms until the eighth century AD.[41]) By the early 1970s, however, the Turkic role in Azeri history had begun to be admitted, so that until the Gorbachev era the Azerbaijani historiography based Azeri identity on a combination of the Medes, the Atropathenes, the Albanians and the Turkic settlers, a formula which helped prevent the emergence of an all-Turkic historiography.[42]

Yet this construction of Azeri identity proved useful to both Baku and Moscow in their policy toward Iran. During most of the Soviet Union's existence, Moscow supported Baku's irredentist claims on northern Iran by arguing that people in both northern and southern Azerbaijan were of a stock closely related to the ancient Atropathenes, and not to the Persians. Since irredentism appealed to the Azeri people as a whole, Baku was only too delighted to play along. The fact that Moscow pursued an irredentist policy toward northern Iran, and that many prominent leaders of the 1945–6 Azerbaijan Republic (in northern Iran) took refuge in Baku and assumed prominent positions in the AzSSR CP, made the claim that greater Azerbaijan was an historical entity a mainstream idea. Hence, unlike the Central Asian peoples, the Azerbaijanis could more easily combine loyalty to the Soviet state with Azerbaijani nationalism, including irredentism.

Baku made use of the same theory to claim that the Armenians living in the mountainous Karabakh (Nagorno-Karabakh) region were not of Armenian stock, but were descendants of the Caucasian Albanians.[43] Accordingly, both the Azeri and the Armenian populations of Karabakh were supposed to have stronger links with Azeris of the Republic of Azerbaijan than with the Armenians of the Republic of Armenia. During the mid-1980s, members of the nascent nationalist elite (for instance, Abulfaz Elchibey) even claimed that the Albanians were of Turkic origin, and hence laid claim to most of the southern Caucasus.[44]

After Stalin's death in 1953, and especially after Khrushchev's 1956 denunciation of Stalinism, Baghirov and his allies were accused of collaborating with Stalin's henchman Beria and of engaging in conspiracy and terrorist activities, and were charged with the very counter-revolutionary activities that they themselves had used to get rid of undesirables. He and others were tried in the Supreme Soviet Military Court in 1956 and were then executed. Baghirov's death and the post-Stalinist relaxation meant the rehabilitation of many native communists, including Nariman Narimanov, who began to be hailed as a true Leninist. A number of banned literary figures were also rehabilitated, among them the poet Mikhail Mushfiq and the playwright Husein Javid, whose works were nevertheless considered too polemical to publish.[45]

The post-Stalin first secretaries of the AzCP pursued policies which permitted more ethno-cultural expression as sanctioned by Moscow. The administrations of Imam Dashdemiroglu Mustafaev (1954–9), Veli Yusufoglu Akhundov (1959–69) and Haydar Aliev (1969–82) implemented policies which responded favourably to ethnocultural demands, made Azeri nationality more pronounced and consolidated the Azeri ethno-linguistic community into an Azeri nation.[46]

Unlike Baghirov, Mustafaev was not a strong leader, but he

succeeded in making Azeri Turkish the official language of the Azerbaijan Republic, and his policy of allowing Azeri migrants from rural areas to settle in Baku, making it an overwhelmingly Azeri city, also favoured indigenous nationality. Mustafaev's opposition to the 1958 language law, which made the learning of a native language optional in schools where the language of the curriculum was Russian, led to his removal after being labelled 'nationalist'.[47] (Prior to 1958, native languages in Russian schools were compulsory as a 'second language' for the natives. The new law led to a more widespread use of Russian.)

Mustafaev's successor, Akhundov (1959–69), implemented the law, but turned a blind eye to low-key literary 'nationalist' works, although he made extensive use of Marxist–Leninist rhetoric.[48] His entourage included the Azerbaijan Communist Party (AzCP) third secretary, Kurbanov, who insisted on delivering speeches to the soviet CP Central Committee in Azeri Turkish. Nevertheless, neither he nor his predecessor could be considered anti-Moscow, and they pursued flexible and accommodating policies towards Moscow in return for which Moscow ignored – deliberately at times, by default at other times – the resurgence of nationalism.

Encouraged by Moscow's lack of interest in the republics' day-to-day affairs as long as they met the production quotas, curbed dissent and paid lip-service to the official ideology, Akhundov tolerated the ever-widening room for manoeuvre of the Azeri literati and historians, who were in a quiet, painstaking and successful process of reclaiming Azerbaijan's past. It should be mentioned that, though Khrushchev was keen on ideological correctness, his de-Stalinization campaign meant that the republics could take issue with Stalin's misdeeds, which quite often acquired anti-Russian characteristics in non-Russian republics.[49]

Akhundov was an ally of former KGB boss Aleksandr Shelepin – Leonid Brezhnev's rival for the party leadership – so when Brezhnev became general secretary of the Soviet CP in 1964, the writing was on the wall for Akhundov. He was accused of corruption, influence-peddling and cover-ups for corruption in Sovkhoz and Kolkhozes, charges which had also been brought against his predecessor. In 1969, Akhundov was replaced by Haydar Aliev, a former head of the KGB in Azerbaijan, who made Akhundov vice-president of the Azerbaijan Academy of Sciences, signifying his demotion.[50]

Aliev, like his predecessor, fought corruption and used Marxist–Leninist rhetoric, but he allowed the continuation of the Azeri cultural revival, provided it was done quietly. Under Aliev, Azeri intellectuals were able to publish books and articles reacquainting Azeris with their past (or imagined past), traditions and culture. Historians were obliged to be more timid because Aliev did not want discussion of the Bolshevization of Azerbaijan, the 1918–20 period of independence, or the Musavat Party. Instead they focused on the distant past, including the period between the eleventh and nineteenth centuries.[51] The literary journals became bolder during the 1970s, and they published articles on the national *Dada Gorgud* epic, on the poets Seyld Nesimi (1369–1417), Mehmed Fuzuli (1498–1556), Shahriyar (1906–88) and on other representatives of the Turco-Persian literary heritage.[52]

Aliev's era can be characterized as one of 'more discipline, more production'. Sizeable increases in industrial and agricultural output were achieved and corruption and bribery were drastically curtailed while ideological orthodoxy and the role of the party were emphasized. He toed the Moscow line on such issues as stressing Russian-language-learning during the 1970s after Brezhnev demanded better Russian-teaching in the non-Slavic republics.[53]

Yet Aliev also tolerated national and cultural revival to the extent that they were sanctioned by Moscow. His era witnessed phenomena such as the transfer of national poet Husein Javid's remains from Siberia to Baku.[54] A few decades earlier such an action would have brought Moscow's wrath down on him but he did not risk much in doing it during the Brezhnev era. Moreover, such acts as the burial of Javid in Baku probably had Soviet leadership's overall blessing, although they may not have been well versed in specific cases. Aliev's magnanimous behaviour was made possible by Brezhnev's policy of allowing the republics to make peace with their past by rectifying some of the most dramatic errors, if not crimes, committed under Stalin.

Aliev can be considered fortunate, because Azerbaijan borders Armenia and Georgia, two republics in which nationalist expression was greater and Moscow's tolerance of it higher. Azerbaijan benefited from Moscow's apparent wish to appear equidistant from each Transcaucasian republic. Whereas Central Asians were able to declare the titular language of their republics as state languages only in 1989, the Azeris enjoyed that right as early as the late 1950s, together with Armenia and Georgia.[55] Similarly, when in April 1978 Georgia – with Moscow's prodding – planned to remove this provision from its constitution, Georgian nationalists took to the streets, and Tblisi had to cancel the plan. (The change would have given Russian a state language status equal to that of Georgian.) Preparations were under way in Armenia and Azerbaijan for a similar change, but they were also cancelled.[56]

Despite the similarities, illegal dissident nationalism appeared in Georgia and Armenia, but it was practically non-existent in Azerbaijan until the late 1980s. The same is true of public nationalist demonstrations. On 24 April 1965 Armenians illegally demonstrated to mark the fiftieth anniversary of the genocide of Armenians by Ottoman Turks, and first secretary Zakov Zarobian chose not to use force to disperse them.[57] Although Moscow sacked him in 1966, there was no witch-hunt for the demonstrators. In Azerbaijan, such a demonstration never occurred. The reason may be that, unlike other people under colonial rule, the Azeri intellectual elite did not express their national aspirations by being assertive and by rejecting the political system. Partly as a result of unique Soviet conditions, which included tight control and centralization, the Azeris chose to use flexibility and accommodation within the system in order to protect their national resilience. Therefore, the lack of *samizdat* activity in Azerbaijan as well as in the other Soviet Muslim republics is not surprising. The Azeris and Central Asians argued privately that they were not as openly assertive as the Armenians or the Georgians because Moscow was more fearful of and less tolerant towards Muslim dissidents. Whatever the reason, through subtle dissidence, the Azeris nevertheless quietly succeeded in reclaiming their past.[58]

As mentioned above, the revival of history was done cautiously and literary and historical works which were too critical of the regime were not published. Among important publications a 1960 novel by Qurban Said (pseudonym of Yusif Vazir Chamanzaminli) about Vagýf (1717–97), who was the chief vizier of Karabakh's Khan Ibrahim. A diplomat of the independent Azerbaijani republic and a Musavat member, Chamanzaminli (1887–1943) wrote a more famous novel, *Ali and Nino*, in which he criticized Moscow's destruction of Azerbaijan's independence in 1920. He left Azerbaijan in 1920 but returned in 1926 and led a quiet life until his death in 1943. Although he was rehabilitated in 1960, *Ali and Nino* was still too risky for the indigenous Azeri leadership, and it was not published until 1990.[59]

The works of Ahmad Ağaoğlu, a prominent pan-Turkist member of the Musavat government of 1918–20 who had escaped to Turkey, where he died in 1939, were also considered too bold, and hence not published. And despite his rehabilitation in the 1980s, his role in the 1918–20 Musavat government was not mentioned in references to him; only his literary works were mentioned. Huseinzadeh Ali (Turan) (1864–1940), also a pan-Turkist, was rehabilitated in the late 1980s but his works were not published.[60]

The Azeri journals also became bolder in the 1970s. In literary and historical journals, such topics as the *Dada Gorgud* epic and the various aspects of the Azerbaijani classics by, among others, Fuzuli and Nasimi were published.[61] In the 1970s, many books were published on the archaeology and architecture of the premodern era and on medieval poetry. Starting in the late 1970s, nineteenth- and early-twentieth-century literature was extensively examined.[62] By the late 1980s, the journals had become bolder still. In 1988 a pro-Musavat poet, Muhammad Hadi (1879–1920) was rehabilitated, and a few of his poems were published, though the journal in which they appeared noted that he had been misled by Musavat's nationalism. In 1988, even the president of the short-lived independent Azerbaijan, Mehmet Emin Rasulzadeh, was the subject of an article in *Edebiyyat va Injasanat*. The author, M. Ismaylov, called for more impartial treatment of Rasulzadeh's role in history, but he did not venture to demand more.[63]

The Significance of Karabakh

The eruption of the Karabakh dispute in 1988 did much to transform the subtle revival of nationalism into an open popular challenge to Soviet rule in Azerbaijan. Although initially the AzCP hoped to deal with the problem through cooperation with Moscow, the Armenian Communist Party's (ACP) embracing of Armenian nationalist demands, and Gorbachev's inability to cope with the crisis, forced the AzCP to tolerate the activities of the Azerbaijani Popular Front (APF). This enabled the APF to organize mass demonstrations, to use the media freely, and by 1990 to establish a parallel administration to implement policies. This shift in the political equilibrium was reflected in the editorial policy of the Azerbaijani Writers' Association's literary journal, *Azerbaijan*. Whereas the journal had contributed to the nationalist revival in the 1960s and 1970s, the most daring step it took then was to publish articles on the history and literature of the early twentieth century. In 1988, however, it began publishing articles on Karabakh's history, Islam, the APF's demands, and the liquidation of Azeri communists in the 1930s. In 1990 Lenin and the twenty-six Baku commissars began to be criticized.[64]

The Nagorno-Karabakh problem changed the political climate of Azerbaijan to a great extent. The Azeris, after the start of the hostilities in 1988, closely followed developments in the Nagorno-Karabakh Autonomous Oblast (NKAO) and Armenia, where the communist political leadership increasingly cooperated with the nationalist ANM. The emergence of the ANM was primarily due to Gorbachev's decision to break the monopoly of the all-Union and republican Communist Parties and allow multi-candidate elections in 1988. In both the Transcaucasus and the Baltics, mass movements (or popular fronts) emerged and put forward ethnocultural demands.[65] In short, democratization in the border republics meant more freedom for nationalist expression.

After the start of the cooperation between the ANM and the ACP, the ANM used mass demonstration and its free access to the media to call for the 'return' of the NKAO to Armenia.[66] The events in Armenia were not lost on the Azeris. Unlike its counterpart in Armenia, the AzCP had not even considered acting against Moscow's wishes and tolerating domestic political dissent. The emergence of the NKAO dispute forced the AzCP to turn a blind eye to the yet-to-be established Azerbaijan Popular Front's (APF) activities. Nevertheless, the AzCP still hoped to regain the NKAO through cooperation with Moscow, which was expected to support Baku against the anti-Moscow nationalist Armenians.

For the Azeri population at large, the possibility of the loss of the NKAO led to a popular emphasis on the republic's sovereignty vis-à-vis Moscow. The newly formed APF could operate in the republic freely in 1989, while the AzCP only months earlier had proscribed all political activities. In short, the 'national dispute' led to popular participation in politics and the emergence of various opposition parties, including the APF. It was interesting to see the wide-ranging participation of a largely apolitical population in demonstrations and political meetings.

Developments in the NKAO and Armenia were almost instantaneously felt, creating reaction in Azerbaijan. In 1987 the nationalists started to collect signatures in Armenia and the NKAO in support of a declaration demanding the unification of Karabakh with Armenia.

Interestingly, the Armenian National Movement, which spearheaded the campaign, had initially been called the Karabakh Committee, symbolizing the significance of Karabakh for Armenian nationalism.[67] In 1988, intercommunal clashes began and they led to ethnic cleansing, first by the Armenians in Armenia and the NKAO, and in due course by the Azeris. By the end of 1988, there were already 100,000 Azeri refugees (Armenian refugees at this stage were about one-tenth of that figure). Ironically, some of the Azeri refugees took part in the anti-Armenian massacre in the city of Sumgait in February 1988.[68]

The events that followed contributed to increasing popular participation in politics, the emergence of various opposition parties, political turnover, and eventually the replacement of the pro-Moscow old guard by anti-Russian nationalists. In November 1988, the Azeris discovered that the Armenian leadership of the NKAO had allocated six hectares of Topkhane, a national park, to Armenia for the construction of an aluminium plant and resort facilities. Topkhane is near Shusha, the only large town in the NKAO predominantly populated by Azeris, and the plan caused immediate public uproar in Azerbaijan, because the Azeris linked the Topkhane project to the ethnic cleansing in the NKAO.[69] During late November and early December 1988, demonstrators occupied Baku's huge Lenin Square for two weeks. Their grievances were perceived by all as so legitimate that the first secretary of the AzCP, Abdurrahman Vazirov, had to attend one of the demonstrations and listen to the demands of his outraged countrymen.[70] In due course, the AzCP cancelled the NKAOs decision to allocate the Topkhane land to Armenia.

In January 1989, the USSR Supreme Soviet decided to relieve the Armenian-dominated NKAO Soviet of its duties and established direct rule over the NKAO. This move was balanced when the new Moscow-appointed administrator of the NKAO, Aleksandr Volskiy, made some pro-Armenian gestures, such as granting the longstanding Armenian (NKAO) demand that Armenian TV be relayed to the NKAO via special transmitters. This in turn led to further demonstrations by the Azeris.[71]

In spring 1989, when the controversy in and around the NKAO was in full swing, the APF was established. It was an umbrella organization bringing together the urban and the rural, the secular as well as the Islamic radicals. Many AzCP members and non-AzCP intellectuals, social democrats, and pan-Turkists joined. There were the minimalists, calling for more sovereignty within the USSR, and also the maximalists, who demanded independence and unification with Iranian Azerbaijan.[72] The APF programme, however, was a compromise which included mostly moderate demands. It called for the 'democratization of society', respect for human and civil rights, and Azerbaijan's political, economic and cultural sovereignty within the USSR. It demanded the restoration of historical place names and the development of economic and cultural ties with Iranian Azerbaijan. It also, like those of many popular fronts elsewhere in the USSR, called for an end to Azerbaijan's economic exploitation by Moscow and equality in terms of trade. Blaming the republic's environmental calamities on Moscow, the APF – perhaps with Topkhane in mind – called for the protection of the environment.[73]

Moscow's inability to keep developments under control, no matter what it tried, contributed to a gradual loss of face by the AzCP, which the public identified with Moscow. In order to cope with its marginalization in the socio-political life of the republic, the AzCP acted on 16 September 1989 to cancel Moscow's direct rule (through the Volskiy Commission) and to re-establish Azerbaijani rule over the NKAO. In response, Gorbachev abolished the Volskiy Commission himself and returned power to the mostly Armenian NKAO Soviet, ordering the local troops to act under Moscow's direct orders. The AzCP was quick to suspend these provisions, placing the oblast under the control of the 'Organizational Committee' headed by the second secretary of the AzCP, Victor Polyanichko, an ethnic Russian. The committee did not include any Armenians from the NKAO.[74] In addition, on 23 september 1989 the Azerbaijan Supreme Soviet declared Azerbaijan 'a sovereign republic' within the USSR and resolved that all Union laws had to be approved by the soviet in order to be enforced in the republic.[75] Both these acts were part of the APF programme, and therefore, instead of augmenting the AzCP's vanishing authority, they probably made the APF more popular, as later events suggest.

In late 1989, the APF began regularly to attend the Azerbaijan Supreme Soviet sessions, and its leaders made speeches to air their remaining demands, and on 5 October 1989, the APF was officially recognized.[76] It also got involved in local government. Local AzCP officials in Jalilabad, Lenkoran and Kachmaz were replaced at the insistence of the APF, and it contributed to the supreme soviet's decision to replace the name of the city of Kirovabad with its historical name, Ganja.[77]

In December 1989, Azeris mostly belonging to Nemat Panakhov's extremist wing of the APF burned the border posts between Iran and Nakhichevan (in the south-west), and in early 1990 the Turkey–Nakhichevan and the Iran–Lenkoran (in the south-east) border posts were damaged.[78] December 1990 saw the Social Democrats, including Leila Yunusova, split from the APF,[79] and Armenian and Azeri conscripts began to desert their units in the Soviet Army and to trickle into their respective republics. They were to constitute the backbone of the national units, some of which took part in the Karabakh hostilities.

On 20 january 1990, Moscow took a drastic step to prevent power from slipping through the hands of the AzCP into those of the APF: the Red Army invaded Baku, causing hundreds of casualties, according to most accounts. During the week preceding the invasion, APF paramilitary units had taken over the local government and police responsibilities in localities throughout the country.[80] The invasion was therefore considered a last-ditch effort by Moscow to stop the APF taking full control of the republic and leading it out of the Soviet Union.

The Azeris saw the invasion differently. However impartial Moscow might have been in the Armeno–Azeri conflict until then, the Azeris' verdict on the invasion was harsh. It was widely believed that Moscow was siding with Armenia and that it had invaded Baku, but not Yerevan – where nationalist agitation was also strong – in order to enable the Armenians to secure the unification of the NKAO with Armenia.

The popular outcry against the invasion was so strong that the next day the communist-dominated Azerbaijan Supreme Soviet – with the participant of the APF, by now outlawed by Moscow – resolved that the Red Army had entered Baku by force and without an invitation from the supreme soviet. It declared the invasion illegal and unconstitutional, and called for the immediate withdrawal of all Soviet troops. On 22 January 1990, those killed in the invasion were given state funerals at the newly named *Azatlik* (Freedom) Cemetery.[81] Official Azerbaijani radio and television invited people to attend the 'martyrs'' funerals, which were organized by the Baku City Soviet Executive Committee, the APF and the Muslim Board of the Transcaucasus. That day and on following days many AzCF members ceremonially burned their membership cards.[82]

In spite of the Soviet invasion, the retrieval of the past resumed in February 1990, when the AzCP Central Committee decided to erect a monument in Moscow dedicated to the Azerbaijani (or Turkish) classical poet Elyas Nizami on the 850th anniversary of his birth in 1141.[83] The Moscow City Soviet Executive Committee approved Baku's suggestion of the location of the monument. Moreover, in the same month Azerbaijan's Academy of Sciences began preparations to adopt the Latin alphabet.[84]

In summer 1990, the first Azerbaijani group left for the Hajj to Mecca.[85] During the year dozens of mosques were reopened and an Islamic journal began to be published. In December 1990 Kirov University was renamed Mehmet Emin Rasulzadeh University (after the president of the 1918–20 independent Azerbaijan), and the country was renamed the Republic of Azerbaijan.[86] During the February 1991 opening of the Azerbaijan Supreme Soviet, Allahshukur Pashazade, head of the Spiritual Directorate of the Muslims of the Transcaucasus, read prayers, and there was a one-minute silence for the victims of the Soviet invasion.[87]

In September 1990 Azerbaijan Supreme Soviet elections were held, the first during the Soviet era in which the opposition Democratic bloc (including the APF) participated. The opposition won twenty-six of the 350 seats, despite many election irregularities and government hinderance of opposition campaigning. September also saw the APF's adoption of a new programme, just over a year after the adoption of its first one. The new programme was more radical in that it called for independence, whereas the first one had only demanded more sovereignty within the USSR. It also called for democratic elections and legal reforms to guarantee the independence of judges and the rights of the accused. It foresaw a total overhaul of the socio-economic system of Azerbaijan, promising to introduce a free-market economy, and the 'de-partyzation' and 'de-ideologization' of the state and society.[88]

Whereas the APF was able to put forward maximalist goals, the AzCP was handicapped by its subservience to Moscow, although in recent months it had challenged Moscow's policy regarding the NKAO. In April 1990, the new first secretary of the AzCP, Ayaz Mutalibov, stated that the AzCP had lost credibility because of its inability to adopt policies independent of Moscow. He said that under his leadership the AzCP was determined to protect national interests and that Moscow should allow the AzCP more latitude to form its own policies.[89]

As if to justify Mutalibov's sincerity, the newly elected but still communist-dominated Azerbaijan Supreme Soviet adopted independent Azerbaijan's flag as the new national flag, and the day of the establishment of independent Azerbaijan (28 May 1918) was declared National Revival Day. Furthermore, the words of Azerbaijan's national anthem were changed to reflect the country's nationalist mood.[90]

Another example of how the NKAO issue changed the political discourse is the debate between the AzCP and the APF regarding the new union treaty Gorbachev wanted to sign with the republics before the August 1991 coup against him scuttled it. The APF and other opposition groups opposed the treaty, regarding it as another means of continuing Moscow's domination over Azerbaijan.[91] Mutalibov, however, considered it necessary, because if Armenia joined it and Azerbaijan did not, he said, Moscow might support the Armenian claim to Karabakh.[92] Since the Democratic bloc had only 26 votes in the supreme soviet, it could not prevent the issue being put to the public, in a referendum, held on 17 march 1991. Despite the APF's strong support in the streets, the majority of the population voted in favour of the new treaty,[93] which the Azerbaijan Supreme Soviet approved on 26 June 1991.

After the abortive anti-Gorbachev coup in August 1991, the new treaty was no longer on anyone's agenda. In October 1991 Mutalibov was quick to support Gorbachev's new brain child, the economic union agreement, when he stressed that it was necessary because it would help Azerbaijan to keep the NKAO.[94] However, the refusal of the Russian Republic, under its new president, Boris Yeltsin, to join the economic union meant the end of the idea. Using the same argument, in December 1991 Mutalibov signed the Commonwealth of Independent States (CIS) collective security treaty, but the supreme soviet refused to ratify it, arguing that there was no sign that the CIS would restore Azeri rule over the NKAO.[95] Undeterred, Mutalibov went to Tashkent to sign the treaty on 15 May 1992, which led to an APF-organized armed revolt and the overthrow of Mutalibov.[96] In the June 1992 presidential elections, Abulfaz Elchibey, the APF candidate who seemed to offer most hope of the return of the NKAO to Azeri rule, was elected in a landslide victory.

Conclusion

In this essay I have suggested that there were strong links between the growth of Azerbaijani nationalism and such factors as the post-Stalin historical and literary nationalist revival; the national elite's tolerance of subtle nationalist expression in the form of the rediscovery of the past; the relative relaxation of controls over political expression during Gorbachev's later years; and the gradual escalation of the tension between Azerbaijan and Armenia over Karabakh.

The existence of these links is explained by reference to socio-political events, international developments, articles and reports in Azerbaijani journals and newspapers pointing to the retrieval of the past, and policy decisions and the statements and arguments of the various parties involved in Azerbaijani politics between 1988 and 1991. The official and unofficial publications are to a great extent indicators of the people's views. More importantly, however, the intellectual elite who wrote for those publications tried to mould public opinion. Links between the events and the views, arguments and theories of that elite show that the assumptions I outlined at the beginning of the essay are valid: the articles written by the elite evolved from being regime-supportive and apolitical to being anti-regime and radical–nationalist within the short period between 1985 and 1991.[97]

There is ample evidence that the first three of the above-mentioned factors, namely the post-Stalin revival, the tolerance of subtle nationalist expression, and Gorbachev's relaxation of controls were responsible for the emergence of a more liberal atmosphere in Azerbaijani historical and literary publications in the mid-1980s. Issues including Moscow's disregard for the environment, emphasis on cotton monoculture, the neglected use of the Azerbaijani language and excessive Russification, the excessive utilization of Azerbaijan's oil for all-Union needs, and the unfavourable terms of trade for the Azerbaijani products all began to be freely discussed in the mid-1980s. Yet the Azerbaijan-Armenian dispute over Nagorno-Karabakh and Moscow's inability or unwillingness to arbitrate drastically changed the political discourse. Starting in 1988, Moscow's policies regarding nationalities, the lack of Azeri sovereignty, and Moscow's perceived tilt toward Yerevan began to be widely discussed.

Not only during the Abulfaz Elçibey presidency (June 1992–June 1993), but also under President Aliev, the themes of independence and sovereignty have been constantly in the forefront of the political discourse. Given the fact that since independence Azerbaijan has been engaged in a virtual interstate war with Armenia and has lost 20 per cent of its territory, this is not surprising.

It is also a fact, however, that the once all-powerful APF no longer enjoys its former popularity, partly because of its failure in 1992–3 to recover the Armenian-occupied territories, but also because these days the Azeri people are more preoccupied with economic hardships, and so are less interested in the APF's rhetoric. This is not to say, however, that Aliev, who was initially perceived to have little interest in the nationalist discourse, did not engage in nation-building. Although he – unlike the APF – avoided anti-Russian or anti-Iranian rhetoric, he has distanced Azerbaijan from Russia by refusing to allow Russian troops to return, either as peace-keepers in Karabakh or as border guards. By manipulating ethnic or national symbols, Aliev has tried to present himself as a national leader in pursuit of national goals. Despite the fact that street demonstrations – which were commonplace during 1988–91 – ceased under Aliev, nationalist discourse is still more widespread in Azerbaijan than in any other Turkic state. This state of affairs is primarily due to the simmering Karabakh dispute and the continuing occupation of Azeri territory by Armenian forces. Hence, it would not be much of a prophesy to say that the persistence of the Armeno–Azeri conflict will ensure that any Azeri president will try not to look too soft on the Karabakh – read 'national' – issue.

Notes

1 Ernest Gellner, *Thought and Change* (Chicago: University of Chicago Press, 1964), p. 164.
2 Alexander J. Motyl, *Sovietology, Rationality, Nationality: Coming to Grips with Nationalism in the USSR* (New York: Columbia University Press, 1990), p. 55.
3 See Eugene Kamenka, 'Nationalism: Ambiguous Legacies and Contingent Futures', *Political Studies*, vol. 41 (1993), special issue, pp. 78–92.
4 See Mark Hagopian's description of nationalism as an ideal in *The Ideals and Ideologies of Modern Politics* (New York: Longman, 1985), pp. 2, 70.
5 Ibid.
6 For various views see Ian Bremmer and Ras Taras, eds., *Nations and Politics in the Soviet Successor States* (New York: Cambridge University Press, 1993); Ronald Grigor Suny, *The Revenge of the Past: Nationalism, Revolution, and the Collapse of the Soviet Union* (Stanford, CA: Stanford University Press, 1993); Motyl, *Sovietology, Rationality, Nationality*.
7 I borrowed this categorization from Suny, *The Revenge of the Past*, pp. 102–22.

8 William Fierman, 'The Soviet Transformation of Central Asia', in Fierman, ed., *Soviet Central Asia: The Failed Transformation* (Boulder, CO: Westview Press, 1991).

9 See Alexander J. Motyl, *Thinking Theoretically About Soviet Nationalities: History and Comparison in the Study of the USSR* (New York: Columbia University Press, 1992).

10 Ibid.

11 Tom Nairn, 'Beyond Big Brother', *New Statesman and Society*, vol. 3, no. 105 (15 June 1990), p. 31.

12 Audrey L. Altstadt, 'Decolonization in Azerbaijan', in Donald Schwartz and Razmik Panossian, eds., *Nationalism in History* (Toronto: University of Toronto Press, 1994).

13 Michael Hechter, *Internal Colonialism* (Berkeley, CA: University of California Press, 1975), p. 49.

14 See John A. Armstrong, 'The Autonomy of Ethnic Identity: Historic Cleavages and Nationality Relations in the USSR', in Alexander J. Motyl, ed., *Thinking Theoretically*, pp. 59–71.

15 Karl Deutsch, *Nationalism and Social Communication* (New York, 1966).

16 Benedict Anderson, *Imagined Communities: Reflections on the Origin and Spread of Nationalism* (New York: Verso, 1991).

17 Partha Chatterjee, *The Nation and Its Fragments: Colonial and Postcolonial Histories* (Princeton, NJ: Princeton University Press, 1993), p. 6.

18 Rupert Emerson, *From Empire to Nation* (1969); Carl J. Friedrich, *Man and His Government* (1963).

19 Ernest Gellner, *Nations and Nationalism* (Ithaca, NY: Cornell University Press, 1983).

20 See Anthony D. Smith, *Theories of Nationalism*, 2nd edn (London: 1983).

21 See James Critchlow, 'Islam and Nationalism in Soviet Central Asia', in Pedro Ramet, ed., *Religion and Nationalism in Soviet and East European Politics* (Durham, NC: Duke University Press, 1989, pp. 198–219).

22 Miroslav Hroch, *Social Preconditions of National Revival in Europe* (Cambridge: Cambridge University Press, 1985), pp. 22–3.

23 Peter Palmer Ekeh, 'Colonialism and the Two Publics in Africa', *Comparative Studies in Society and History*, vol. 17 (1975), p. 108.

24 See Christopher Clapham, *Third World Politics* (Madison, WI: University of Wisconsin Press, 1985).

25 Chantal Lemercier Quelqujay, 'Islam and Identity in Azerbaijan', *Central Asian Survey*, vol. 3 (1984), no. 2, pp. 33, 50; Audrey L. Altstadt, 'Azerbaijani Turks' Response to Russian Conquests', *Studies in Comparative Communism*, vol. 19 (1986), nos. 3–4, pp. 267–86.

26 Suny, *The Revenge of the Past*, p. 22.

27 Ronald G. Suny, *The Baku Commune, 1917–1918: Class and Nationality*

in the Russian Revolution (Princeton, NJ: Princeton University Press, 1972), p. 14.

28 Tadeusz Swietochowski, *Russian Azerbaijan, 1905–1920: The Shaping of National Identity in a Muslim Community* (New York: Cambridge University Press, 1985), p. 60.

29 Ibid, p. 69.

30 Altstadt, 'Azerbaijani Turks' Response', p. 271.

31 Audrey L. Altstadt, 'O Patria Mia: National Conflict in Mountainous Karabakh', in Raymond Duncan and Paul Holman, eds., *Ethnic Nationalism & Regional Conflicts: The Former Soviet Union and Yugoslavia* (Boulder, CO: Westview Press, 1994), p. 129.

32 Audrey L. Altstadt, *The Azerbaijani Turks: Power and Identity Under Russian Rule* (Stanford, CA: Hoover Institution Press, 1992), pp. 47, 72–3.

33 Swietochowski, *Russian Azerbaijan*, pp. 52, 88–92.

34 Ibid, pp. 163–5.

35 Ibid, pp. 165–7.

36 Altstadt, *The Azerbaijani Turks*, p. 134.

37 Ibid, pp. 131–2, 141–2.

38 Ibid, p. 152.

39 Ibid, p. 161.

40 Stephen H. Astourian, 'In Search of their Forefathers: National Identity and the Historiography and Politics of Armenian and Azerbaijani Ethnogenesis', in Donald Schwartz and Razmik Panossian, eds., *Nationalism and History* (Toronto: University of Toronto Press, 1994), p. 55.

42 Alstadt, 'O Patria Mia', p. 113.

43 See 'Albaniya', in *Azerbaijan Soviet Ensiklopediyasi* (Baku: [n.d.]), p. 216.

44 See Bakhtiyar Vahabzada and Sulayman Aliyarov's letter in 'Redaksiyamizin Pochtudan', *Azerbaijan* (Baku), no. 2 (1988), pp. 188–9; Mehmet Emin Rasulzadeh's 1928 article 'Gafgasiya Turklari', reprinted in *Azerbaijan*, no. 12 (1990), p. 143; Abulfaz Aliev (Elchibey), 'Tarikhin Darin Gatlarina Doghru', *Azerbaijan*, no. 10 (1989), p. 130.

45 Altstadt, *The Azerbaijani Turks*, p. 169; Abbasali Djavadi, 'Glasnost and Soviet Azerbaijani Literature', *Central Asian Survey*, vol. 9 (1990), no. 1, p. 98.

46 See Steven L. Burg, 'Nationality Elites and Political Change in the Soviet Union', in Lumobyr Hajda and Mark Beissinger, eds., *The Nationalities Factor in Soviet Politics and Society* (Boulder, CO: Westview Press, 1990), pp. 24–42; Shireen T. Hunter, *The Transcaucasus in Transition* (Washington, DC: Center for Strategic and International Studies, 1994), p. 13.

47 Stephen E. Hegaard, 'Nationalism in Azerbaijan in the Era of Brezhnev', in George W. Simmonds, ed., *Nationalism in the USSR and Eastern*

Europe in the Era of Brezhnev and Kosygin (Detroit, MI: University of Detroit Press, 1977), p. 191.

48 Azade Ayşe Rorlich, 'Not by History Alone: The Retrieval of the Past among the Tatars and the Azeris', *Central Asian Survey*, vol. 3 (1984), no. 2, p. 91.

49 Ibid.

50 Ibid, p. 93.

51 Djavadi, 'Glasnost and Soviet Azerbaijani Literature', pp. 100–2.

52 See Ziya Buniatov, *Gosudartsvo Atabekov Azerbaidzhana, 1136–1225 gody* (Baku, 1978); Sh. Farzaliev's monograph on Khasan Bek Rumlu's *Akhsan at-Attavarith (The Best of Histories)* in Sh. Farzaliev, *Akhan at-Tavarith Khasan beka Rumlu kak istochnik po istorii Azerbaidzhana* (Baku, 1981); A Jafarzada, *Baku–1051* (Baku, 1981), p. 262.

53 Suny, 'Transcaucasia', pp. 232–41.

54 Husein Javid was a native communist who was accused of jadidism during the Stalinist purges. He died in Siberia in 1941. See S. Enders Wimbush, 'Why Geidar Aliev', *Central Asian Survey*, vol. 1 (1983), no. 4, p. 5.

55 See Mahmut Ismailov's article in *Azerbaijan* (Baku, 1986), no. 6.

56 Alstadt, 'O Patria Mia', p. 113.

57 Suny, *The Revenge of the Past*, p. 122.

58 Raoul Motika, 'Glasnost in der Sowjetrepublik Aserbaidschan am Beispiel der Zeitschrift Azerbaijan', *Orient* (Hamburg), vol. 32 (1991), no. 4, p. 576.

59 Rorlich, 'Not by History Alone', p. 96.

60 See Altstadt, *The Azerbaijani Turks*, pp. 185–91; Rorlich, 'Not by History Alone'.

61 See Aliyarov, 'Redaksiyamizin', p. 182.

62 Motika, 'Glasnost', p. 580.

63 Ibid, p. 581.

64 *Central Asia and Caucasus Chronicle*, vol. 8 (1989), no. 5, p. 1.

65 Motyl, *Thinking Theoretically.*

66 Agence France-Presse, Paris, in English, in *Foreign Broadcast Information Service, Soviet Union* (hereafter *FBIS/SU*), 31 May 1988, p. 42.

67 See Yerevan International Service in Armenian, 26 February 1988, in FBIS/SU, 29 February 1988, p. 64.

68 *Bakinskiy Rabochiy* in Russian, 18 May 1988, p. 1.

69 *Pravda*, Moscow, in Russian, 21 November 1988, p. 4, in FBIS/SU, 21 November 1988, p. 59.

70 Baku Domestic Service in Azeri, 29 December 1988, in FBIS/SU, 30 December 1988, p. 37.

71 *Izvestiya*, Moscow, 21 january 1989, p. 1, in FBIS/SU, 23 January 1989, p. 62; International Service in Armenian, Yerevan, 12 March 1989, in FBIS/SU, 14 March 1989, p. 54.

72 *Baikskiy Rabochiy*, Baku, in Russian, 16 December 1989, p. 4, in FBIS/SU, 25 January 1990, p. 53.
73 For the APF programme, see *Central Asia and Caucasus Chronicle*, vol. 8 (1989), no. 4, pp. 7–9; Audrey L. Altstadt, 'Decolonization in Azerbaijan', pp. 101–2.
74 Baku Domestic Service in Azeri, 18 September 1989, in FBIS/SU, 19 September 1989, pp. 48–9.
75 *Central Asia and Caucasus Chronicle*, vol. 8 (1989), no. 5, p. 1.
76 Moscow Television Service in Russian, 5 October 1989, in FBIS/SU, 6 October 1989, p. 42.
77 In 1935 Ganja was renamed Kirovabad in honour of Sergey Kirov, who had served in the Transcaucasus. For the name change see Baku Domestic Service in Azeri, 30 December 1989, in FBIS/SU, 2 January 1990, p. 49.
78 Moscow Television Service in Russian, 2 January 1990, in FBIS/SU, 3 January 1990, p. 32.
79 Agence France-Presse, Paris, in English, 2 January 1990, in FBIS/SU, 2 January 1990, p. 47.
80 *Pravda*, Moscow, in Russian, 16 February 1990, p. 8, in FBIS/SU, 20 February 1990, pp. 83–7.
81 Baku Domestic Service in Azeri, 21 January 1990, in FBIS/SU, 22 January 1990, p. 101.
82 Moscow Television Service in Russian, 21 January 1990, in FBIS/SU, 22 January 1990, pp. 78–9.
83 Baku Domestic Service in Azeri, 10 February 1990, in FBIS/SU, 14 February 1990, p. 96.
84 *Central Asia and Caucasus Chronicle*, vol. 8 (1989), no. 5, p. 1.
85 Tass, Moscow, in English, 22 November 1990, in FBIS/SU, 29 November, 1990, p. 95.
86 Baku Domestic Service in Azeri, 21 January 1990, in FBIS/SU, 28 June 1990, p. 121.
87 *Tercüman*, Istanbul, 7 December 1990, p. 8; Tass International Service in Russian, Moscow, 5 February 1991, in FBIS/SU, 6 February 1991, p. 99.
88 See *Azadlyk*, Baku, 8 September 1990, in Audrey L. Altstadt, 'Baku 1991: One Year after Black January', *AACAR Bulletin*, vol. 4 (1991), no. 1, p. 8.
89 *Bakinskiy Rabochiy*, in Russian, 13 April 1990, p. 1, in FBIS/SU, 27 April 1990, p. 103.
90 *Rabochaya Tribuna*, in Russian, 20 February 1991, p. 2, in FBIS/SU, 25 February 1991, p. 92.
91 See *Azerbaijan*, Baku, 4 May 1990; *Azadlyk*, 22 November 1990.
92 Domestic Service in Russian, Moscow, 9 March 1991, in FBIS/SU, 11 March 1991, pp. 83–4.

93 See Agence France-Presse, Paris, 19 October 1991 in FBIS/SU, 21 October 1991, p. 91. If the referendum was not rigged, the Azeri voters agreed with the AzCP's thesis that, if Azerbaijan did not join the new union, Moscow might support Armenia's unification with Karabakh.

94 Mutalibov could not, however, prevent the declaration of independence in September 1991.

95 Radio Baku, in Azeri, 21 December 1991, in FBIS/SU, 27 December 1991, p. 63.

96 Hunter, *The Transcaucasian in Transition*, pp. 73–4.

97 The articles include Azamat Rustamov, 'Dada Gorkut'la Bagly Yer Adlary', *Elm va Hayat*, no. 9 (1987); Kamal Veliyev, 'Bir Daha Dada Gorgud Shairlari Hakkynda', *Azerbaijan*, no. 11 (1981); Mahmut Ismaylov, 'Tariximiz va Tadqiqatimyz', *Adabiyyat va Injasanat*, 15 July 1988; R. Allahverdiyev, 'Bashlyja Istimaqat Uzra', *Azerbaijan Kommunisti*, no. 9 (1986); Akif Huseynov, 'Nashrimiz va Kechmishimiz', *Azerbaijan*, no. 10 (1982); Zemfira Verdiyeva, 'Mavzumuz: Tarikhimiz, Abidalarimiz, Darsliklarimiz', *Azerbaijan*, no. 6 (1988); Mehmed Dadashzade, 'Dada Gorgud Dastanlarynda Azerbaijan Ethnografiyasýna Dair Bazi Malumatlar', *Azerbaijanyn Ethnografik Mechmuasi*, no. 3 (1977). Books which show the evolution include T. I. Hajiev and K. N. Veliyev, *Azerbaijan Dili Tarikhi: Ocherklar va Materiallar* (Baku: Maarif, 1983); Sabir Rustamkhanly, *Omur Kitaby* (Baku: Genjlik, 1988); *Azerbaijan Filologiya Masalalari*, vol. 2 (Baku: Institute of Philology, Azerbaijan Academy of Sciences, 1984); V. Allahverdiyev and S. Mehdiyev, *Azerbaijan Demokratik Respublikasý: Azerbaijan Hokumatý, 1918–1920* (Baku: Genchlik, 1990); Mirali Seidov, *Azerbaijan Khalgynyn Soikokunu Dushunarkan* (Baku: Yazychy, 1990); Ali Saladdin, *Azerbaijan She ri va Folklor, 19–20 Asrlar* (Baku: Elm, 1982).

3· Recasting Oneself, Rejecting the Other: Pan-Turkism and Iranian Nationalism

Touraj Atabaki

Twentieth-century historiography on nation–state correlation and nationalism has to a large extent been shaped by a eurocentric ethno-linguistic discourse, where 'ethnicity and language' become the central, increasingly the decisive or even the only, criteria of potential nationhood,[1] or as Karl Renner asserts:

> once a certain degree of European development has been reached, the linguistic and cultural communities of people, having silently matured throughout the centuries, emerge from the world of passive existence as people (*Passiver Volkheit*). They become conscious of themselves as a force with historical destiny. They demand control over the state, as the highest available instrument of power, and strive for their political self-determination. The birthday of the political idea of the nation and the birth-year of this new consciousness, is 1789, the year of the French Revolution.[2]

However, what this perception of the nation-state largely neglects is the fact that the construction of a bounded territorial entity (or what is generally referred to as nation-state-building) has often entailed components other than ethnic or linguistic bonds. Collective imagination, political allegiances, reconstructing and reinterpreting history, the invention of necessary historical traditions to justify and give coherence to the emerging modern state: all these are often major factors in bringing groups of people together and strengthening or even forming their common sense of identity and political solidarity.

In some cases the mere application of ancient, historically resonant names and traditions is enough to evoke a consensus of political legitimacy. Consequently, the social connotations of certain key socio-political phrases, as well as geographic terms, become an important element in reshaping the geographic boundaries of emerging sovereign states.

As far as Iran is concerned, it is widely argued that Iranian nationalism was born as a state ideology in the Reza Shah era, based on philological nationalism and as a result of his innovative success in creating a modern nation-state in Iran. However, what is often neglected is that Iranian nationalism has its roots in the political upheavals of the nineteenth century and the disintegration immediately following the Constitutional revolution of 1905–9. It was during this period that Iranism gradually took shape as a defensive discourse for constructing a bounded territorial entity – the 'pure Iran' standing against all others. Consequently, over time there emerged among the country's intelligentsia a political xenophobia which contributed to the formation of Iranian defensive nationalism. It is noteworthy that, contrary to what one might expect, many of the leading agents of the construction of an Iranian bounded territorial entity came from non-Persian-speaking ethnic minorities, and the foremost were the Azerbaijanis, rather than the nation's titular ethnic group, the Persians.

The intention of this essay is to throw further light on the complex origins of Iranian nationalism. While examining the various loyalties of the Iranian non-Persian intelligentsia, I shall sketch the measures adopted by such groups when defending their real or imagined identities against the early-twentieth-century irredentist ideology of neighbouring states.

The Outbreak of World War I

For many Iranians the thirteen months of 'lesser despotism' of June 1908–July 1909 which followed Muhammad 'Ali Shah's coup was the most crucial period of their country's constitutional history: the entire country, except for Azerbaijan, was subjugated to the new regime. By sending in the army and imposing economic restrictions, the central government strove to bring the Azerbaijanis, too, to their knees. However, while famine spread across the province, the Azerbaijani constitutionalists set up barricades in Tabriz and prepared to offer armed resistance. When the government in Tehran was eventually overthrown, the constitutionalists found themselves in a nearly unique position with the attention of the entire nation fixed on them. Gradually the belief arose among Iranians that, although the Constitutional Revolution had been born in Tehran, it had been baptized in Tabriz and the Constitution had no chance of surviving without Azerbaijan. Moreover, Azerbaijan was seen as the most important centre where any future progressive political changes would originate. This appraisal of the cardinal role played by the Azerbaijanis in restoring constitutionalism in Iran left Azerbaijani constitutionalists with a strong consciousness of being the protectors of the country's territorial integrity, a consciousness which still persists.

When World War I erupted, political chaos and confusion swept across Iran. Successive governments proved incapable of solving the country's escalating problems and implementing fundamental reforms. Indeed, not only did the outbreak of the war fail to stop political disintegration in Iran, but increased foreign pressure caused the long-standing rift in Iranian politics to widen. As early as October 1910, Britain had delivered an ultimatum to Iran concerning the security of southern Iran. In so doing, Britain set an example for the Russians to follow. Russian troops had already occupied the northern provinces. In November 1911 the tsarist government presented its own ultimatum to Iran, which amounted to nothing less than an attempt to reduce the north of the country to the status of a semi-dependent colony.[3] However, while the Iranian parliament, which enjoyed the support of the crowds in the street, resisted the Russian ultimatum, the fragile Iranian government decided to accept it and dissolve the parliament. This seemed the only effective measure available to the deputies in the face of the crisis that had arisen.[4] Meanwhile, the occupation of the north and south of Iran by Russian and British troops was to provoke the Ottoman forces to invade western and north-western Iran early in the war. If we add to this list of disasters the activities of German agents, especially among the southern tribes, we begin to get an idea of how impotent the Iranian government was during this period.

The Iranian government's reaction to the outbreak of the war was to declare Iran's strict neutrality in the *farman* of 1 November 1914. On the other hand, what sense was there in the government's announcing its neutrality when a sizeable part of Iran's territory was occupied by the Entente forces? When Mostowfi ol-Mamalik, the prime minister, approached the Russian authorities and asked that they withdraw their troops from Azerbaijan because their presence gave the Turks a pretext for invading Iran, 'the Russian minister appreciated the Iranian viewpoint but inquired what guarantees could be given that after the withdrawal of Russian forces, the Turks would not bring in theirs.'[5] Consequently, Azerbaijan became one of the major battlefields of the war. As part of their military strategy, the Russians, British and Ottomans all pursued policies which aimed at stirring up or aggravating the existing animosities between the different ethnic and religious groupings in the province. Promises were made with regard to setting up a sovereign state for Kurds, Assyrians, Armenians and Azerbaijani Muslims. Such demagogic manipulations led to the most bloody and barbaric confrontations among these ethnic and religious groups.

Soon after the outbreak of World War I, the Ottoman Empire, with the encouragement of Enver Pasha, the Ottoman minister of war, sided with Germany. Enver Pasha, judged that doing so gave the Ottomans a good chance of surviving and perhaps even of making some gains from Russia. He also declared a jihad, inciting Muslims to rise up against British and Russian rule in India, Iran, the Caucasus and Central Asia. To him, the Russians were not only *kafir* (infidels), but also invaders who had occupied areas south of the Caucasus which were considered part of the Islamic–Turkic homeland. Enver Pasha played a leading part in negotiating a secret German–Ottoman treaty, signed on 2 August 1914; in October the Ottoman fleet entered the Black Sea, bombarded Odessa and the Crimean ports, and sank Russian ships. In addition, Ottoman forces were deployed along the Caucasus frontier with Russia, where severe fighting began in the harsh mountain terrain.

The ultimate strategic objective for the Ottomans was to capture the Baku oilfields and northern Iran in order to penetrate Central Asia and Afghanistan, not only as a threat to British India, but also to extend the Ottoman Empire to what were referred as its natural boundaries:

> We should not forget that the reason for our entrance into the world war is not only to save our country from the danger threatening it. No, we pursue an even more immediate goal – the realization of our ideal, which demands that, having shattered our Muscovite enemy, we lead our empire to its natural boundaries, which would encompass and unite all our related people.[6]

In December 1914, a Russian advance towards Erzurum was countered by the Ottomans, but, in battles at Sarıkamış in January 1915 the Ottomans, ill-clad and ill-supplied for the Caucasian winter, suffered their greatest defeat of the war.

In the south, other Ottoman forces, which had invaded the city of Maraghan in late November 1914, moved to Tabriz on 14 January. Since the Russian army was still stationed in Tabriz, confrontation between two armies seemed inevitable. Although the Russian troops avoided a military confrontation and evacuated Tabriz, the Ottomans were unable to maintain their hold on the city and were expelled by a Russian counter-invasion in March 1915.[7] The defeat at Sarıkamış was indeed a turning-point in the Ottomans' policy of expanding east. Throughout the remaining years of the war they adopted a low profile in the region. It was only at the end of the World War I, and following the Russian Revolution, that the Ottomans were able to return to Iran.

Pan-Turkism and Iran's Response to It

Although it took some years for the Ottomans to realize their dream of installing themselves in the region north as well as south of the Araxes river, the pan-Turkist uproar reached Baku as early as 1908, when the Young Turk Committee of Union and Progress (CUP) launched their coup, which brought an end to the despotic era of Abdülhamid. When Abdülhamid abdicated, pan-Islamism, which he had supported, was flavoured throughout the heartland of the empire by Turkic national sentiment. Like the people who initiated pan-Turkism, the pioneers of propagating pan-Turkism among the Turkic peoples came from the Russian Empire, having been influenced by the model of nineteenth-century pan-Slavism.

As early as 1904, Yusuf Akçuroglu (later known as Yusuf Akçura), a Tatar from the Russian Empire, published a pamphlet called *Üç Tarz-i Siyâset* (Three Kinds of Policies), which soon came to be known as the manifesto of the pan-Turkists. In this famous declaration, which was originally printed in Cairo by Turks in exile, Akçura discussed the inherent historical obstacles blocking the advance of pan-Ottomanism and pan-Islamism and advocated *İttihad-i Etrak* (Unity of Turks), or as he later called it, *Türkçülük* (Turkism),[8] as the sole concept capable of sustaining the *Türk milleti* (Turkish nation).

He admitted that he 'does not know if the idea still had adherents outside the Ottoman Empire', especially in *Qafqaziya ve şimali Iran* (the Caucasus and northern Iran), but he hoped that in the near future his views on Turkish identity would attract the support of many Turks wherever they lived.[9]

İttihad-i Etrak was soon adopted as a policy by political parties and 'cultural organizations' in the Ottoman Empire. In 1908, *Türk Dernegi* (the Turkish Society) was founded in Istanbul to study the 'past and present activities and circumstances of all the people called *Türk*'.[10] In its declaration issued on 25 December 1908, the society pledged to 'encourage the use of Ottoman-Turkish among foreign peoples. At first, Turks in the Balkan states, Austria, Russia, Iran, Africa, Central Asia and China will be familiarized with Ottoman-Turkish'. Furthermore, 'languages in Azerbaijan, Kashgar, Bukhara, Khiva, etc., will be reformed to be like Ottoman-Turkish for the benefit of Ottoman trade'.[11] *Türk Dernegi* was followed by another society called *Türk Ocagi* (Turkish Hearth). In its manifesto, written in 1912, this society proclaimed as its chief aim 'to advance the national education and raise the scientific, social and economic level of the Turks who are the foremost of the peoples of Islam, and to strive for the betterment of the Turkish race and language'.[12]

The pioneers of pan-Turkism in Caucasian Azerbaijan, however, were those of the Azerbaijani elite living in Istanbul who were disillusioned by the stagnation of the Iranian constitutional movement, the failure of the Russian revolution of 1905, and the crisis in the European social democratic movement. Some, who were sympathetic to the Iranian reformist movement, turned their gaze from Tabriz and Tehran to Istanbul. The Istanbul of the Young Turks, with its call for unity among the Turkic peoples, was a new haven for such elites from tsarist Russia. With a growing sense of their isolation, they turned to studying ethnic culture and history and its accompanying political importance. The outlook of Ali Husaynzade, Ahmad Aghayev and, later, Muhammad Amin Rasulzade was immediately welcomed by the CUP, and some of them were even given government positions in the new Ottoman regime. When *Türk Yurdu* (Turkish Homeland), the main journal propagating pan-Turkism in the Ottoman Empire was launched in Istanbul, they were among the most prominent contributors to it. In one of his editorials Ahmad Aghayev even reproached the Ottomans for calling the Iranian Azerbaijanis, Iranians, rather than Turks.[13] Muhammad Amin Rasulzade in a series of articles entitled 'Iran Türkleri' (the Iranian Turks), contributed a descriptive analysis of the Iranian Turkic minorities and their distinctive national identities.[14]

During the war, pan-Turkist activities in Baku, which was still under tsarist rule, were mainly confined to the publication of certain periodicals. While maintaining their absolute loyalty in the tsarist cause in the war, periodicals such as *Yeni Füyuzat* (New Abundance) and *Şâlâlé* (Cascade), adopted as their chief mission the purification of the Azerbaijani language, Arabic and Persian vocabulary was to be purged, and words of pure Turkic origin were to be substituted, as was being done in nationalist circles in the Ottoman Empire. Whereas news about the activities of pan-Turkist organizations in the empire was often covered in editorials by 'Isa Bey Azurbeyli, the editor of Şâlâlé, the question of Iranian Azerbaijan remained neglected by such periodicals, and it seemed that in their hidden agenda the forging of firmer ties with the Ottomans had priority over unification with the Iranian Azerbaijanis.[15]

However, the attitude toward Turkism in the Caucasus was somewhat altered when in 1913 an amnesty was declared in Baku on the occasion of the three hundredth anniversary of the Romanov dynasty. Political activists such as the committed social democrat Rasulzade, who some years earlier had launched the leading newspaper *Iran-e Now* in Tehran, were then able to return to live within tsarist territory. On his return to Baku, Rasulzade began to publish his own newspaper. The first issue of *Achiq Söz* (Candid Speech) appeared in October 1915 and publication continued until March 1918. Under the tsars the newspaper called itself 'a Turkish political, social and literary paper' and adopted a standpoint close to that of the tsarist empire, endorsing the latter's war policy. At the same time, it paid a certain amount of attention to Iran and Iranian Azerbaijan. When it had occasion to cover Iranian news, it voiced its sympathy for the Iranian Democrats.[16] After the Russian Revolution, however, it changed its attitude, and abruptly adopted an openly pro-Ottoman policy, calling for *türklamé, islamlamé va mu'asirllamé* (Turkicization, Islamicization and modernization).

On 18 October 1917, a branch of *Türk Ocağı* was founded in Baku. Among the aspirations of the new society, which claimed that its activities were confined exclusively to the cultural domain, was the desire to 'acquaint the younger generation with their historical Turkic heritage and to consolidate their Turkic consciousness through setting up schools, organizing conferences and publishing books'.[17] *Achiq Söz* not only welcomed the new society but reported extensively on its activities, covered its frequent gatherings in Baku, and published lectures delivered at its conferences. Most of these lengthy articles were on different aspects of the history and culture of the Muslim peoples of the southern Caucasus. It seems that at this stage no one in Baku was interested in applying the term 'Azerbaijan' to the territory south of the Caucasus. '*Türk milleti*' and '*Qafqaziya müsalman Xalqi*' (the Muslim people of the Caucasus) were often employed to designate the inhabitants of the region. The first Constituent Assembly, which was established in Baku on 29 April 1917, was even called the General Assembly of the Caucasian Muslims.

One result of the political upheavals in Moscow, which eventually ended with the Bolshevik takeover in October 1917, was the creation of a power vacuum in the Caucasus. A month later, the Transcaucasian Commissariat was established in Tblisi, and it proclaimed 'the right of Caucasian nations to self-determination'. By then it was obvious that the Armenian Dashnakists and Georgian Mensheviks were poised to establish their power over a large part of the region. The Baku Musavatists, who enjoyed an absolute majority in the Baku Constituent Assembly, realized that the time had come for swift political action. With the old tsarist empire gone, the Musavatists were counting on the Ottomans, who were now viewed as the uncontested dominant power in the region. The goal of the Musavatists in their contest with the Armenians and the Georgians was to win control over as much territory as possible. They claimed 'besides the Baku and Ganja province, the Muslim population of Daghestan, the northern Caucasus, the Georgian-speaking Muslim Inghilios of Zakataly, the Turkish inhabitants of the province of Erivan and Kars, and even the Georgian-speaking Muslim Ajars of the southern shore of the Black Sea'.[18] Furthermore, since the majority of Azerbaijani-speaking people lived in a large region within northern Iran, their ultimate hope was to persuade the Azerbaijani leaders in Iran to support their proposed project for unity. Consequently, in October 1917 an emissary arrived in Tabriz, approached the local politicians and advocated that they separate from Iran and join with Baku in a great federation. However, their proposal was rejected by the Azerbaijani Democrats.[19]

Following this failure, in an editorial published in *Achiq Söz*, in January 1918 the Musavatists for the first time tackled the question of

Iranian Azerbaijan. In a rather haughty style, the author defined the historical boundaries of Azerbaijan as stretching to the Caucasian mountains in the north and to Kirmanshah in the south, with Tbilisi forming the western frontier and the Caspian Sea the eastern. The Russian expansionists and the Iranian ruling class were blamed for having adopted policies that resulted in the dismemberment of the nation of Azerbaijan. Furthermore, according to the author, it was the 'natural right of the south Caucasian Muslims to call their territory Azerbaijan' and to hope that 'one day their brothers in the south could join them'.[20]

Interestingly enough, the first reaction to this irredentist propaganda came from a group of Iranian Democrats residing in Baku. Since the beginning of the century, the flourishing economy of the Caucasus had attracted many Iranians, most of whom were Azerbaijanis or Azerbaijani-speakers from the north of Iran. But although they spoke the same language, they did not readily assimilate. Throughout the Caucasus region they were known as '*hamshahri*' (fellow countrymen) and they maintained a sense of separate identity which marked them out as different from the local population.[21]

Of the various organizations that existed among the Iranian community in Baku, the local branch of the Iranian Democrat Party was the most eminent and active. The party's Baku Committee was founded in 1914 and its members were recruited from the Iranian community in Baku and the adjacent regions. In their perception the view expounded in the *Achiq Söz* editorial was nothing less than a pan-Turkist plot which menaced Iran's sovereignty and territorial integrity. Disturbed by such attempts to undermine Iranian unity, they soon inaugurated their own political campaign in the region. On 10 February 1918, the Democrats launched the publication of a bilingual newspaper, *Azarbayjan, Joz -e la-yanfakk-e Iran* (Azerbaijan, an Inseparable Part of Iran).[22] '*Azarbayjan*' was printed in big letters on the masthead with '*Joz -e la-yanfakk-e Iran*' printed in much smaller letters inside the 'n' of *Azarbayjan*'. Later on Salamullah Javid, a political activist in Baku, acknowledged that 'the decision to publish the newspaper was taken by the Democrats at the local level and was a direct response to irredentist propaganda initiated by *Achiq Söz*'.[23]

In addition to promoting political change and reform in Iran, the newspaper declared as its task 'displaying the country's glorious past and its historical continuity',[24] as well as 'hindering any attempt to diminish the national consciousness of Iranians'.[25] While glorifying the name of Azerbaijan and its 'key position in Iranian history', the publication frequently referred to 'the many centuries during which Azerbaijan governed all of Iran'. Similarly, it stressed that Azerbaijan had a shared history with the rest of Iran, and strove to foster self-confidence and the feeling of belonging to territorial Iran. Pointing to the geographical front-line position of the province, the newspaper 'declared it to be the duty of Azerbaijanis' to confront the hostile outsiders, and to safeguard the country's 'national pride' and 'territorial integrity'. Though the newspaper never named these outsiders, or 'intruders', as they were called, it considered that 'their intention has always been to undermine Iran's territorial integrity and political sovereignty'. Moreover, by representing Azerbaijanis as the main champions of the Iranian Constitutional Revolution, it attempted to portray them as the sole guardians of Iran as a bounded territorial entity.

In a multi-ethnic society like Iran, where Persians form the titular ethnic group, a minority of Azerbaijanis living outside Iran, but within their linguistic territory, promoted a sense of Iranian state-patriotism and territorial nationalism rather than their own ethno-nationalism. Their political loyalty and attachment to a constructed political reliability therefore took precedence over their other loyalties, in particular their ethnic loyalty. Likewise, they apparently believed in the nineteenth-century notion of a 'historical nation' in which the *Staatsvolk* (state-people) was associated with the state. In their view, the Iranians, just as the dispersed members of a Greater Russia or a Greater Germany did, made up a community associated with a territorial state. Consequently they attempted to uphold their territorial/Iranian identity in the face of pan-Turkist propaganda by 'shaping a significant and unbroken link with a seminal past that could fill the gap between the nation's origin and its actuality'.[26] For them, as Nipperdey has correctly pointed out, romantic nationalism provided the driving force for political action: 'cultural identity with its claims for what ought to be, demanded political consequences: a common state, the only context in which they [the people] could develop, the only force that could protect them and the only real possibility for integrating individuals into a nation'.[27]

With a persuasive political agenda, *Azarbayjan, Joz -e la-yanfakk-e Iran* pursued what in its first issue it had proclaimed to be its duty, and continued to publish even after the takeover of Baku by the Bolsheviks known as the Baku Commune. However, it was forced to close down in May 1918 when the Musavatists regained power and formed their national government. In their turn the Musavatists, who had been obliged to stop publishing *Achiq Söz* during the previous five months, in September 1918 launched their new gazette *Azerbayjan*. By adopting the same name for their publication that the Iranian Democrats in Baku had used four months earlier, the Musavatists demonstrated their firm attachment to the name they intended to give their future independent state.

The Return of the Ottomans

After World War I, the political arena in Anatolia as well as the Caucasus was significantly altered. The tsarist empire had been swept away by the winds of revolution and the Ottomans were striving to put together the jigsaw pieces of their empire. If during their first short-lived invasion the Ottomans had not had time to disseminate their pan-Turkist propaganda among the Iranian Azerbaijanis, as a result of the Russian Revolution of 1917 and the fall of their old foe, the CUP were now able to initiate a new pan-Turkist campaign in northern Iran. As noted by a member of the British diplomatic service: Turkey are hand in glove with the Tatars of Transcaucasia (Baku) and these have put in claims to Azerbaijan on their own account. ... Northern Persia is essential to Turkey as a link with the Turanians of Central Asia.[28]

In the middle of April 1918, the Ottoman army invaded Azerbaijan for the second time. Yusuf Zia,[29] a local coordinator of the activities of the *Teşkilât-i Mahsusa* (Special Organization)[30] in the region, was appointed political adviser to the Ottoman contingent in Iran. Soon, the *Teşkilât-i Mahsusa* introduced a small pan-Turkist party in Tabriz[31], together with the publication of an Azerbaijani-language newspaper called *Azarabadegan*, which was the Ottomans' main instrument for propagating pan-Turkism throughout the province. The editorship of the newspaper was offered to Taqi Rafcat, a local Azerbaijani who later became known for his vanguard role in effecting innovations in Persian literature.

Contrary to their expectations, however, the Ottomans did not achieve impressive success in Azerbaijan. Although the province remained under quasi-occupation by Ottoman troops for months, attempting to win endorsement for pan-Turkism ended in failure.

The Ottomans had never enjoyed the support of local political parties, ever since their arrival in Tabriz, and their relations with the local Democrats had been particularly strained. With the passage of time relations with the Democrats deteriorated to the point, where the Ottomans went as far as to arrest the Democrats' popular radical leader, Muhammad Khiyabani, together with his two comrades Nowbari and Badamchi, and sent them to Kars in exile.[32] Khiyabani being accused of 'collaborating with the Armenians against the forces of Islam',[33] the immediate result of their intervention was to whip up serious anti-Ottoman sentiment among the Democrats, who were preparing to take control of the province.

The summer of 1918 appeared to be a honeymoon period for the Ottomans after stationing their troops on Iranian soil. Occupying the area north of the Araxes was the next logical step on their agenda. With the seizure of Baku in September 1918, it seemed that their Turanian dream was gradually being realized: the region both north and south of the Araxes was now under their control. However, with the end of the war approaching, and an escalating political problem at home, not to mention the food crisis, the CUP leadership was obliged to give priority to the centre of its envisaged empire rather than to the periphery. A direct consequence of the large-scale export of cattle and grain from the newly occupied territories to the Ottoman interior was a mounting resentment among the local population. On 23 September 1918, an Ottoman–German protocol was signed, confirming the territorial integrity of Iran, but the Ottomans suffered a setback on their western front when Bulgaria was forced to surrender on 30 September. It was then obvious that pursuing the war any further was impossible for the Ottomans. On 9 October, the CUP government fell and the new government of Izzet Pasha signed an armistice with the Allies.

Returning to Tabriz from exile on 24 June 1920, Khiyabani announced the formation of a local government. The announcement took place with pomp and ceremony in the 'Ali Qapi', the central government's provincial headquarters. In a country where the political culture was dominated by xenophobia, one of the key issues for Khiyabani and his fellow Democrats was how to dissociate themselves as completely as possible from the foreign powers. Their relations with the Ottomans, in view of the latter's actions against Khiyabani, remained cold and distant. But what concerned them even more urgently was how to defend their position in face of the political upheavals sweeping through the Caucasus.

On 27 May 1918, when the new Republic of Azerbaijan was founded on the territory north of the Araxes River and south-east of Transcaucasia, the adoption of the name 'Azerbaijan' caused consternation in Iran, especially among Azerbaijani intellectuals. Khiyabani and his fellow Democrats, in order to dissociate themselves from the Transcaucasians, decided to change the name of Iranian Azerbaijan to *Azadistan* (Land of Freedom).[34] By way of justifying this decision, they referred to the important 'heroic role' Azerbaijan had played in the struggle to establish the Constitution in Iran which, in their view, warranted adopting the name *Azadistan*.[35]

From Territorial to Titular Nationalism

The fall of the Musavatists in 1920s, which was a result of close collaboration between the Bolsheviks and the CUP leadership, caused considerable disillusion among the Azerbaijani pro-Ottoman intelligentsia. However profitable this cooperation was for the Bolsheviks, the old guard of the Ottoman Unionists in the region, by adopting different measures, were still striving to realize their old dream. As an intelligence British office remarked:

> It will be remembered that the unfortunate 'Musavat' government of Baku was successfully overturned by the Communists mainly as a result of the assistance given by the numerous Turkish Unionists. The infiltration of Unionists in the Turkish Communist Party in Baku still continues; they thus seek to establish complete control in course of time, and to gain control of Georgia and Azerbaijan in order to connect them up with their schemes in Central Asia. ... The Unionists' plan therefore is to continue the alliance with Russia so long as it enables them to advance their own plans, which are being energetically pursued.[36]

The final consolidation of Soviet power in the Caucasus, which was eventually realized by the subjugating of Georgia on March 1921, paved the way for a shift in diplomatic manoeuvering by the newly born Soviet administration. In February the Soviet–Iranian Treaty was concluded, and it was followed by the signing of a peace treaty with Turkey in March 1921. Having extended its southern border to the Araxes river, the Soviet regime adopted a restrained policy towards Iran, officially forbidding any nationalist claims on Iranian territory.

The tragic outcome of Khiyabani's revolt, which was followed by the suppression of the uprisings in Khorasan and Gilan, left the Democrats in Iran in total disarray. A group of them, mainly from non-Azerbaijani background, were enthralled by pan-Islamism, as propagated by the late Ottomans as a means of winning over a non-Turkic people in the region. Another tendency within the Democrats found it difficult to subscribe to the regional movement launched by their party comrades. Subsequently, a new group of reform-minded intellectuals gradually emerged on the Iranian political scene. Their mode of understanding society was based on socio-political ideas of West European origin. Despite the diversity of their political views, what singled out them from the home-grown variety of educated or learned individuals was the model of society that they took for granted. The West European model presupposed a coherent, class-layered society, which by definition was organized around the distinctive concepts of *nation* and *state*. They were convinced that only a strong centralized government based in the capital would be capable of implementing reform throughout Iran, while preserving the nation's territorial integrity. Likewise they believed that modernization and modern state-building in Iran would require low cultural diversity and a high degree of ethnic homogeneity. Only when Iran fulfilled the preconditions for a nation-state as defined by them, when 'empirically almost all the residents of a state identify with the one subjective idea of the nation, and that nation is virtually contiguous',[37] could they realistically cherish hopes of safeguarding Iranian territorial integrity.

In the recently born state of Turkey, the *Türk Ocağı* activists strove to find a new home under the self-restrained Kemalist regime. In 1923, the Turkish magazine *Yeni Mecmu a* (the New Journal) reported on a conference about Azerbaijan, held by Türk Ocağı in Istanbul. During the conference, Roshani Barkin, an ex-member of Teşkilât-i Mahsusa and an eminent pan-Turkist, condemned the Iranian government for its oppressive and tyrannical policies towards the Azerbaijanis living in Iran. He called on all Azerbaijanis in Iran to unite with the new-born Republic of Turkey.[38]

In reply *Iranshahr* (Land of Iran), a journal published in Berlin, and the Tehran-based journal *Ayandeh* (The Future) ran a series of articles denouncing pan-Turkism and became the pioneers of the newly launched titular nationalism in Iran. While *Iranshahr* attempted to provide historical underpinning, *Ayandeh* took on the task of propounding the necessary conditions for the 'unification' and 'Persianization' of all Iranians as one nation.[39] Advocating the elimination of regional differences in 'language, clothing, customs and suchlike', *Ayandeh* demanded 'national unity' based on the standardized, homogeneous and centrally sustained high culture of the titular ethnic group:

> Kurds, Lors, Qashwa'is, Arabs, Turks, Turkmens, etc., shall not differ from one another by wearing different clothes or speaking a different language. In my opinion, until national unity is achieved in Iran, with regard to customs, clothing, and so forth, the possibility of our political independence and geographical integrity being endangered will always remain.[40]

Their insistence on raising the status of Persian above that of a *lingua franca* and cleansing its vocabulary of loan words, especially those from Turkish and Arabic, provided the newly constructed sentiment with a form of philological nationalism. Later, philologists were to be inspired to create grotesque and far-fetched neologisms such as '*kas nadanad-sikhaki*', to replace '*mahramana-mostagim*' (direct-confidential). Moreover, their campaign of purification naturally went beyond the linguistic field and pervaded the realm of Iranian history as well. By rewriting history, a 'pure Iran' with a long historical identity was created, an Iran purged of all 'foreign' and 'uncivilized elements' within its borders. Such an identity ultimately depended on negative stereotypes of non-Iranians. The Turks and later the Arabs, who were referred in nationalist discourse as the 'yellow and green hazards',[41] served as the indispensable 'others' in the construction of the new Iranian identity. With the passage of time, the proponents of this form of revivalist nationalism became the founders of a trend in Iranian historiography known above all for its emphasis on continuity in Iranian culture and its concern to uphold the country's pre-Islamic values.

Furthermore, by adopting the Western European model of modern nation-state-building under an absolutist ruler, the Iranian nationalists in their manifesto advocated bureaucratic efficiency, clear territorial demarcation, and a homogenized and territorially fixed population, who were to be taxed, conscripted into the army and administered in such a way as to be transformed into modern 'citizens'. When Reza Shah ascended the throne, he wholeheartedly endorsed all the demands voiced by these nationalists. Indeed, the blueprint for his 'one country, one nation' project was already on his desk.

Conclusion

The most important political development affecting the Middle East at the beginning of the twentieth century was the collapse of the Ottoman and the Russian empires. The idea of a greater homeland for all Turks was propagated by pan-Turkism, which was adopted almost at once as a main ideological pillar by the Committee of Union and Progress and somewhat later by other political caucuses in what remained of the Ottoman Empire. On the eve of World War I, pan-Turkist propaganda focused chiefly on the Turkic-speaking peoples of the southern Caucasus, in Iranian Azerbaijan and Turkistan in Central Asia, with the ultimate purpose of persuading them all to secede from the larger political entities to which they belonged and to join the new pan-Turkic homeland. Interestingly, it was this latter appeal to Iranian Azerbaijanis which, contrary to pan-Turkist intentions, caused a small group of Azerbaijani intellectuals to become the most vociferous advocates of Iran's territorial integrity and sovereignty.

If in Europe 'romantic nationalism responded to the damage likely to be caused by modernism by providing a new and larger sense of belonging, an all-encompassing totality, which brought about new social ties, identity and meaning, and a new sense of history from one's origin on to an illustrious future',[42] in Iran after the Constitutional movement romantic nationalism was adopted by the Azerbaijani Democrats as a reaction to the irredentist policies threatening the country's territorial integrity. In their view, assuring territorial integrity was a necessary first step on the road to establishing the rule of law in society and a competent modern state which would safeguard collective as well as individual rights. It was within this context that their political loyalty outweighed their other ethnic or regional affinities. The failure of the Democrats in the arena of Iranian politics after the Constitutional movement and the start of modern state-building paved the way for the emergence of the titular ethnic group's cultural nationalism. Whereas the adoption of integrationist policies preserved Iran's geographic integrity and provided the majority of Iranians with a secure and firm *national* identity, the blatant ignoring of other demands of the Constitutional movement, such as the call for formation of society based on law and order, left the country still searching for a *political* identity.

Notes

1 E. J. Hobsbawm, *Nation and Nationalism since 1780: Programme, Myth, Reality* (Cambridge: Cambridge University Press, 1990), p. 102.
2 K. Renner, *Staat und Nation*, p. 89, quoted by Hobsbawm, ibid., p. 101.
3 For the details of the ultimatum, see A. Kasravi, *Tarikh-e Hijdah Saleh-e Azarbayjan*, 9th edn (Tehran: Amir Kabir, 1978), vol. 1, pp. 235–40.
4 R. Ramazine, *The Foreign Policy of Iran* (Charlottesville: University Press of Virginia, 1966), pp. 103–8.
5 Ramazani, *The Foreign Policy of Iran*, p. 115.
6 S. A. Zenkovsky, *Pan-Turkism and Islam in Russia* (Cambridge, MA: Harvard University Press, 1960), pp. 127–8.
7 R. Orbay, 'Hatiralar', *Yakinn Tarihimiz*, cilt I (Istanbul: Türkpetrol, 1963), pp. 16–29.
8 Y. Akçuroglu, ed., *Türk Yıl, 1928* (Istanbul: Yeni Metba'a, 1928), p. 396.
9 Y. Akçuroglu, *Üç Tarz-i Siyâset* (Cairo: Metba'a-i Qadr, 1909), pp. 11–12.
10 B. Lewis, *The Emergence of Modern Turkey* (London: Oxford University Press, 1962), p. 343.
11 M. Arai, *Turkish Nationalism in the Young Turk Era* (Leiden: E.J. Brill, 1992), p. 20.
12 Ibid, p. 344.
13 Türk 'Ãlemi *Türk Yurdu* Birici Cilt 1327–1328 (Istanbul: Tanin Matba'asi, 1328/1912), p. 16.
14 'Iran Türkleri', *Türk Yurdu* Birici Cilt 1327–1328 (Istanbul: Tanin Matba'asi, 1328/1912), pp. 106–11, 428–32, 551–6, 648–56, 670–72, 755–60.
15 See, for example, *Şâlâlé*, 17 January 1914.
16 See, for example, *Achiq Söz*, 20 August 1917.
17 *Achiq Söz*, 18 October 1917. Among the founders of Türk Ocağı was Abdullah Şa'iq, the younger brother of Yusuf Zia. For Yusuf Zia, see note 29.
18 Zenkovsky, *Pan-Turkism and Islam in Russia*, p. 262.
19 FO 371/4358, 1918.
20 *Achiq Söz*, 17 January 1918.

21 On the process of self-identification, see Thomas Hylland Eriksen, *Ethnicity and Nationalism: Anthropoligical Perspectives* (London: Pluto Press, 1993), pp. 9–10.

22 Mohammad Khan Tarbiyat was the founder of the Democrat Party's Baku committee, and the director of Iranian Etehhad school in Baku. Other members: Mirza Mahmud Khan Parvaresh, Mirza 'Abdollah 'Abdolahzadeh, Shaykh Baqir Shirazi, Azhdar 'Alizadeh, Hosayn Khayyat, Hosayn Mahmuzadeh, Mir Hosayn Motazavi, Mirza 'Aliqoli (from Ashqabad, who later became the editor of the newspaper *Azarbayjan, Joz -e layanfakk-e Iran*), Mir Jafar Javadzadeh Pishavari, Haji Mo'atlem Ja'farzadeh Kalkhali, Mirza Aqa Valizadeh, Sayfollah Ibrahimzadeh, 'Ali Akbar Ooku'i (founder of Iranian gilde, labours executive committee). Because of his political activities Parvarish had to leave Baku in 1916; he went illegally to Iran. After the Russian Revolution of February 1917, the Democrat Party began to operate legally. See S. Javid, *Iran Sosyal Demokrat (Adalat) Firqasi Haqqinda Khataralarim* (Tehran: Lithography, 1980), pp. 9–10. The other Iranian societies and organizations in Baku included the 'Iran Independent party', pro-Iranian government, Javid p. 11. 'Sanduq-e Ta'avon-e Madrisa-e Etehad-e Iraniyan-e Baku', Javid, p. 13. 'Jam'iyat-e Ma'arif-el Iran' (an Adalat party front), Javid p. 17. 'Ijtima'iyun-Inqilabiyun (Sosyal-Revolutioner). 'Ali Bayramov, was killed by Musavatists during their reign, Javid, p. 19. Furthermore, the Iranians had two schools: Ettehad in the city centre and Tamadon (in the Sabunchi district). In March 1918, following the conflict between Musavatists and the Baku Commune, almost all Iranian societies were liquidated. Javid, pp. 14–15.

23 Ibid, p. 10.

24 On the origin of reconstructing Iran's pre-Islamic history in the nationalist discourse, see M. Tavaqoli-Targhi, 'Contested Memories: Narrative Structure and Allegorical Meaning of Iran's pre-Islamic History', *Iranian Studies*, vol. 29, nos. 1–2 (1996), pp. 149–175.

25 *Azarbayjan Joz -e layanfakk-e Iran*, nos. 2 and 3, 2 and 6 February 1918.

26 I. Gershoni, 'Imagining and Reimagining the Past: The Use of History by Egyptian Nationalist Writers, 1919–1952', *History & Memory*, vol. 4, no. 2 (fall-winter 1992), p. 7.

27 T. Nipperdey, 'In Search of Identity: Romantic Nationalism, its Intellectual, Political and Social Background', in J. C. Eade, ed., *Romantic Nationalism in Europe* (Australian National University, 1983), p. 11.

28 FO 371/4358, 1918.

29 Yusuf Zia Talibzada was born in Burchali in Georgia in 1877. His father was a high-ranking mulla in the Caucasus region. When Yusuf was a child his mother took him, together with his brother 'Abdullâh, later 'Abdullâh Şa'iq to Mashhad to study. His teacher there was a dissident

Anatolian Turk called Zia, whose name Yusuf adopted. After finishing elementary school in Mashhad, he went to Kerbela and became a mulla. Returning to Baku in 1899, he started his career in the service of Haj Zaynolabidin Taqiov, at whose order he translated *Hashf al-Haqaiq* into Azerbaijani. Three copies of the book was presented to the Shah of Iran, the Amir of Afghanistan and the Ottoman Sultan. Yusuf Zia was asked to take the Sultan's copy to Istanbul. In 1907 he went to Istanbul and joined the CUP. He served with the Ottoman forces in the 1912 Balkan war and received the title of Pasha. He spent periods as an Ottoman secret agent in Iranian Azerbaijan. Following the Bolshevik takeover he temporarily joined the Bolsheviks and spent some time in Nakhjivan. Later he joined Enver Pasha in Turkistan and became his deputy. Following the death of Enver, while attempting to escape to Afghanistan he was drowned in the Panj river.

30 For a detailed study of *Teşkilât-i Mahsusa*'s activities in Iran, the Caucasus and Central Asia', in Tabaki, ed., *The Great War in Iran* (St Antony's Publications, forthcoming).

31 FO 371/4358, 1918.

32 Kasravi, *Tarikh-e Hejdah Saleh-e Azarbayjan*, vol. 2.

33 Ibid.

34 Kasravi, *Tarikh-e Hejdah Saleh-e Azarbayjan*, vol. 2, p. 872.

35 Azar, A. op. cit., p. 299.

36 FO 371/6342, 1921.

37 J. J. Linz and A. Stepan, *Problems of Democratic Transition and Consolidation, Southern Europe, South America, and post-Communist Europe* (London: Johns Hopkins University Press, 1996), p. 25.

38 Türk Ocağında Konfirans', *Yeni Mecmu a*, no. 81, 2 August 1923, pp. 317–8.

39 See, for example, *Ayandeh*, nos. 1 (1925), 8 (1926); *Iranshahr*, no. 2 (1923). The magazine *Iranshahr* was first published in Berlin, in June 1922. The editor, Hosayn Kazemzadeh, maintained close contact with intellectuals in Europe who were involved with Iranian studies, and his magazine was soon exercising a powerful influence in political and intellectual circles in Iran. During the five years of *Iranshahr*'s existence, forty-eight issues appeared and special attention was often paid to Azerbaijan. Indeed, there were nine long articles devoted to the subject.

40 Afshar, M., 'Aghaz-nameh', *Ayandeh*, no. 1 1925.

41 Afshar, M., 'Khatar-i zard', *Ayandeh*, no. 24 (1927).

42 Nipperdey, 'In Search of Identity', p. 15.

4· Nations Imagined and Fragmented: Bengali Ethnicity and the Break up of Pakistan

Tazeen M. Murshid

This essay explores the contextual and fragmented nature of Bengali identity in the 1940s and 1950s and attempts to understand the Bengali experience of option for nationhood. Identity politics in twentieth-century Bengal, which must be viewed in the context of the politics of Partition and its legacies, created the option for nationhood among Muslims several times. In the 1940s they had the possibility to be Indian, Pakistani or Bengali (in a United Bengal), and in the 1970s to be Pakistani, Bengali or Bangladeshi. Nationhood in each instance was manipulated from above. The British imposed it in the form of the 1947 Partition of India, which gave rise to the successor states of India and Pakistan and laid the foundations for the eventual emergence of Bangladesh in 1971.

In 1947, Bengal Muslims became Pakistani despite strong attachments to the idea of coexisting with Hindus within a juridical state called United Bengal. The unmaking of the Pakistani nation which began soon afterwards was also owed to intervention at the top. The growing discontent with the centralizing nation-building policies of the Pakistani state elite gave rise to Bengali ethnicity, which was fuelled by experiences of cultural difference and economic marginalization. Their dissatisfaction was reflected in the political choices made by Bengalis: they rejected the 1951 Basic Principles Committee Report, which visualized a strong centre that would leave East Bengal at the mercy of West Pakistani authority; they protested against the Urdu-only state language policy, which they regarded as exclusionary of Bengali aspirations, and which in turn provoked state intervention in the form of police firing on dissident students in 1952. These and other acts of state intimidation led to a loss of confidence in the party that led the movement for independence from British rule and culminated in the election defeat of the Muslim League in East Bengal in 1954.[1]

This study is placed within the wider background of nationalist endeavours in India which may be explained in terms of the impact of modernity, that is, the influence of new ideas such as the rights of man, democracy and self-governance. The rise of ethno-religious and nationalist struggles in twentieth-century India was both reactive to colonial policies of containment of Indian aspirations, and proactive in the nationalistic visualization of new utopias, such as Gandhi's *Ramrajya*, the glorious kingdom of Rama, and Jinnah's *Khulafi-i-Rashidun*, the age of the rightly guided Caliphs. While Gandhi stood for composite Indian nationalism and Jinnah for Muslim rights, both invoked concepts of a golden age. But these were utopias in conflict because of the tension between competing groups, the Hindus and Muslims, defined as communities in colonial literature, each vying for the largesse of the state.[2]

Identity politics surfaced first in nineteenth-century Bengal, which had, incidentally, experienced the longest period of British colonial rule and exposure to Western ideas. It was played out at its fiercest in the 1940s both in the Punjab and in Bengal: the 1946 election verdict indicated the stark polarization of Hindus and Muslims, who had by now become separate 'nations'. The subsequent communal violence depicted in Partition riots, gave way to the division of India in 1947 and the creation of two new territorial states: Pakistan, as a homeland for Muslims ostensibly based on religion, and India, supposedly rooted in secular values and a plural ethos.[3] Through an examination of the case of Bengal, I shall challenge the explanatory value of the two-nation theory or 'clash of civilizations' as the basis for Pakistan.[4] Further, I shall argue that the exercise of option may at times be unavoidable, although narrow nationalism may be self-defeating, in that persistent problems of ethnicity can not be ruled out.

The case of Bengal demonstrates that state formation and nation formation are neither simultaneous nor chronological. They follow various trajectories. The imagined nation seeks territorial boundaries through the mediation of nationalists. The juridical state, once formed, continues to reinvent the nation in order to justify its existence, reinterpret old ideologies and forge new alliances. But in the process new forces are unleashed which follow their own logic, culminating in the formulation of new nations, once again.[5] It is in this context that the emergence of Bangladesh as an independent state in 1971 can be understood, and for that matter the continued debate about Bengali versus Bangladeshi identity, in which 'Bengali' stands for the composite identity of Hindus and Muslims and 'Bangladeshi' emphasizes the distinctions between the two, invoking the concerns that led to Partition in the first place.

Given such fluidity in the politics of identification, it is inevitable that problems of ethnicity will persist in some form or other. This is because the nationalist project is to strive towards a congruity of borders between the imagined nation and the juridical state.[6] However, many nationalities and ethno-linguistic communities remain divided by international boundaries. The Partition of India and the birth of Pakistan did not resolve this issue, although in rhetorical terms they created the expectation that they would be a panacea for all problems tracing Indian Muslims. Part of the problem lay in the fact that Partition entailed the partition of the Muslim-majority provinces of the Punjab and Bengal. It thus rendered the people residing in East Bengal and West Punjab into parts of the imagined Pakistani nation; it also made them significant majorities of the fragmented Bengali and Punjabi nations.

In Bengal, however, nations were being recast at a rapid pace. This is reflected in the abortive attempt by Muslims, with the support of some Hindus, to create a sovereign independent Bengal only weeks before the division, emphasizing their Bengali rather than Muslim identity; in the emergence of independent Bangladesh out of the eastern wing of Pakistan a quarter of a century later in a similar vein; and in the demand of a quarter of a million Biharis to be repatriated to Pakistan, to which they owed allegiance ideologically. They were, however, forced to remain in Bangladesh as refugees or 'stranded Pakistanis' because of Pakistan's refusal to accede to the logic of Partition and accept those who opted for it, albeit a second time in the wake of the separation of East Pakistan.[7] These examples of nationalist projects chart alternative discourses in identity politics whereby the nation or nation-state is accepted, rejected or reformulated. The fluid nature of identity formulations in Bengal, emphasizing alternately the exclusive and then the composite culture of Bengali Hindus and Muslims, complicates any straightforward analysis of the Pakistan movement and the relevance of the two-nation theory, or 'clash of civilizations', as the basis for state formation and national identity in Pakistan.

All this gives rise to two important questions. First, what are the conditions that lead to 'opting out of the nation' in the form of nationalistic discourses, resistance to the hegemony of the state, movements for autonomy or secession? Second, are there alternative solutions to Partition and the creation of new, ever-smaller states, for example, through an emphasis on citizenship rights, pluralism and liberal-democratic state structures? These questions inform the discussions that follow. My emphasis, however, is on the exploration of the experiences of the Partition for Bengalis. This is done, first, by positioning them in relation to the United Bengal movement and, second, by examining what Pakistan meant for them in the early years, and in the period of their subsequent disillusionment with it.

United Bengal

The movement for a sovereign United Bengal with minority safeguards reflects the ambivalence of the Muslim leadership in Bengal regarding the concept of Pakistan and its relevance to their everyday reality. While the charm of Pakistan was that it meant all things to all people, Bengali Muslims were not prepared to cut all links with Bengali Hindus. The United Bengal idea was propagated at the penultimate moment, amid great opposition from the British, the Congress and the Hindu Mahasabha, which doomed it to failure.

The ambivalence is most notable in the actions of Husain Suhrawardy, the chief minister of Bengal. After several years of campaigning for Pakistan and winning a landslide victory for the Muslim league in Bengal in 1946, which was essentially regarded as a vote for Pakistan, he made what appeared to be a volte face the following year. In May 1947, with Sarat Chandra Bose, founder of the Socialist Republican Party, he put forward a scheme for a sovereign United Bengal, with the tacit approval of Jinnah and the blessing of Gandhi, at least initially. The plan envisaged Bengal as a free and independent state, where elections would be held on the basis of joint electorates and adult franchise. Seats would be reserved for Hindus according to population proportion. Other minds behind the plan were ministers Fazlur Rahman and Mohammad Ali, Abul Hashim, Abdul Malik, M. L. A., Kiran Shankar Roy and Satyaranjan Bakshi.[8]

Their reasons highlight the economic, political and cultural unities of the region. Suhrawardy emphasized the economic rationale of his proposal and argued that a United Bengal would be strong and prosperous, whereas Partition of Bengal would cause 'the doom of Hindus and Muslims alike'.[9] Abul Hashim, who belonged to the left wing of the Muslim League, took strength from the 'common culture and tradition' that had evolved in Bengal while Hindus and Muslims had preserved 'their respective entities'. He feared that Partition of Bengal would only serve the interests of alien Anglo-American capital, which was suspicious of the growing socialist tendencies in Bengal and wished to destroy them.[10] Sarat Chandra Bose argued along similar lines, adding that Partition would 'accentuate and aggravate' communal differences. He thought it would be 'suicidal to the cause of Indian independence and also to the cause of social progress'.[11] Khwaja Nazimuddin of the Bengal Muslim League supported the move as being 'in the best interests of its people'.[12]

Others who did not want the Partition of Bengal included members of the Krishak Praja Party and the Community Party, the humanist scholar Humayun Kabir and the politician A. K. Fazlul Huq. But, essentially, they wanted to preserve the Indian union and keep intact the provinces of Punjab and Bengal along the line of nationalist Indians. Humayun Kabir argued that the demand for United Bengal would have to be carefully justified. Mawlana Akram Khan, editor of *Masik Mohammadi* wanted Bengal to be part of Pakistan, and so found the scheme unacceptable.[13]

The proponents of the scheme were prepared for Hindu scepticism, for in a united India they would be in a majority, but in a united Bengal they would not. In order to allay their fears of Muslim domination in a United Bengal, Suhrawardy assured them that they would be able to maintain their advantages, both because of their current economic and political strength and also because they could secure their own future safeguards. Abul Hashim was happy to agree to a formula of 50:50 share in political power and economic privileges.

The United Bengal scheme was a departure from previous proposals, which had visualized the boundaries of Muslim-majority Bengal within the Pakistan scheme. In response to Jinnah's request in 1944, the Bengal Provincial Muslim League leaders had put forward three alternative schemes on the future form, shape and boundaries of East Pakistan: Raghib Ahsan's proposal for a confederation or federation of Bengal, Assam and Jharkhando of Chotanagpur; Fazlur Rahman's East Pakistan composed of Bengal and the Surma valley of Assam along the Curzon Partition line, to ensure a Muslim majority; and Hamidul Huq Chowdhury's plan for a United Bengal and Assam as part of Pakistan.[14]

The proponents of the United Bengal scheme, however, were keen to show that the demand for it did not undermine Pakistan's claims. Rather, it was an endorsement of the idea of self-determination visualized in the Lahore Resolution. Abul Hashim argued that the Lahore Resolution

> never contemplated the creation of any Akhand Muslim State or any artificial Muslim majority. ... It merely demands complete sovereignty for those countries of India which are known to the world as Muslim majority countries, and by implication demands complete sovereignty and right of self-determination of all the nations and countries of India. It gives Bengal and other cultural units of India complete sovereignty while keeping open the possibility of creating an Indian international on a purely voluntary basis for the benefit of all.[15]

He thus explained that the plan for a United Bengal was in the spirit of the Lahore Resolution which recognized the right to self-determination by the various nations and cultural units of India. However, his recognition of Bengal as a cultural unit stands in two different social orders. At the same time, like Jinnah he argued that India was composed of 'nations and countries', thus complicating the analysis.

Suhrawardy had very little time 'to have talks with the opposition and educate them to the advantages of unpartitioned Bengal'.[16] He had asked Mountbatten for two months 'to convert Bengal to the idea'. He was optimistic about his success. As Mountbatten reported on their meeting, 'he could tell me now that given enough time he was confident that he could get Bengal to remain as a complete entity. He told me that he could get Jinnah to agree that it need not join Pakistan if it was prepared to remain united'.[17] But Mountbatten 'wanted above everything a united India'; if that was not possible, he wanted the Cabinet Mission plan, failing which the provinces were to decide by rote about the transfer of power.[18] So, to Suhrawardy's great distress, Mountbatten reluctantly agreed to give him only a month within which to see if he could raise general support for his scheme.

When the matter was placed before the Bengal Constituent Assemblies, the Hindu members voted for the Partition of Bengal, a sharp contrast to their movement for the annulment of the first Partition of Bengal in 1905. In another vote, they opted for a united India.

Indeed, there was no endorsement of this proposal from the Hindu Mahasabha, from the influential Congress deputy Sardar Patel, or from Nehru. Even Gandhi withdrew his support. They possibly feared that, once Bengal became independent, 'a way would be found to associate it with Pakistan later'.[19] It was also argued that the grounds for a united Bengal also applied to a united India, so if India was to be Partitioned the same logic ought to be applied to the Muslim-majority regions of Bengal and the Punjab – but, significantly, not to regions where they were in a minority. Essentially, the Bengali Hindus were not keen to be in a political system dominated by Muslims. As the Mountbatten Papers record, in April 1947 'there was no doubt that, until recently, there had been a very strong sense of union in Bengal – but this had lately been overcome among non-Muslims'.[20]

The Muslim response was diametrically opposite. In one instance, the Muslim members voted for a sovereign United Bengal. In a separate vote, they opted for the Partition of India. The voting pattern suggests that they were not committed to the idea of a communal divide, but feared Hindu domination at the centre. It reflects the fragmented nature of Bengali identity, both for Muslims and for Hindus, and complicates the explanation of the emergence of Pakistan in terms of a 'clash of civilizations'.

The United Bengal scheme failed because the Raj, committed to a united India and therefore to greater territorial concessions to it, submitted to pressure from the Congress and the Mahasabha to Partition Bengal, as it conceded to Sikh pressure to Partition the Punjab. It leads one to the conclusion that the essential struggle between the two communities was for territory and advantages, although other issues, such as concern for the preservation of cultural and economic unities, also played a role, albeit a small one.

Given this denouement, it is relevant to examine how the Muslims of Bengal negotiated their Pakistani identity, which greatly emphasized Islam at the state level and the distinctions between Hindus and Muslims. There are two ways of doing so. One is to assess their immediate responses to and experience of Pakistan in the context of Partition, and their attachment to the idea of a composite Bengali identity reflected in their support for a United Bengal. The other is to examine their responses to the policies of the Pakistan state which aimed to forge a Pakistani nation, but tended to exclude certain segments of society, provoking a backlash.

Negotiating a Pakistani Identity

In the new state of Pakistan, the immediate task before the leadership was one of nation formation. Although the loss of West Bengal, particularly of Calcutta, was lamented by the intelligentsia,[21] their greater concern was to give form to this nation and stake their claims to the new state. It is partly in this context that one can begin to comprehend their want of engagement with the past and the dearth of literature about their experiences of Partition. Begum Shaista Ikramullah was one of the few who wrote eye-witness accounts of the carnage during the great Calcutta killings of 1946 which began on Direct Action Day, declared by Jinnah to 'win' Pakistan. But that is in a recent publication.[22] It is possible that the trauma was far too painful to write about at the time, for forgetfulness is a part of the process of dealing with the memory of pain. Or perhaps it was not traumatic but cathartic. The worst had already happened during the riots of the year before, and the climax was reached in the form of a 'moth-eaten Pakistan'. Moreover, in the aftermath of Partition, the borders were initially quite porous[23] and there was no strong ill-will against Hindus. The only way forward was to look to the future and face the challenges. The intelligentsia virtually refused to confront the past to make sense of the great change that had befallen them, until borders were being sealed off a few years later, constraining the free flow of goods and people. Only then did the realization dawn on many that a new political entity had come into being, that Pakistan was not to be found all over India, as some had imagined.[24] On the other hand, for large numbers the creation of Pakistan was a euphoric event, for it held great promise of advantages, the end of Hindu domination and a real prospect of self-determination.

To a great extent, the meaning or relevance of Pakistan for Bengalis was determined by their socio-economic conditions, political interests, and the desire for nation-building, driven by the instinct to belong. The Muslims of Bengal were generally less affluent than the Hindus of the region. To them, Pakistan offered great opportunities for economic advancement. The losses, such as that of the city of Calcutta, appeared to be far outweighed by the gains. Pakistan 'became a question of bread and butter' comments the writer Ali Kabir in an interview. He was a college student in 1947. 'The top-class students like Zillur Rahman Siddiqui, Sarwar Murshid and

Habibur Rahman would have survived in India, but I would have had to go into the legal profession,' he said, implying that that was something that anybody could do. Indeed, for the migrant with a modicum of educational qualifications, there were tremendous prospects for upward mobility.[25] In the 1950s and 1960s it was possible to hold quite senior appointments as teachers, medical professionals and civil servants with few formal qualifications. According to the 1961 census, 31.5 per cent of teachers had secondary education and 43 per cent were matriculates; only 11 per cent held degrees.[26] This indicates that a fair proportion had only primary education or less. About a third of those engaged in business or administrative duties were educated up to primary level. It was also possible for matriculates to obtain employment in government services.[27] Under the circumstances, Bengalis did not want to look back to a past when they were not well off, and when opportunities for upward mobility had dried up in urban centres like Calcutta.

Certainly, the Muslims wanted Pakistan. In political terms it offered the middle classes possibilities for greater participation in the decision-making process, for Partition signified the end of Hindu overlordship. Pakistan was a new entity. Although the leadership had applied the rhetoric of 'Islam in danger' to rally support for it, no attempt was made to create an Islamic state. While there was some expectation that it should be an ideological state, the policies of the leadership were essentially secular, in that Jinnah visualized a non-discriminatory state. The intelligentsia were acutely aware of the tasks of nation-building that lay ahead, and so set about giving shape to this new nation by founding journals and articulating their views of a just social order.[28] The liberal intelligentsia visualized a secular world wherein Bengali would have its rightful place as the language of the majority. They also projected a vision of a just, egalitarian and democratic order, and were willing to take on the state for its failures in these matters. For their part, the religious intelligentsia argued for a system based on Islamic principles. Among the journals considered progressive were *Mukti*, *New Values* and *Saogat*. *Azad* and *Mohammadi* toed the official line and so were considered conservative. The boldness with which they articulated their vision has not been matched by subsequent generations.

For the migrants from India, the importance of Pakistan was centred around the need to find a refuge, a home, and take advantage of the new opportunities opening up. Some fled from political persecution, others from intolerable personal predicaments; yet others sought to escape from communal violence. People emigrated for many reasons, but most of them searched 'for a sense of belonging'.[29] Even those who were non-communal and believed in Hindu–Muslim harmony acknowledged that Pakistan was 'home'. Herein lies a paradox of Partition.

The anecdotal examples below illustrate some of these experiences. They are based on interviews with middle-class families who have successfully established roots in their new homes. Sayeeda Khatun's experience was one of trying to find a home for her family and of ensuring financial security for them. Though not a typical case, it offers some insight into the practical considerations behind emigration, although her immediate family, being communist, was not keen on Partition. Born in Burdwan in 1916 into a *zamindari* family, she was married to Syed Sulaiman Ali, an income tax officer in 1930. Her husband came from Bagerhat, Khulna, in eastern Bengal. He died only seven years later, at the age of 42. So Sayeeda Khatun lived in a joint household with her brothers, but frequently visited her father-in-law in Khulna. After Partition, her four successful brothers, some of whom were communists, decided to remain in West Bengal, but gave away their eastern family estates to the two sisters who had married men from East Bengal. Sayeeda continued to live in West Bengal, however, while her two sons studied in Burdwan and later in Calcutta. Only after her sons finished their education did she send them to Pakistan and later joined them: 'I thought there would be good employment opportunities for the boys. After all, it was their country' ('Bhablam chakri bakrir shubidha habe, nijer desh to?'). But on reflection she added, 'Partition has been inconvenient. We used to come here before. The people of this country all used to work over there' ('Partition howate ashubidhai hoyeche. Age to ashtam to. Edesher lokera shobai odikei chakri-bakri korto.').[30] She was referring to disruption caused to the economic and administrative infrastructure, as well as the problems of travel visas, the requirement which most embodied the Partition.

Bibi Khatimunnessa (1900–74), another widow, came from an educated, landed family in Murshidabad who had no strong political affiliations; she also sought a home in Pakistan. She had rather more compelling personal reasons for sending her daughters on ahead, before following suit. Bitter disputes over property inheritance after the death of her husband, and the threat of physical violence from rival claimants, led her to opt for Pakistan and exchange what was salvageable of the property. She, too, fled in search of security, but not from Hindu persecutors. Indeed, her immediate protector was a Hindu policeman who escorted her to a shelter, whence she never returned to her bridal home.[31]

Some people fled India for political reasons in order to ensure personal safety. Habibur Rahman, retired chief justice of Bangladesh, noted that his father, a Zila Muslim League branch secretary, had incurred the wrath of the Congress leadership when he demonstrated in favour of Kashmir's right to self-determination. Following his arrest, imprisonment and release, the family considered it prudent to leave. They emigrated reluctantly on 31 December 1947. Yet Rahman, a young man of sixteen or seventeen with leftist leanings, had addressed a Muslim League gathering and had said, 'Ye azadi jhuta hai' ('This is a false independence'). His reason was that the successor states acquired dominion status and joined the British Commonwealth.[32]

It is notable that the influence of the communists in Bengal among the emergent middle classes was very strong. They were unwilling to treat Partition as final or the new borders as fixed. They therefore stayed put in their original homes, although they often sent away some members of their families, especially the women and children, to safety.

Many people opted for Pakistan but found it hard to leave Calcutta; among them was the politician Abul Mansur Admad, who bitterly resented Hindu separatism.[33] Others wanted to stay but changed their minds when threatened with violence or Hindu contempt. The process of migration was slow, long-drawn-out and done in stages, spurred on by intermittent communal rioting. The exodus of Hindus, too, was gradual. Their proportion of the population dropped from 22 per cent in 1951 to only 18 per cent in 1961, a sharp contrast to the total exchange of population in the Punjab.[34] For them, too, emigration was provoked by fears for physical security and experience of harassment, as well as scepticism about economic prospects in East Bengal.[35]

Dislocation marked by fear and insecurity was a common experience of Partition. However, referring to the migrants generally from West Bengal, Habibur Rahman observed: 'They were not at all sorry to leave' ('Oder phele ashte aeto tuku kharap laglo na').[36] While the comment needs to be treated with some caution, there is some truth in it. The Muslim experience thus provides a contrast to the Hindu experience of migration, as reflected in literature, which is one of uprootedness and poverty, living in squalor in refugee camps, and remembering with loss and nostalgia, the smell, sights and sounds of the daily rituals of home life.[37]

For divided families, the experience of dislocation was compounded by the loss of freedom of movement and of unrestricted travel across the newly constructed borders. At one level, the borders were quite porous and people could slip in and out unnoticed. Those permitted to travel led a charmed life, with frequent shopping sprees across the border. But for prominent politicians, communists, leftists and Hindu professionals, 'Partition meant the loss of contact with friends and relatives on the other side'.[38] In most instances the Pakistan authorities refused to give travel permits in a bid to contain communism and weaken ties between the two Bengals.

Thus, one aspect of nation formation was to relocate the relationship between Hindus and Muslims. While at the state level this aimed to drive a wedge between the two to emphasize the distinctiveness of Pakistan, at the common level the attitude to Hindus was inclusionary, though ambiguous in relation to the past. There was some resentment of past treatment by Hindus, but no ill-will against them.[39] Friendships were recollected and missed, as was the intellectual and cultural life of Calcutta.[40] Some have commented on the segregation at educational establishments: living in separate halls of residence, having separate kitchens, and playing for separate teams, all of which prevented the rise of comradeship.[41] The poet Shamsur Rahman, a student at Dhaka Intermediate College in 1946–7, deeply regrets the Partition 'as a stupendous tragedy'. Although he has no recollection of direct personal communal experiences, he did find certain collective acts of discrimination at school discomfiting. He remembers that at Pogosa School, Dhaka, only twenty out of nine hundred boys were Muslim. 'There were separate aluminium glasses for us left outside the classroom; their bronze glasses were kept inside. It was irritating/insulting' ('Amader jonye alada aekta glass chhilo, aluminiuimer, sheta baire rakha hoto, oder kashar glass bhetore rakha hoto . . . baro peeradayak chhilo'). But he counterpoises this experience with his account of the kindness he was shown by his Hindu teacher of English at Dacca University, Amiya Bhushan Chakrabarty, who permitted him to use his personal library. After Partition, 'during riots we [students] used to guard his house'.[42] In her memoirs, A. G. Stock, who was a visiting professor at Dacca University, remarked on the 'generosity' of Bengalis to the Hindus in Dhaka at that time. She noted that if word got around that a Hindu teacher was being persecuted by the authorities, students rallied to his support.[43] There was thus a clear disjunction between the state and the people in their attitude to minorities.

For the Bengal political leadership, Partition entailed an immediate jockeying for power between the centre and the provinces. The central leadership, headed by Jinnah, sought to curtail the influence of Husain Suhrawardy, a popular and able leader who had until recently been chief minister of Bengal. He was ousted from parliament on the technicality that he had delayed taking up residence in East Bengal. In fact, he had been deported when he attempted to gain entry within the six-month period stipulated. Such central machinations to weaken the province were to be a recurring feature of Pakistani politics. Thus the expected share of Bengali political participation in decision-making did not materialize in reality, because of the unstated policy of excluding Bengalis adopted by the Punjabi-dominated centre.

Zillur Rahman Siddiqui's reflections sum up the experience of Partition and its aftermath for a large segment of society. 'I campaigned for Pakistan alongside other Muslim students. It was the done thing among youths. But at sixteen I was not politically conscious then. Pakistan held promise of a bright future. In young minds there was no critical questioning of this assumption. ... The reality of Pakistan dawned after 1947, when the state policies began to alienate Bengalis.' The impact of subsequent social and political developments has been such that as Habibur Rahman notes, in the post-liberation period, 'we want to forget Pakistan' ('amra Pakistan bhule jete chai'), meaning that the Bengali intelligentsia do not wish to confront their past engagement with the Pakistan idea.

The Legacies of Partition

It is in the context of the reality of Pakistan and the legacies of Partition that its achievements can be questioned. It was a tragedy in that Partition created new problems of ethnicity and minority rights: it gave rise to Bengali ethnicity, culminating in the emergence of independent Bangladesh; in Chittagong it provoked the Chakmas into resistance which evolved into a movement for land rights. The breakup of Pakistan left in its wake half a million Biharis as 'stranded

Pakistanis' in Bangladesh, of whom a quarter of a million still lived in squalid camps decades later, waiting to be repatriated to Pakistan.

The Pakistani state failed to capitalize on the sense of belonging that had characterized the initial Bengali response to Pakistan. Instead, it alienated Bengalis by pursuing a policy of one nation, one language and one culture, to the detriment of Bengali interests. At the same time, it dubbed assertions of Bengali economic interests acts of 'provincialism', and therefore treacherous. Bengalis were thus being struck in the areas that had most attracted them to Pakistan. But the language issue, probably more than any other, galvanized Bengali opinion against the state, particularly after the 1952 gunning down by police of students protesting against the policy to introduce Urdu as the only state language of Pakistan. There were more protests – 'Ora amar mukher katha kaira nite chae' ('They want to take away my words') – and more reprisals. Increasingly, the state came to be viewed as repressive and without legitimacy as it failed to accommodate Bengali cultural and political aspirations, through for instance, formal electoral and representational channels.[44] Bengali ethnicity was mobilized into a movement for autonomy in the 1960s under the charismatic leadership of Sheikh Mujibar Rahman, who offered his six-point formula as 'our right to live'.

I shall not dwell at length on the factors that led to the dismemberment of Pakistan, as they have been widely discussed elsewhere.[45] One is struck, however, by the similarities at many levels between this event and the Partition. Each was preceded by the growth of the middle class accompanied by a restriction of opportunities, marked by intense competition. Conditions were therefore ripe for the rise of ethno-religious nationalism. The struggle in each instance was for territory and economic advantages. The language of mobilization was couched in terms of a golden age: the establishment of the Khulafa-i-Rashidun in Pakistan and of Sonar Bangla, or Golden Bengal, in Bangladesh. The former visualized a just social order that can be explained as a response to a felt discrimination. The latter conjured up images of plenty against the backdrop of hunger and deprivation. A refrain of the Bengali nationalist movement was 'Sonar bangla shashan keno?' ('Why is Golden Bengal a field of the dead?'). In each instance, these developments were marred by suspicion of the 'other', whose motives became increasingly incomprehensible. The leaderships of the Congress and of the Muslim League mistrusted each other as much as the Bengali and Punjabi elite doubted each other. As argued earlier, the endgame of 'opting out of the nation' was in each instance influenced by the experience of violence and threat to physical security: communal riots in the 1940s and Pakistan army action on a sleeping population in March 1971 in the eastern wing. Each event left behind problems as legacies for the future, indicating that these options were not final solutions.

The stranded Biharis in Bangladesh represent the ultimate paradox of Partition. Large numbers had migrated to East Bengal during colonial rule, some to work on the railways, others to escape hardship and communal conflict in Bihar. A major exodus occurred following the November 1946 Bihar riots. They were among the 'most determined' to resist Hindu domination and establish Pakistan. They 'were both small in numbers and poor in status, and they had been thrashed by the Congress there more than in any other Province'.[46] Their experience of communal violence convinced them that their future was not safe in India. After Partition, an estimated one million emigrated.

In Pakistan, they were strong allies of the Punjab-dominated central government and received official patronage for their loyalty. Many worked as small traders, clerks, civil servants, skilled railway and mill workers, and doctors. Many replaced educated Hindus in administrative jobs and in mills after their exodus. In the 1950s, they supported the government's language policy, which privileged Urdu as the national language. In the 1960s, they opposed the regional autonomy movement in Bengal, which visualized a decentralized structure with greater economic and political powers of decision-making in the provinces. Eventually, in 1971, a significant number took up arms in defence of Pakistan and Islam. The Pakistan military refused to let the majority party, the Awami League, form a government although it had won a landslide victory in the first ever national elections in 1970. Unfortunately, it had no following in the western wing. In March 1971 Biharis generally supported the army action against unwary Bengalis, code-named 'Operation Searchlight'. Many joined the auxiliary forces of the Pakistan army, some under duress. One wing of the Razakars, known as 'Al-Shams' was composed entirely of young Biharis.[47] Their surrender to the combined forces of the Indian army and the Mukti Bahini was a major blow to the Biharis, who lost their political identity overnight and became stateless.

After the breakup of Pakistan, about a million Biharis were left in Bangladesh spread over sixty-six refugee camps. Approximately half a million (539,669) persons opted for Pakistan. Of these, less than half

(163,072) were repatriated through a process of lengthy negotiations.[48] The Pakistan government repatriated 126,941 of them at its own expense, but they were mostly dependants and relations of Pakistani army officers and civil servants. As for the rest, Pakistan has made periodic gestures to accept and accommodate some to satisfy internal political demands, but not in any sustained fashion. Pakistan fears that the Biharis would only swell the ranks of the *muhajirs* in Karachi, who continue to be seen as outsiders by many native-born, and as a threat to the social fabric because they originally came from India. Thus Pakistan has made a distinction between its subjects based on their socio-political status.

The remaining optees live in camps throughout Bangladesh in congestion and poverty. Each family is allocated a room 6 feet by 6 feet irrespective of family size and a ration of wheat of 2 kilos and 418 grams per adult per month.[49] In terms of socio-economic status they quickly slid from middle- to lower-class positions to being poor, eking out a living through the charity of a rejected state.[50] Fifty years after Partition and twenty-seven years after the breakup of Pakistan, a quarter of a million 'stranded Pakistanis' had not yet been provided with a home in Pakistan. Despite this betrayal, the Biharis still want to go to Pakistan, their ideological homeland. They regard it as a moral right. Their plight provides a sharp contrast to the experience of Bengali migrants to Pakistan. In the long run the Biharis lost out, became stateless, homeless and poor, getting the very opposite of the promises Pakistan made them at the outset. The Bengalis, on the other hand, gained an independent state and achieved a greater sense of security. As Abul Mansur Ahmed wrote, this was the intended culmination of the original Lahore Resolution.[51]

Conclusion

In conclusion, I would like to sum up some of my key arguments. The politics of identity has created the possibility for nationhood several times in Bengal since the 1940s. Only some materialized, but there were great limitations. Contrary to popular expectations, the emergence of Pakistan did not resolve outstanding problems of ethnicity and minority rights. The Pakistan union failed because Bengalis were not represented in the government structure well enough to have a stake in the Pakistan ideology. There was therefore a lack of Bengali support for the Pakistani nation-building project. The alternatives were not quite attainable, either. The path to an Indian union was foreclosed by the failure of the Congress Party to accommodate Muslim interests as articulated by Jinnah. Similarly, the United Bengal scheme failed because the Hindus and Muslims did not create a common platform of economic and political interests, nor project their shared cultural heritage. The symbiosis that had allowed cooperation and coexistence among them had broken down. They had for all intents and purposes become 'separate nations'.

The rise of the Pakistan demand and that of Bengali ethnicity have certain features in common. The desire for separate nationhood was fostered by political elites who galvanized group solidarity by drawing on the shared linguistic and cultural heritage of the group and focusing on their feelings of discrimination, neglect and disparity in relation to their significant 'other'. But this alone did not cause the imagined nation to strive for statehood. Feelings of marginality, together with fears for physical safety, spurred them to exercise their option for territorial separation. Thus the option for nationhood was based on ideas of self-determination.

The fact that the option emerged several times for Bengalis indicates their complex but fluid identity. In particular, it demonstrates the instrumental character of identity formulation. To a large extent it was manipulated from above: Pakistan was imposed by Mountbatten and Bangladesh by the Pakistani generals Yahya Khan and Tikka Khan. While alternate discourses in identity politics gave rise to reconstituted nations and selves, perceptions of advantages and interests determined their sustainability and transformation into nations bounded by juridical states.

The exercise of option, however, was not a final solution. The appeal of Pakistan to immigrants from India was that it gave them a 'sense of belonging', a 'home'. Yet its impact has been strikingly different upon the fortunes of Bengalis and Biharis. Bengalis, who might have been quite happy to coexist with Hindus in a United Bengal, found a new home in the form of the new state of Bangladesh. But the Biharis, whose efforts had made Pakistan possible, lost the only home they had and became stateless. The Biharis in Bangladesh call themselves 'stranded Pakistanis' and await the fulfilment of the Pakistan dream and repatriation to Pakistan.

The subsequent debate in Bangladesh over Bengali versus Bangladeshi identity indicates another dimension of 'option' in the form of oppositional politics, that is, resistance to the hegemony of the state and political rhetoric to establish the legitimacy of the state. Political elites have engaged in the continued reformulation of national identity not necessarily to enlarge their territorial jurisdiction but perhaps to enlarge their ideological domain. Thus the nation-building project pursued in Bangladesh is not dissimilar to that adopted by Pakistan, except that the ideologues and the subject populations are of the same 'ethnic' stock. Hence, it has given rise to identity politics based on struggles for ideology and legitimacy.

Acknowledgements

The author would like to thank the participants in the workshop on 'Opting Out of the Nation', held in Antalya, Turkey, on 13–16 November 1997, and the South Asia History seminar held at the School of Oriental and African Studies, London, for their lively discussions of this paper; and, in particular, Professor Willem van Schendel for his comments on an earlier draft.

Notes

1 East Bengal was renamed East Pakistan in the 1956 constitution to reflect the post-Partition reality. For a discussion of Bengali discontent giving rise to the autonomy movement, see, for example, Badruddin Umar, *Bhasha andolana o tatkalin rajniti* (Dhaka: 1975).

2 For a discussion of the phrase 'utopias in conflict', see A. T. Embree, *Utopias in Conflict: Religion and Nationalism in Modern India* (Delhi: Oxford University Press, 19920, pp. 1–18.

3 Pakistan was comprised of the territories of western Punjab, North-west Frontier province, Sindh, Baluchistan and eastern Bengal, Kashmir was, and still is, a disputed area. Part of it is under Pakistani jurisdiction as Azad ('Liberated') Kashmir; the remainder is referred to as 'occupied Kashmir', since India controls it, contrary to the rule of self-determination which was the basis of Partition.

4 This theory, which is the rationale for the Pakistan ideology as propagated by the Muslim League, stipulates that Hindus and Muslims are two different nations which have always lived in mutual antagonism and are better off territorially divided. The theory finds its counterpart in the idea of 'the clash of civilizations' propounded in a 1994 *Foreign*

Affairs essay of that title by Samuel P. Huntington of Harvard University, as an explanation for ethnic and nationalistic conflicts.

5 For a discussion of some of these theoretical issues, see Tazeen M. Murshid, 'State Nation Identity: The Quest for Legitimacy in Bangladesh', *South Asia*, vol. 20, no. 2 (December 1997), pp. 1–5.

6 Ernest Gellner, *Nations and Nationalism* (Oxford: Blackwell, 1983); E. J. Hobsbawm, *Nations and Nationalism since 1780; Programme, Myth and Reality* (Cambridge: Cambridge University Press, 1990), p. 9.

7 Pakistan fears a Sindhi backlash because *muhajirs*, or refugees, tend to conglomerate in Karachi, its capital, thus disturbing its demographic balance.

8 Sarat Chandra Bose, 'I Warned my Countrymen', cited in Pradip Kumar Lahiri, *Bengal Muslin Thoughts, 1818–1947: Its Liberal and Rational Trends* (Calcutta: K. P. Bagchi, 1991), pp. 151, 163.

9 *The Statesman*, 8 May 1947.

10 *Star of India*, 30 April 1947.

11 *The Statesman*, 21 May 1947.

12 Ibid, 23 April 1947.

13 Lahiri, *Bengal Muslim Thought*, pp. 152–5.

14 Raghib Ahsan, *A note on the Inner History of the United Bengal Scheme* (Draft Bengal Pact), cited in Mohammad H. R. Talukdar, ed., *Memoirs of Huseyn Shaheed Suhrawardy (With a Brief Account of his Life and Work)* (Dhaka: University Press, 1987), p. 28.

15 *Star of India*, 30 April 1947; Lahiri, *Bengal Muslim Thought*, p. 149.

16 Minutes of Lord Ismay and Rear-Admiral Viscount Mountbatten of Burma, Mountbatten Papers, Official Correspondence Files; Interviews, 26 April 1947, in *TP 10*, no, 228, p. 450.

17 Record of interview between Rear-Admiral Lord Mountbatten of Burma and Mr Suhrawardy, Mountbatten Papers, Viceroy's Interview, no. 98.

18 Ibid.

19 Minutes of Viceroy's Sixth Meeting, 22 April 1947, Mountbatten Papers, no. 194, in Nicholas Mansergh and Penderal Moon, eds., *Transfer of Power, 1942–47*, vol. 10: *The Mountbatten Viceroyalty: Formulation of a Plan*, 22 March–30 may 1947, pp. 363–4.

20 Ibid, p. 364.

21 Interviews with writer Ali Kabir, poet Shamsur Rahman, academic Zillur Rahman Siddiqui and others, Dhaka, August 1997.

22 Shaista Ikramullah, *Husayn Shaheed Suhrawardy: A Biography* (Karachi: Oxford University Press, 1995).

23 In an interview in August 1997, Professor Zillur Rahman Siddiqui, retired vice-chancellor of Jahangimagar University, noted that there was a continuous flow of goods, music, films, literature and books.

24 Interview with Justice S. A. Masud, Calcutta, January 1985.

25 Tazeen M. Murshid, *The Sacred and the Secular: Bengal Muslim Discourses, 1871–1977* (Calcutta: Oxford University Press, 1995), pp. 237–8, 242–3.
26 *1961 Population Census of Pakistan*, vol. 5, Table 4, p. 206.
27 Ibid.
28 For a discussion of the intellectual stirrings, see A. G. Stock, *Memoirs of Dacca University, 1947–51* (Dacca [Dhaka]: Green Book House, 1973), p. 52. For the views of the liberal intelligentsia, see 'Editorial', *New Values*, vol. 1, no. 1 (September 1949); 'Letters to the Editor', *Pakistan Observer*, 1 March 1951. For the orthodox position, see *Al-Islam*, 1, 15 October 1961.
29 Interview with the writer Ali Kabir, August 1997.
30 Interview, Shaka, August 1997.
31 The story was recounted by her granddaughter, who at the age of four witnessed the events and still recollects them vividly, interview with Mastura Huq, December 1997.
32 Interview with Habibur Rahman, Dhaka, August 1997. Now a retired chief justice, he was then a student at Presidency College and had had family home in Murshidabad. His family's decision to emigrate was determined by external factors; central to this was concern for family security.
33 Abul Mansur Ahmad, *Atmakatha* (Dacca [Dhaka]:, 1978).
34 *1961 Population Census.*
35 Speech by Professor Raj Chakravarty, 6 March 1948, *Constituent Assembly Debates, Pakistan*, pp. 269–71; speech by Peter Paul Gomez, 21 February 1956, *Constitutional Assembly Debates*, pp. 3372–3.
36 Interview with Habibur Rahman, Dhaka, August 1997.
37 Dipesh Chakrabarty, 'Remembered Villages: Representations of Hindu-Bengali Memories in the Aftermath of Partition', *South Asia*, special issue, vol. 18 (1995), pp. 109–29.
38 Interviews with a number of people including retired Supreme Court judge Debendrath Bhattacharya (*b* 1916), Nirmal Sen, of the Community Party of Bangladesh, and others, such as Shamsur Rahman and Professor Siddiqui, Dhaka, August 1997.
39 Ahmad, *Atmakatha.*
40 Interview with Professor Siddiqui.
41 Interview with Professor Mahmood of Calcutta University, Calcutta, January 1985.
42 Interview with Shamsur Rahman.
43 Stock, *Memoirs of Dacca University.*
44 The first national general election was held in 1971 after twenty-four years of independence.
45 Raunaq Jahan, *Pakistan: Failure in National Integration* (Dacca [Dhaka]:

Oxford University Press, 1973); Hasan Zaheer, *The Separation of East Pakistan* (Karachi: Oxford University Press, 1994).

46 Lumley to Linlithgow, 15 January 1942, in Nicholas Mansergh, Lumby and Penderel Moon, eds., *Constitutional Relations between Britain and India: The Transfer of Power, 1942–47* (London: HMSO, 1970), vol. 1, no. 13, p. 27.

47 Ben Whitaker, Iain Guest and David Ennals, *The Biharis in Bangladesh* (London: Minority Rights Group, 1982), p. 8.

48 Ministry of Relief and Rehabilitation, *Bangladeshe atkapara abangali sankranta* [The Latest Situation Report on the Stranded non Bengalis in Bangladesh] (Dhaka: Government of Bangladesh, 1997), p. 2.

49 Ibid.

50 Tazeen M. Murshid, 'A Forgotten Minority: The Biharis in Bangladesh. Policy Options for the Repatriation and Resettlement of "Stranded Pakistanis", European Institute of Asian studies, Briefing Paper BP 98/05, pp. 7–8.

51 Abul Mansur Ahmed, *The End of a Betrayal and the Restoration of the Lahore Resolution* (Dhaka: 1978).

5· Who Speaks for the Nation? Nationalist Rhetoric and the Challenge of Cultural Pluralism in Bangladesh

Willem van Schendel

If there is one thing which has dominated public debates in Bangladesh since its birth in 1971, it is the issue of national identity. Today a consensus on this question is much less evident than when Bangladesh came into existence. Passionate but inconclusive discussions take place in newspapers and at political gatherings, during academic meetings and on the Internet, and at private get-togethers. Different interpretations of what it means to be Bangladeshi have become the cornerstone of party politicking, ensuring that national identity remains the hottest issue in national politics. Why is this so? How exactly is national identity debated? What purposes does the debate serve? And what are its implications? These are among the most urgent questions in contemporary Bangladesh.

One way of approaching the subject is to look at questions which are highlighted and ones which are suppressed in the debate. Among the former are ethnicity, religion and sovereignty; among the latter equity, democracy and citizens' rights. In this essay I examine one approach to national identity which addresses the second set. The essay is largely concerned with exploring this approach by means of a case study, examining its critique of the current debate, and concluding that a stable Bangladeshi national identity cannot be constructed without foregrounding the issues raised by proponents of this approach.

Bengalis, Bangladeshis and Muslims: A National Debate

The birth of Bangladesh in 1971 heralded a new phase in South Asian nationalism because it created the first modern regional state in what had been British India. The two successor states to colonial rule had been territorially all-embracing in their nationalist programmes. India was built on the ambition to keep the colony united, and projected 'Indianness' as an encompassing identity onto its citizens. Pakistan, on the other hand, was based on the notion that all Muslims in British India formed a nation, and should have their own state. These conflicting nationalisms inevitably clashed, led to the partitioning of British India, and forced India and Pakistan to live with a political reality which fell short of their territorial ambitions.

But Bangladesh was different. It was built on a nationalism which was decidedly regional, linked with one particular linguistic group, and free from expansionist designs on its neighbours. In this sense, the nationalism that gave rise to Bangladesh was the first to transcend the colonial mould, both because its mental map was no longer the British colony and because it ignored that kingpin of late-colonial politics, communalism – the juxtaposition of two separate religious communities: Hindus and Muslims. No wonder many people in South Asia and beyond greeted Bangladeshi statehood with enthusiasm and relief: they saw it as the first flowering of a post-communalism which might spread throughout the subcontinent. And no wonder that this challenge to well-established parameters of enmity and identification in the subcontinent caused concern to power-holders in both India and Pakistan – it signalled to other regional movements that independent statehood was not impossible.

Bengali nationalism had been gathering momentum as a counter-ideology from the early 1950s. After 1971 it became a state ideology and was enshrined in the constitution of Bangladesh. This important change meant that the dream of Bangladesh was now put to the test of political reality. Despite the enormous relief that swept the country and the great expectations of the early 1970s, by the middle of that decade the mass appeal of Bengali nationalism was fading fast. The new power-holders who identified so strongly with it were seen to be incapable of establishing a more just, equitable and safe society, and their proclamations of 'nationalism, secularism, socialism and democracy' began to ring hollow in the ears of growing numbers of compatriots. The ensuing political crisis threw up different ideological responses.

First, there was an attempt by those who identified strongly with the nationalist cause but did not occupy positions of power to re-appropriate and salvage the nationalism that had created Bangladesh, and free it from its new associations with authoritarianism, military rule and narrow party politics. This struggle, mainly by former freedom fighters, students, intellectuals and others in what had become the national elite, has continued since the mid-1970s, and was particularly intense in the years leading up to the fall of the Ershad regime in 1990. It seeks to recover the liberating potential of nationalism, maintain the post-colonial, post-communalist vision which empowered the movement for Bangladesh, and bring the institutions of state and civil society more closely in line with that vision.[1] Let us call this response 'renewal nationalism'. It would be a mistake to see renewal nationalism merely as a continuation of the 'old' oppositional Bengali nationalism of the Pakistan period; the crucial difference is that renewal nationalism seeks to redefine Bengali nationalism in opposition to a state elite which claims the very same ideology as its *raison d être.* Renewal nationalism employs symbols of the old nationalism to new ends. It uses the powerful 'old' symbols of an independent, self-reliant, secular and democratic Bangladesh – for example Language Day (21 February[2]), Independence Day (26 March[3]) and Victory Day (16 December[4]) – to discredit the authoritarianism and injustice of the new rulers. It argues that in their quest for power and links with international capital, the (military) rulers of Bangladesh since 1975 have manipulated these symbols to create a false dichotomy between 'Bengali' and 'Bangladeshi' nationalism.[5] Renewal nationalism is far from monolithic, however, because the 'vision of Bangladesh' has always been interpreted in a variety of ways, from conservative to radical.[6]

Others sought a very different way out of the ideological crisis of the mid-1970s. Among those who were disillusioned with the corruption of public life and the exclusion of so many from the new state, a new 'moral politics' gained popularity. It gathered strength in the 1980s and 1990s among middling peasants and a squeezed urban middle class, but also among the disgruntled children of the state elite who were looking for an ideological alternative to the discredited nationalism of their elders and who sought to establish new links with 'the people'. This ideology, given coherence by an Islamic idiom, brought about a fusion between 'old communalism' and new ideas about Islam as a model for creating a state which was more moral, accountable and self-reliant. Far from being archaic or traditional, this response, which we can call 'political Islam', is innovative, not only in its discourse but equally in the eclectic use it makes of old and new means of communication, styles of organization, institutional frameworks, and international connections.[7] Political Islam, too, is anything but monolithic; Islamists come in many hues, ranging from reactionary to utopian.

Political Islam celebrates the unity of all believers and seeks to refashion Bangladeshi society and the Bangladeshi state according to religious precepts. Its symbols are the Arabic language, the Qur'an, highly gendered codes of dress, behaviour and morality, and the celebration of Islamic festivals. It is post-nationalist in the sense that it goes beyond the nationalism that lay at the foundation of the state of Bangladesh. But political Islam claims for Muslims a community identity which is hard to distinguish from nationhood and which has been described as religious nationalism. It posits that the 'Muslim community' is under attack, no longer so much from Hindus as from an external enemy – the tutelage and corrupting influence of 'the West' – and an internal one – Bangladeshi secularism.[8] Islamists assert the moral superiority of the 'muscular' Islam to which they aspire. Only by organizing and emancipating themselves as Muslims can Bengali Muslims overcome the political, economic and cultural crisis facing them at the end of the twentieth century.

Today nationalism is in deep crisis. There is still no uncontested sense of nation in Bangladesh. Neither Bengaliness nor Islamism has come to be accepted as 'natural'. Although they continue to vie for support, few people in Bangladesh have been willing to sacrifice their allegiance to either their ethnic group or their religious community. Even though it seems inevitable that some form of 'Bangladeshiness' should eventually develop, the compromise that is on offer now is far from universally accepted. The literature on contemporary Bangladeshi politics pays much attention to the two responses sketched above, and to the intense struggle in which these have been locked over the last twenty-five years. It explores how these responses and struggles are connected with successive rulers' use of military rule and manipulation of 'national' and 'Islamic' symbols in their pursuit for power and open-door policies.[9] This essay, however, is not concerned with this important debate. Instead, it examines another response to the crisis of nationalism, which has received little attention so far.

Cultural Pluralism: An Emerging Challenge

Since the early 1980s, political developments have forced a third interpretation into the debate. It is still being ignored by many participants but it appears to be gaining ground. I shall refer to this challenge as the 'cultural pluralist' interpretation.[10]

What makes the pluralist interpretation of nation and history in Bangladesh important is that it challenges five basic assumptions underlying the current debate. First, it refuses to accept that it is, or could ever be, a debate between Bengalis, that is, members of a relatively well defined linguistic and ethnic group. It insists on the cultural plurality of the inhabitants of Bangladesh. Second, it attacks the assumption that the debate is one between cultural equals. It emphasizes the unequal power relations between cultural groups in Bangladesh, and aims at exposing the political uses of ignoring this reality. Third, it refuses to accept the communalist, religio-political parameters set for the debate: it rejects the binary opposition between Muslim and Hindu on which the debate on nationalism and identity in Bangladesh, and in much of South Asia, hinges. Instead, it demands that participants in the debate take cognizance of a plurality of religio-political identities. Fourth, the pluralist interpretation challenges the assumption that Bangladeshi citizenship extends to all inhabitants of Bangladesh. It argues powerfully that citizenship and the rights and duties that go with it have been restricted to certain groups, excluding many others. And fifth, it argues that those who came to power on the crest of the popular struggle for Bangladesh, and their successors, misused this power to establish a highly authoritarian and centralized state, quite different from the state imagined by those who fought for an independent, self-reliant Bangladesh. Let us take a closer look at these challenges.

Bengalis and Others

As the twenty-first century begins, the territory of Bangladesh is inhabited by some 130 million people. Apart from holders of foreign passports, they are all Bangladeshis in the sense that they are administered by the state of Bangladesh, and are classified as belonging to that state in the international political arena. The vast majority of these individuals identify themselves as Bengalis, that is, speakers of the Bengali language and sharers in a culture which they identify as Bengali. What it means to be a Bengali has never been fixed, of course – it changes with time and circumstances. Speaking very generally, for Bengali-speakers in Bangladesh, self-identification as Bengali was strengthened in the course of the twentieth century. This is not to say that it has not been contested as a major identity informing both self-perception and behaviour. The most powerful contenders have been 'Indian' (in the first half of the twentieth century), 'Pakistani' and 'Muslim' (from the 1930s), and 'Bangladeshi' (since the 1970s). Events since the late 1940s have boosted self-perception as Bengali, first as an 'injured identity' struggling for recognition, and later as a victorious one. This has meant extension in two dimensions. On the one hand, the notion of Bengaliness has taken on a more emotive and consciously political character in Bangladesh for many people who had always identified themselves as Bengali, and who were seen as such by others. On the other hand, it has spread to groups who, at the beginning of the twentieth century, did not identify themselves as strongly as Bengalis as they do now. An example is the large population of northern Bangladesh usually referred to as 'Rajbangshis' who, in reaction to Bengali upper-caste social disdain and colonial ethnographers' descriptions of them being part of a large 'semi-Hinduized' 'Dravidian tribe', campaigned to be accepted as Bengali Hindus of Kshatriya status during the colonial period.[11]

Today, Bengali self-identification is so preponderant in Bangladesh that other self-identifications are usually not taken into account at all. And yet, there are many groups who have not come to identify themselves as Bengalis; nor are they identified as such by those who see themselves as Bengalis. These groups cannot be lumped together into a single category unless it is the negative one of 'non-Bengali'. Although they tend to be equated with 'tribes' (a term to which I shall return shortly), they include various other groups which are usually considered to be 'outside society' but not 'tribal', such as the so-called Biharis and the Bede.[12] The exact size of the different 'non-Bengali' groups in Bangladesh is not known, and those putting forward the pluralist interpretation seriously question the official figures for the 'tribal population': according to them, these figures suffer from distinct under-enumeration, both of individuals and of entire groups.[13] Even so, it is clear that the largest among at least sixty-odd 'non-Bengali' groups in Bangladesh are those who identify themselves as Chakmas, Santals, Marmas, Tripuras, Mandis (Garos) and Biharis.

It is mainly from some of these groups that the pluralist interpretation of Bangladesh history is now being put forward, sometimes articulated only vaguely outside their own circle, but increasingly in formats and media which reach a wider national, and indeed international, audience. The main argument is against the assumption that Bengali nation and Bangladeshi state are coterminous, and that Bangladeshi history can be equated with the history of Bengalis.[14]

Cultural Inequality

The pluralist discourse insists that the modern history of Bangladesh is too often seen as a drama played out between the East Bengali Muslim middle class and successive states – British India, Pakistan, Bangladesh. But Bangladesh is much more than a 'bourgeois project', the outcome of middle-class movements, and it is essential to pay more attention to the agency of other groups in its history.[15] In the country's early years, attempts were made to highlight the roles of peasants and workers in the formation of contemporary Bangladeshi society, but this trend has weakened in recent years. Today the more innovative pluralist interpretations of Bangladeshi history appear to deal with the non-Bengali groups in the country. The pluralist argument is that unequal power relations within the state of Bangladesh, and within its political and academic communities, have allowed Bengalis to dominate discussions completely and to ignore, marginalize, distort and silence other voices systematically. Pluralists urge participants in national debates to stop disregarding and censoring non-Bengali voices and views, and to start taking these seriously, as legitimate and valuable in their own right. At times, a parallel is drawn with the marginalization and repression of Bengali interpretations of history and destiny under the Pakistan regime.[16]

It is undeniable that, generally, Bangladeshi intellectuals, politicians and 'opinion-leaders' have ignored such calls. They have found it more difficult to close their ears completely, however, since the eruption of armed conflict in the Chittagong Hill Tracts, the region with the highest concentration of non-Bengali people in Bangladesh. This conflict remains regionalized and does not threaten the centre of the state – militarily, politically, culturally, or financially.[17] As a result, it has also remained marginal to national debates and few intellectuals have felt a need to address its implications for the future of the state or interpretations of the past.[18] The *communis opinio* remains very much that of Sheikh Mujibur Rahman, Bangladesh's first prime minister, who, at a public meeting in Rangamati, the administrative headquarters of the Chittagong Hill Tracts, in 1975, 'addressed the tribals as brethren and told them to become Bengalis, to forget the colonial past and join the mainstream of Bengali culture'.[19] This attitude was typical of the inclusive, and from their point of view magnanimous, notion of Bengali nationhood held by the founding fathers of Bangladesh. The constitution of 1972 stated that 'by nationalism all citizens of Bangladesh are Bengali', and a famous poster of 1971 read 'Hindus of Bengal, Christians of Bengal, Buddhists of Bengal, Muslims of Bengal – We Are All Bengalis'.[20] The pluralists' argument is that, by ignoring the sharply unequal power relations between cultural groups in Bangladesh, such attitudes serve a clear political purpose: the cultural homogenization of Bangladesh by means of throttling non-Bengali cultural expressions.

Beyond the Communal Mindset

The pluralist interpretation is particularly strong in its refusal to accept religio-political ('communal') interpretations of the past. History-writing, of both the nationalist and the Islamist persuasion, pitches two giant wrestlers against each other: The Hindu and The Muslim. Even though these are often described as Bengali Hindu and Bengali Muslim, or Hindu Bengali and Muslim Bengali, it is in religious terms that the struggles of modern history are almost universally conceptualized. Some nationalist and transnationalist thinkers in Bangladesh have criticized communal interpretations, but a truly non-communal interpretation of history has scarcely developed. The pluralist interpretation draws attention to two facts. First, there were other players in Bangladeshi history, even in socio-religious terms (Buddhists, Christians, believers in many local religions), who are totally ignored in dominant writings. Second, the privileging of religious categories can distort our reading of history. It creates very broad categories (for example, 'the Muslims of Bengal') which may cover up more than they reveal. Region, class, educational background, gender, age, ideological leanings – all are assumed to have been derivative of, or less important than, religious identity. In other words, the intricacies and complex shifts of modern history in Bengal tend to be collapsed into a unidimensional and static, ahistorical dichotomy. This style of thinking was of great political use to the ruling elites of the colonial and post-colonial states, and to academic historians who saw themselves as assistants in the task of nation-building, but has little relevance for those who wish to bring out the plurality of identities that went into the making of modern Bangladesh. The image of the two giant wrestlers must be rejected because it hides from history those connections, dimensions, ambiguities and struggles which the pluralist interpretation seeks to foreground.

The Limits of Citizenship

A crucial challenge thrown up by the pluralists is their questioning of the assumption of universal citizenship that underlies nationalist narratives. Pluralists seek to show that citizens' rights have remained quite restricted under the Bangladesh state and its precursors, that the vast majority of inhabitants are treated as subjects rather than citizens, and that the rhetoric of nationalism serves to cover up this reality. In the 'People's Republic of Bangladesh', the pluralist argument runs, state power has been captured by a minute politico-military elite which has neither extended civil liberties such as equality before the law, freedom of expression, or the principle of democratic representation, nor shown great eagerness to expand universal education or provide basic needs such as food, shelter and social security to all Bangladeshis. It is fair to say that many members of this elite consider only themselves to be 'society', and perceive others in Bangladesh as pre-social, as people who have not really concluded the process towards civilization and individuation, as 'blurred beings' who do not stand out from the corporate groups (such as 'peasants' or 'tribes') to which they belong, and who are ruled by 'custom'.

Various subsections of this elite have struggled for supremacy since 1971 and they have all been determined to uphold exclusionary policies.[21] They could afford this because they could draw on large, increasing, and largely unaccountable external resources in the form of aid (including military aid) which made them less dependent on internal resources and less accountable to the other inhabitants of the country. They have refused to share with others the power to distribute these resources, and they have had to pay a high price for it:

political life in Bangladesh has been extremely volatile and violent because of recurrent demands for a more equitable division of resources as well as citizen's rights. The country has seen a spectacular growth in non-governmental organizations, many of which are in the business of giving voice to these demands. The pluralist interpretation foregrounds these struggles, pointing to routine violations of civil and human rights, the violence which successive governments have unleashed upon those who express dissent, and the weakness of institutions to safeguard social security, democracy, equality before the law, and mass education.

In other words, cultural pluralists, many of whom belong to relatively deprived groups, seek to expose the fangs behind the beatific smile of official nationalist discourse, and to debunk its imagery of kinship with its claim to harmony, equality and shared interests. In the same vein, pluralists critique the core claim of political Islam: the unity of all believers. Although there may be a unity of all believers in the spiritual sense (despite many doctrinal differences), such unity is hardly in evidence in social, political or economic terms, nor has it been in the past. Pluralists argue that, apart from the exclusion of non-believers, Islamist politicians employ the image of 'brotherhood' to hide points of view and policies which exclude many 'brothers' and 'sisters'. In short, pluralists point to the exclusionary practices behind the inclusionary language of both nationalists and Islamists. They assert that the image of the nation (whether ethnic or religious) as being beleaguered by a hostile outside world, and therefore bound to suppress internal divisions, is used to ride roughshod over the legitimate demands of many inhabitants of Bangladesh.

A Centralized State

Finally, pluralists not only argue that the state in Bangladesh is undemocratic and authoritarian, a charge also made by many disgruntled 'renewal nationalists', but also insist that it has become too highly centralized, an insight shared by many foreign donors who have attempted to persuade successive governments in Dhaka to introduce local government in various forms. These attempts have largely failed, and no devolution of power has taken place. Pluralists argue that this is because the state elite feels too threatened by popular forces (nationalist, Islamist or pluralist) to let go. Within the state elite, the military and the central bureaucrats have been dominant since the late

1970s, and they counter any demands for decentralization with an ostensible concern for national integrity and security. Pluralists are suspicious of this; to them it is the ruling elite, not the state, which might be weakened if Bangladesh adopted a more decentralized structure of administration.[22]

Chakma Visions of a Pluralist Bangladesh

Exploring the pluralist interpretation can be done in different ways. Here I am concerned with just one body of evidence: that which has been created by writers who identify themselves as Chakmas. The reason for this choice is twofold: Chakma writings form the largest collection of material with a sustained pluralist vision on Bangladesh, and these writings have become more articulate than any other pluralist writing in Bangladesh as a result of political developments in the Chittagong Hill Tracts, the home of the vast majority of Chakmas, in the second half of the twentieth century. It should be pointed out that Chakmas make up no more than half the non-Bengali population of the Chittagong hills; all the other groups (the largest of which are the Marmas and the Tripuras) have also been caught up in the current upheaval there.

The term 'Chakma' to denote certain inhabitants of the Chittagong hills dates back to at least the mid-sixteenth century.[23] Today Chakmas form the largest non-Bengali group in Bangladesh, and they consider Bangladesh their homeland. During the past half-century, however, four major upheavals have prompted Chakmas to rethink their relationship with the state. Three of these forced groups of Chakmas (and others) to leave their country.

The first upheaval was the Partition of India and Pakistan in 1947, when the Chittagong hills were awarded to East Pakistan (now Bangladesh) and those who opposed the merger fled to India, forming distinct groups in the Indian states of Tripura and Mizoram.[24] The second upheaval is known to Chakmas as *Bara Parang*, or the Great Exodus: tens of thousands of developmental refugees, uprooted by the creation of the Kaptai hydroelectric project in the early 1960s, fled to India, where most were eventually settled in the state of Arunachal Pradesh.[25] The third was the war of 1971, in which Bangladesh broke away from Pakistan. Although it did not lead to permanent migration by Chakmas (with the significant exception of the Chakma Raja, or

Chakma Chief, and part of his family), their falling victim to indiscriminate violence during and immediately after the war left a lasting imprint on their relationship with the emerging state of Bangladesh.[26] And finally, militarization and repression by the Bangladesh army forced tens of thousands of Chakmas to seek political refuge abroad from the mid-1980s. The majority have been living in refugee camps in Tripura up to 1998, but the 'Chakma diaspora' has now spread to other Indian states and well beyond South Asia.[27]

These experiences shaped late-twentieth-century Chakma thinking about Bangladesh society and the place of Chakmas in it. Chakmas had never identified themselves as Bengalis but in the colonial period (1860–1947), during which they were ruled from Bengal, the Chakma elite came to rely more and more on the Bengali cultural model.[28] However, their position weakened considerably in the states of Pakistan and Bangladesh after 1947, and this caused them to distance themselves from the Bengali cultural model and begin a search for new symbols of identity. Two different patterns emerged. One sought to unite various non-Bengali groups under a new heading, and the other tried to highlight the specificity of Chakmas and 'Chakmaness'.

Non-Bengaliness as a Unifier

This pattern of identity politics developed strongly among Chakmas in Bangladesh. It took two forms which we can call the 'regional' and the 'country-wide' project, respectively. Both developed from the 1970s. The regional project manifested itself most clearly in the emergence of the term 'Jumma people' or 'Jumma nation' to refer to all original inhabitants of the Chittagong hills, that is, more than ten distinct groups, but excluding immigrant Bengalis.[29] The term was popularized by the JSS,[30] the only regional political party, which is dominated by Chakmas. It highlights the hill people's cultural separateness from Bengalis, their shared possession of a Jumma homeland – the Chittagong Hill Tracts – a shared history of oppression and marginalization, and the need to develop an 'indigenous cultural model'.[31]

The country-wide form of identity politics seeks to unify groups across Bangladesh on the basis of either their non-Bengaliness or their marginalized position. These attempts have given birth to a lively debate among these groups on how to identify themselves. Should they elect to be referred to in Bengali, the contact language, as *adibasi* (original inhabitants, aborigines), *upajati* (tribals, sub-nations), *sampraday* (communities), or *pahari* (hill people)? None of these seems to find favour, and there appears to be a growing tendency to insist on *jati* (nations, peoples), or, avoiding the stigmatization of Bengali terms, as 'indigenous populations'.[32]

So far, the country-wide form of identity politics has been less successful than the regional one. Two reasons can be suggested. First, the circumstances and historical experiences of different non-Bengali groups in Bangladesh vary considerably, and many of them have hardly been in touch with one another in the past. This makes a united front difficult to create and maintain. Second, there have been attempts to mobilize 'the religious and ethnic minorities, who have been made second class citizens of the country' against the 'majority chauvinism [which] is evident in almost every sphere of socio-political life'.[33] Such mobilization involves large numbers of Bengali Hindus and Christians, and small numbers of Bengali Buddhists, and cuts across attempts at mobilizing people on the basis of non-Bengaliness.

Chakmaness as a Unifier

The other option for Chakmas wishing to distance themselves from the Bengali cultural model has been to emphasize the boundaries between those who are Chakmas and those who are not. Remarkably, this option has not been very popular with Chakmas in Bangladesh; they went from distinctly Chakma organizations in the early years of the twentieth century to more inclusive regional organizations after Partition.[34] Today organizations which are numerically dominated by Chakmas tend to refer to themselves as organizations of 'hill people', 'Jummas', the 'Chittagong Hill Tracts', or, in the case of religious organizations, 'Buddhists'.

By contrast, the Chakma diaspora in India has been more interested in Chakmaness as a unifier. Thus in India a World Chakma Conference was organized in 1993, and the All-India Chakma Cultural Conference (AICCC), meeting in November 1995, demanded an end to the oppression of Chakmas in Mizoram and Arunachal Pradesh, improvement of the position of Chakmas in Assam, the introduction of the Chakma language in its own script in primary schools in Tripura, and the Indian government's recognition of Chakma as a classified language. It also requested the government of India to provide full rations to the refugees from Bangladesh in the camps in Tripura, significantly referring to these refugees as 'Jummas'.[35]

There are three reasons why the Chakma identity was more attractive to Chakmas living in India than to those living in Bangladesh. First, the majority of Chakmas in India are (descendents of) the political and developmental refugees of the 1940s and 1960s, and they have no links with Bangladesh, which came into existence in 1971, or the 'Jumma' concept, which developed in the 1970s and 1980s in response to militarization and state oppression. Equally important, they were in India, a country which encourages self-organization on 'tribal' grounds because of its well-established policy of positive discrimination in favour of 'scheduled tribes'. By contrast, Bangladesh has never developed such a policy.[36] In several Indian states Chakmas had been recognized as a 'scheduled tribe' before the arrival of newcomers from what is now Bangladesh. Third, those Chakmas who arrived in India well after Partition were treated as inferior 'refugees' and had little chance of integrating into local society.[37] In this political environment, it made good sense to identify oneself as Chakma: doing so gave access to state resources which were completely unavailable in Bangladesh. In other words, the use of Chakmaness as a unifier was a direct adaptation to what the Indian state had to offer.[38]

Resisting Bengali Cultural Hegemonism

In Chakma writings in Bangladesh, cultural self-assertion has been a continual theme. For example, a series of periodicals, starting with *Gairika* in 1936, foreshadowed in cultural terms the emergence of the regional model that Chakmas adopted as a political instrument from the 1970s. Authors from different ethnic backgrounds in the Chittagong Hill Tracts were included in these periodicals, which directed themselves to both a non-Bengali and a Bengali audience.[39] The publications presented regional 'tribal' voices as legitimate and civilized, demanded that non-Bengali cultural expressions be taken seriously, and asserted that Bengali contempt of such expressions was based on deep ignorance.[40] Those who contributed articles and poetry shared a concern that their own culture might be crushed by the dominance of a Bengali culture which was largely oblivious of it, and which at best bestowed a benevolent but misguided and misinformed paternalism on it. In other words, these publications presented statements of cultural assertion and increasingly self-confident calls to come to terms with the fact that Bangladesh is a multicultural society:

there are other voices speaking for the 'nation' and these challenge the monopoly claimed by Bengali culture.[41]

A Critique of Communalism

Chakma writings also serve as good examples of the pluralist interpretation because they refuse to accept the religio-political ('communal') interpretations of the past that are so common in Bangladeshi debates. Chakmas, being neither Muslims nor Hindus but overwhelmingly Buddhists, have always been uncomfortable with Hindu–Muslim communalism. During the colonial period they sought to distance themselves from it but the strategy proved increasingly futile as the communalist mindset took hold of Bengal's dominant politicians.

Both in the movement for Pakistan (up to 1947) and in the movement for Bangladesh (1952–71), Chakmas found themselves caught in the middle, because both presented them with a no-win situation. Their interpretations of the modern history of Bangladesh are largely a defence against hegemonic readings of that history which depict Chakmas as traitors, first to the movement for Pakistan, then to the movement for Bangladesh, and finally to the state of Bangladesh. Communalist elements are legion in these hegemonic readings, for example, the emphasis on what has become the prime symbol of Chakma unreliability in many accounts of the formation of Pakistan: the raising of the Indian flag at Rangamati on 15 August 1947 when it was still unclear whether the Chittagong Hill Tracts had been 'awarded' to India or Pakistan. 'This treasonable act was righted by Pakistani police forces',[42] but it is rarely mentioned that Marmas (the second largest non-Bengali group) raised the Burmese flag in Bandarban (in the southern Chittagong Hill Tracts) on that same confused day. In the construction of a Pakistani identity, Burma (or, in communalist terms, 'Buddhists') played no role, whereas India (and Hindus) became the villain of the piece.[43] Similarly, Chakma indecision and attempted neutrality during the war of 1971 led to their being portrayed in later Bangladeshi readings of history as siding with the villain of that piece, Pakistan. And finally, with the resurgence of fears of India in post-1971 Bangladesh, Chakmas were once again depicted as conspirators and agents of 'a foreign country', the standard communalist term for India.[44] In other words, no honourable place was allowed for Chakmas in the heroic nationalist narratives of either the Pakistan or the Bangladesh period. Local memories were loaded with shame and recrimination as the supposed complicity of Chakmas (and others) with enemies of the state was used to bring out in full relief the heroism of first the Pakistani and then the Bengali nation.

In recent years Chakma authors have demonstrated that this allocation of shame is inseparable from the nationalist narrative, and their demand for rehabilitation implies a fundamental critique of that narrative. They argue that the defamation of supposedly 'non-loyal' groups is self-serving, misleading and based on a wilful disregard of the historical record. They have begun to put up a spirited defence of Chakmas in processes of state formation since colonial times, arguing that the communalist perspective leaves no room for players in Bangladeshi history other than Muslims and Hindus, and that the nationalist narrative totally disregards the impact of actions of Bangladeshi citizens belonging to other socio-religious and ethnic groups. And more importantly, they discard the idea that religious or ethnic identity is more significant than other identities, notably those based on region, regional language and powerlessness vis-à-vis the state. Each of these categories invites different, pluralist, 'post-nationalist', 'post-communalist' readings of the history of Bangladesh. Each points to the plurality of identities that went into the making of modern Bangladesh and suggests a much more complicated way of looking at Bangladeshi history than has been prevalent till now. If this approach is taken seriously, it reveals a multitude of connections and struggles, both local and global, which we need to understand in order to make better sense of how contemporary Bangladeshi society came into existence. In other words, what recent Chakma writings contribute to the national debate is an indication that the two heroic master narratives of Bangladeshi history – the 'Emancipation of the Muslim'[45] and the 'Struggle for Bengali Nationhood'[46] – are insufficient for understanding the formation of contemporary Bangladeshi society.[47]

Demanding Citizenship

The nationalist narrative assumes that citizenship and its rights and duties are shared by all Bangladeshis. Pluralist interpretations, on the other hand, assume that this is a myth, that citizens' rights have hardly spread beyond a tiny elite, and that the nationalist rhetoric of harmony, equality and shared interests serves to mask political realities which are starkly different. According to this view, it is precisely the thwarting of citizens' rights and the recurrent demand for them that have made cultural, economic and political life as volatile as it has been throughout the years of Bangladesh's existence.

Once again, Chakma accounts of recent history provide a good example, although by no means the only one.[48] Inevitably, the armed revolt in the Chittagong Hill Tracts, which broke out in the early years of Bangladesh and continues to this day, has loomed large in the consciousness of Chakma writers and has given their writings a special edge. To them, the conflict is merely the latest phase in a long struggle to attain citizens' rights, and their analyses have shown a distinct tendency to become more inclusive. What they saw essentially as a Chakma struggle for cultural and political rights till the 1960s was reconceptualized as the struggle of all Jumma people of the Chittagong hills in the 1970s. And several Chakma authors have now widened the scope further by adopting the term 'indigenous people'. This term, which stems from an international discourse on the limits to modern citizenship,[49] relates local issues directly to the nature of the state and its dealings with *all* the inhabitants of its territory.

Chakma writers are now asking questions about civil liberties in Bangladesh which go well beyond regional or 'minority' issues and are therefore of direct interest to the national debate on citizenship. What about equality before the law, the right of assembly, freedom of expression, and the principle of democratic representation? What about education, social security and 'basic needs'? To what extent is the relationship between Chakmas and the state of Bangladesh exceptional, and to what extent is it representative of the relationship between all Bangladeshis and their state? What are the mechanisms by which the state has restricted citizenship? Do these mechanisms differ for different groups and periods, and, if so, how? Such questions are now beginning to be explored, and pluralists argue that they cannot be resolved from a nationalist point of view. Any connected history of citizenship, and indeed the state, in Bangladesh will have to explain why successive governments are on record as unleashing violence on those who expressed dissent – whether in the streets of Dhaka, the villages of the Chittagong hills, or elsewhere – failing to punish those responsible, routinely violating civil and human rights, and weakening the institutions of democratic representation and participation. To understand all this, a cultural pluralist perspective on the recent history of Bangladesh is essential.

A Critique of Overcentralization

The state elite of Bangladesh presides over a considerably centralized machinery of administration and control. It has rebuked or quietly sabotaged several campaigns to allow more equal power-sharing among the various echelons of government, and to develop a more accountable and democratic style of government. Centralization has been presented as a national duty, and as the only way to preserve national integrity and security. Any challenge to this ideological legitimation meets with a swift response.

Pluralists contend that such overcentralization has created many problems for ordinary Bangladeshis. A good example is the uprising in the Chittagong Hill Tracts, a regional 'problem' which could have been resolved long ago by granting a form of regional autonomy. The reaction of the state elite has been the opposite: invoking the unitary nature of the state, hinting darkly at foreign powers wishing to dismember Bangladesh, and claiming that regional autonomy would require a change in the constitution for which there was too little support, it has sent in the army. Not surprisingly, the leaders of the uprising have clung to an equally legalistic position, pointing to the region's history of separate administration under British rule and the fact that the document in which this autonomy was guaranteed (the Chittagong Hill Tracts Regulation of 1900) has never been rescinded. In historical accounts, Chakma writers have placed great emphasis on this colonial Regulation, showing its 'separate but equal' approach in the best possible light, and playing down the racism embedded in it. In effect, these writers challenge the government's assertion that Bangladesh has ever been a unitary state.[50] A crucial issue is the long-standing legal pluralism between the Hill Tracts and the rest of Bangladesh. Land rights in particular have become the focus of a powerful argument against the unitary aspirations of the overcentralized state.[51] These writers argue that without a return to a more pluriform administration – in reality rather than merely on paper – the revolt in the Chittagong hills will continue.[52]

A Peace Deal

In December 1997 the government of Bangladesh and the leaders of the uprising signed a peace agreement in which the long-standing administrative pluralism between the Chittagong Hill Tracts and the rest of Bangladesh was reaffirmed. Institutions such as the Hill District Council (with the right to collect taxes, appeal laws passed by Parliament, and administer 'tribal law'), the three administrative Circles (not identical with districts) with their three hereditary Circle Chiefs and the Hill District Police are unique to the region. Most significantly, the agreement states that if the new apex institution, the Regional Council,

> finds any rule of the 1900 CHT Regulation and other related laws, rules and ordinances contradictory to the 1989 Hill District Council Acts then the government shall remove that inconsistency by law according to recommendation of and in consultation with the Regional Council.[53]

This recognition of administrative pluralism did not satisfy a group of young Chakmas. They turned against the peace treaty on tactical grounds. Feeling that it blocked the road to further autonomy and significant decentralisation of the state, they formed a new political party.[54] Other groups demanded full citizenship: the Jumma Peoples Network, the apex body of overseas Jummas, denounced the agreement for failing 'to address fundamental problems of the indigenous Jumma peoples, like constitutional recognition of their distinct identity, land rights, full autonomy to the CHT's [Chittagong Hill Tracts] and withdrawal of illegal settlers and the armed forces.'[55] The theme of cultural hegemony was addressed by the Rangamati Declaration of December 1998 which demanded primary education 'in the mother tongues of the indigenous peoples of the Chittagong Hill Tracts' as well as 'courses on the languages and cultures of the indigenous peoples of the Chittagong Hill Tracts.' It also demanded that 'the existing inaccurate and disrespectful references to the languages and cultures of the indigenous peoples of the Chittagong Hill Tracts in the national educational curriculums be corrected in consultation with the leaders and representatives of the peoples concerned.'[56]

As we have seen, the peace treaty was as unpalatable for many Bangladeshi politicians: 'critics of the treaty point out that this has compromised state sovereignty; it is inconsistent with the unitary character of the state, as such it is unconstitutional'.[57] More evocatively, these politicians communicated their concerns to the electorate in terms of a nation being sold down the river. In the campaign against the 'anti-people agreement', the opposition portrayed themselves publicly as protectors of the nation.[58] The Chittagong Hill Tracts peace agreement threw into sharp focus the issues of national identity, nationalist ideology, pluralism, citizenship and exclusion which Chakma writers had been addressing for years. Suddenly, Chakma voices were being picked up by the media in Dhaka, thereby opening a window to their integration into national public debates.[59]

Pluralist Challenges and Nationalist Rhetoric

At the beginning of the twenty-first century, nationalist ideologies are here to stay. They seem indispensable for most, if not all, of us. They give meaning to our social environment and provide guidelines to our behaviour. But all over the world, nationalism has also come to be seen as a dangerously Janus-like ideology which may instil a sense of pride, belonging and sacrifice for the common good, or may lead to war, bloodshed and destruction.

Most people in Bangladesh focus firmly on the positive face of nationalism. For them, it continues to be a liberation ideology which brought self-esteem and emancipation from political subordination in the recent past, and which holds the promise of further emancipation in the future. But it is clear that, although liberation nationalism may have won the war of independence, it dismally failed to win the peace that followed.

Until 1971, Bengali nationalism was an anti-systemic political programme within the state of Pakistan, the tool of a social movement which gathered force and radicalized mainly as a result of the intransigent conservatism of the Pakistani state elite. In the war of 1971 nationalists were widely considered to be using violence in self-defence, and therefore legitimately, against a genocidal state. After 1971, however, Bengali nationalism was quickly appropriated by the new Bangladeshi state elite, which found nationalist phraseology useful to legitimize its power and policies, discredit its critics as unpatriotic, and discipline the 'lower orders'. The promise of social reform vanished, dreams of democracy and social justice evaporated, and nationalist rhetoric in Bangladesh went the way of Pakistani nationalism after 1947: it came to support ruthless accumulation, authoritarian developmentalism, cultural hegemonism, selective xenophobia and frequent military rule. As nationalism became an ideological tool in the hands of a state elite which was soon widely considered to be self-serving, nationalism showed its other face, that of conservatism, protection of vested interests and repressive violence.

We have seen that there were two ways open to those opposing this trend. One was to stick with the nationalist paradigm but insist on its emancipatory potential. This was the way of the renewal nationalists. The other was to acknowledge that the nationalism which had empowered the struggle for Bangladesh was quite insufficient to fire new social movements which might lead to greater social justice and equity in independent Bangladesh.

The two examples of this second trend to which I have referred in this paper, political Islam and cultural pluralism, are diametrically opposed in many respects but they share an attitude which can be called 'transnational'. They reflect, in very different ways, the perceived bankruptcy of Bengali nationalism as an emancipatory force in contemporary Bangladesh and the awareness that within a generation Bangladesh has been transformed from a relatively inward-looking rural hinterland into a state society characterized by a multitude of international links and influences – political, economic, ecological and cultural. This is especially true of the state elite, propelled from the relative obscurity of a provincial satrapy into the exhilaration of international exposure. What distinguished Bangladesh from many other cultures around the world which underwent transnationalization at the same time was the sheer suddenness with which this process accelerated after 1971 – especially as a result of international aid, trade and diplomacy, and a revolution in communications and transport. As many Bangladeshis became more aware of the outside world, that world came to impinge increasingly on Bangladeshi self-images. It is not surprising that transnational ideologies came to exert more influence, and that they point to the silences in nationalist discourses.

Nationalists have tended to dismiss these ideologies as throwbacks, atavisms, or foreign grafts that will not hold. Thus, political Islam is frequently portrayed as 'medieval', 'antiquated', 'fascist', 'reactionary', or 'incompatible with Bengali culture'. I would argue that it is better understood as a radical and new critique of contemporary conservative nationalism in Bangladesh and the political practices that go under its cover. In other words, it is rooted locally, in the accumulation practices and ideological justifications of an elite which has ensconced itself in an overcentralized state, but attacks these from the high moral ground of transnational Islam. Political Islam may be preponderantly right-wing, intolerant, anti-democratic and prone to violence, but in that it differs only in degree from dominant forms of establishment nationalism. To many Bangladeshis, its appeal lies precisely in its looking beyond a discredited 'nation' for moral inspiration.

Similarly, nationalists tend to brush aside pluralism as the mere musings of tribals and other disgruntled marginals who are yet to join the 'mainstream' of society. Or, worse, pluralism is discredited as the outcome of machinations by external powers eager to destroy the nation. It is true that some pluralists appear to fall prey to the 'matrioshka syndrome' and propound forms of (sub)nationalism that hold little promise of innovation.[60] It is also true that pluralists are relatively few in number. But in questions of nationalism, numbers have often proved to be less significant than creative imagination. What is important is that the appeal of pluralism in Bangladesh is increasingly its criticism of the undemocratic, repressive and intolerant behaviour of establishment nationalists, as well as its suggestion that Bangladeshis need to look outside the country for indications of how cultural pluralist solutions might take care of Bangladeshi problems.

In other words, pluralism in Bangladesh, too, is a response to the practices employed by a state elite which has captured and developed an overcentralized state. As such, it presents uncanny parallels with Bengali critiques of erstwhile United Pakistan. Colonial rule had depended partly on what has recently been called 'decentralized despotism', which relies heavily on the politics of indirect rule, the manufacture of native rulers and the dogma of customary law.[61] All over the decolonized world the new post-colonial rulers have tried unsuccessfully to come to terms with this legacy of colonialism. In both Pakistan and Bangladesh, the state elite attempted to overcome it by building a strong, unitary state and a robust nationalism. This option has failed twice.

There can be no doubt that ignoring the challenges of pluralism, or repressing their expression, does not make them go away. But whereas successive governments in Dhaka have sought to accommodate, or at least appease, Islamists, they have judged it unnecessary to do so in the case of pluralists.[62] It would seem that this policy might eventually blow up in their face. Once more, the crisis in the Chittagong Hill Tracts can serve as an example. Until 1997, Dhaka authorities tried to defuse that crisis largely by a policy of military deployment, counter-insurgency, the terror of occasional mass killings, everyday intimidation, physical isolation, disinformation, and stalling through inconclusive negotiations. These repressive policies worked fairly well in terms of keeping the issue low on the political agenda inside Bangladesh, but they have resulted in considerable political damage to the country's international image.

Outside Bangladesh, the crisis in the hills has led to a decisive change in attitudes towards the country. Before the mid-1980s the government was successful in presenting itself in the international arena as a victim of world economic forces, natural disasters and a gruesome war of independence. It was seen predominantly as an 'innocent state' struggling hard to overcome huge odds. After news about militarization, refugees and a string of massacres in the Chittagong Hill Tracts began to circulate abroad, however, this image became tarnished. The state of Bangladesh lost its innocence in the eyes of international bodies and many donor governments. It was perceived as systematically and wilfully violating human rights, and even engaging in genocide and ethnocide. Since the mid-1980s it has had to defend itself frequently against such accusations in international forums. The political damage thus inflicted on Bangladesh's international image appears to be more extensive than is commonly realized inside the country. Foreign political pressure was a major force behind the peace treaty the government signed with the JSS in December 1997. It led to furiously anti-pluralist reactions from the parliamentary opposition, as well as to many Chakmas expressing their disillusionment with a settlement which fell far short of their pluralist hopes. In this climate, the implementation of the main points of the agreement became delayed, perhaps indefinitely.

It is one of the paradoxes of nationalism that it presents itself as entirely homegrown but is in fact deeply influenced by international factors. The emergence of transnational challenges to nationalist ideologies is also a worldwide phenomenon. As the sun rises over the twenty-first century, states' claims to nationality, territoriality and sovereignty are under siege all over the world. Seeking legitimacy on the basis of shared traditions and history is still possible, but such legitimacy is increasingly short-lived and contested. The tenet of nationalism – to represent the true, immutable essence of a group of people – clashes with a growing awareness that all human groups are temporary and transient.

In Bangladesh, nationalism emerged from the encounter of local sensibilities and two centuries of European domination and accumulation. The shapes it took were influenced by a long-term process of globalization and European models just as much as by local developments. The speeding-up of globalization in the late twentieth century, however, makes inevitable the continual reassessment of local nationalisms. Alternative views of the nation, the state, and group identities develop and force themselves onto national agendas. Because of their recent history, Bangladeshis are acutely aware of the power of such views. When their critique of the authoritarian and undemocratic character of the Pakistan state was brushed aside by its rulers, they opted out of the 'Pakistani nation' and the state of Pakistan came unstuck. Now the rulers of Bangladesh have developed many of the same reflexes to critiques of their own authoritarianism, their dogma of the unitary state, and their claim to being the guardians of the nation. This parallel should not be discounted, because it tells us much about the continuities between the two states and the use made of nationalism to prop up strategies of centralized control and accumulation.

The cultural pluralist argument is straightforward: there is no hope for a fruitful exploration of national identity in Bangladesh as long as the explorers remain entangled in the two old heroic master narratives, that of the 'Struggle for Bengali Nationhood' and that of the 'Emancipation of the Muslim'. Neither ethnic nor religious nationalism has been able to construct a stable national identity. On the contrary, the two narratives, which continue to lock so many in such a fierce battle, have drawn attention away from what many perceive as Bangladesh's greatest obstacles to long-term stability: inequity (between rich and poor, men and women, Bengalis and non-Bengalis, Muslims and non-Muslims), low economic growth and political instability. A pluralist understanding of Bangladesh society might go some way towards reducing political instability and focusing much-needed attention upon inequities and stagnation, and their causes.

Since 1971, however, the willingness to countenance the pluralist argument has decreased. Bengali nationalism, not very sensitive to pluralist expressions and claims to begin with, has grown increasingly impatient of them. This can be seen across the board, whether we look at pluralism in terms of class, religion, language, gender, lifestyle or region. It is important to remember that the example presented in this essay explores merely one dimension of this trend. If nationalism is an indispensable crutch, it should at least be refashioned to minimize social tensions leading to large-scale social and individual damage. A debate is necessary to find out if nationalism in Bangladesh can be redefined ('pluralized') so that it can rekindle the liberating intentions of the movement for Bangladesh.

A Post-nationalist Debate?

Today there is a growing awareness that the conceptual apparatus of the social sciences is no longer adequate for analysing the social transformations in which we are all caught up. One of the 'nineteenth-century fallacies' that are being discarded is the idea that the world divides into distinct 'nations' or 'societies', each with its more or less autonomous culture, government, economy and solidarity.[63] The relevance of the nation-state as a political project and as a unit of social analysis has become more contested than ever, and the very stridency of contemporary nationalist discourses can be understood as a defensive reaction, an attempt to resist transformations which are beyond the power of single states to control. The nation-state is being threatened by transnational processes (globalization, migration and 'global concerns' such as the environment, development and human rights) as well as by the subnational claims of region, religion and class. The creation of new multiform identities demands that we take a fresh look at the toolkit of the social sciences. And as the 'nation' is being reconsidered, so are related categories such as 'tribe' and 'peasant'.[64]

We have seen that the concept of 'tribe' belongs to a nationalist narrative which seeks to disempower and marginalize. By stressing the 'primitiveness', 'isolation' and 'backwardness' of people identified as 'tribal', this narrative denies them both voice and agency. They are seen as at best proto-national, capable of being allowed to join the nation only to the extent in which they assimilate, that is, shed their 'tribal' characteristics. Till that time, their exclusion is justified by their difference. This narrative is completely oblivious of the possibility of these groups making and unmaking identities which differ from the ascribed one.

It is here that the discourse on indigenous populations turns out to be highly disruptive of both the concept of tribe and the political authority of the nation-state. Nationalists consider 'tribals' to be their wards, 'fragments' of the nation to be incorporated in the course of progress and development,[65] and deeply rooted in a particular (inaccessible, remote, marginal) territory and a primordial lifestyle. But 'tribals' in Bangladesh do not behave according to this scenario. The treatment meted out has moved them to keep on re-defining their position. In this process they use the political discourse of sovereignty and self-determination – which has empowered South Asian nationalisms throughout the twentieth century – to a new end: creating the Bangladeshi representation of a transnational category, 'indigenous people'. No longer willing to accept the status of fragments living 'out there' in isolation, waiting for the magic kiss of life from the Bengali nation, they have embarked on a policy of forging international links which allow them to bypass their self-appointed guardians. Their new identity can no longer be contained within a national framework: the persisting nationalist image of 'tribals' as simple-minded, happy-go-lucky, uncivilized children of nature is way out of touch with the reality of jet-setting international lobbyists which many of them have become. They make active use of the enormous new opportunities offered by globalization, transnationalization, communications networking and 'diasporization' to reach out, beyond the state of Bangladesh, to other 'indigenous peoples' in similar positions vis-à-vis other nation-states. In this process of inscribing themselves into world history, they contribute to the creation of a new social category whose politics are truly global.

It is important to realize that this category employs the universalist rhetoric of rights and at the same time links up with local symbols and understandings of the world. This is particularly transparent in the emergence of pluralist views of the past. The crucial significance of the pluralist challenge lies in its independent conceptualization of 'time' and 'space'; pluralist visions base themselves on time frames and historical geographies which differ fundamentally from nationalist ones.[66] The study of pluralist views of the past in Bangladesh remains a *terra incognita;* post- and transnationalist historiographies have not yet entered the academy. 'Tribals' are still routinely seen as somehow 'outside Bangladesh history', as people without history rather than as the very participants and products of the history of Bangladesh in the making. As a result, the creation of post-national cultural symbols has gone largely undetected. For example, in their search for a common identity and culture which challenges the nationalist hegemony, Jummas have adapted old rituals and symbols (such as the Bizu festival, local dress, 'tribal' languages) and offered new ones (such as the 'Jumma' identity, a Jumma flag) to an emerging 'post-national' public. It is from such innovations that 'indigenous' identities and views of the past are being manufactured.

Historians of Bangladesh have an important role to play in overcoming monolithic perceptions of the past and the mythologies spun around the 'great events' of state formation. A basic question is how certain groups have come to claim the right to speak for the nation, pushing others to the margins. Why is it that the 'nation' today speaks with such a male, urban, educated, Bengali, Muslim, military-bureaucratic voice? The pluralist vision provides a mirror to reflect nationalist pretensions. Events in the Chittagong Hill Tracts, in particular, provide insights into how the nation is represented and how its aspirations are authorized:

> As the claims to nationhood metastasize into the evils of ethnic cleansing and genocide, the task of intellectuals to remind us all of the imaginary quality of much of the ideology and history that has gone into the making of nations becomes all the more acute.[67]

Obviously, contemporary political disputes in Bangladesh revolve not just round visions of the future of the nation-state or the relationship between Muslims and others. They are fundamentally conflicts about what constitutes the 'common history' and the 'common destiny' of the inhabitants of the country. What is worthy of being remembered, and what must be suppressed and forgotten? Which version of history should be canonized? Are alternative memories to be silenced and, if so, how is the evidence of such memories to be hidden, ignored or destroyed? In this sense, the history of Bangladesh, like all histories, is 'made' by groups of people jostling to get their particular interpretation of history accepted as convincing.

Not surprisingly, this task is felt to be far too important, and too urgent, to be left largely to professional historians. In Bangladesh, it is the state elite and their political adversaries who are perhaps the most energetic creators of such interpretations. Their search is for a 'usable past', an interpretation of history which reflects and legitimizes their social position or their political project, and which mobilizes social support for it. They seek, in a phrase recently coined by Anthony Smith, to enforce a specific 'territorialization of memory' to legitimize their desire for territorial power.[68] The study of history is always a study in power relations, a comment on the exercise of power, and itself an example of the exercise of power. Professional historians are not disinterested, although in their search for a 'usable past', the politics of knowledge are disciplined by academic standards of substantive evidence, reasoned argument and peer scrutiny. The need for independent professional historical work on Bangladesh is shown dramatically every time such work becomes contested because it is felt to have a direct impact on current ideologies and positions of power. But much historical work which is less conspicuous can be equally powerful in analysing the symbols of domination, challenging cherished historical myths, defying the territorialization and periodization of memory, exposing the suppression of alternative histories, and providing new insights into the social transformations which have given birth to today's society.[69]

Such work is needed to generate a post-nationalist debate on Bangladesh. In this period of transnationalization and a widespread feeling that the Bangladeshi nationalist project has not succeeded, public debates must go well beyond getting Bengali nationalism right. What is required first of all is a rethinking of the parameters of debates on identity, and the pluralist critique can be used as an important springboard in that process. Its most useful contribution may be its insistence on the inadequacy of binary oppositions in our thinking about the history of Bangladesh. The categories 'Muslim' and 'non-Muslim', or 'Bengali' and 'non-Bengali', are ultimately self-defeating, because they obscure a multiplicity of groups and alliances which compete for power and self-expression, and which cannot be contained in essentialized religious and ethnic oppositions. Using the pluralist critique also implies confronting the downside of nationalist narratives of Bangladeshi history as they have developed since 1971. How, and in whose hands, have these come to sanction programmes of public action with devastating effects on Bangladeshis labelled as outside, or opposed to, the nation? It can be argued that these effects include not only the drawing of the boundaries of citizenship to exclude most Bangladeshis but also the wilful destruction of symbols of cultural pluralism and political dissent, the expulsion of certain groups of inhabitants, and mass killings.

We may be witnessing the beginning of a new intellectual project: the writing of post-nationalist histories of Bangladesh which emphasize the relative malleability of identities and the transitory nature of their territorial expression. Such a project may help in defining new, more pluralistic, inclusive and democratic notions of what it could mean to be a Bangladeshi citizen in the twenty-first century.

Acknowledgements

I wish to thank B. K. Jahangir, Sirajul Islam, Meghna Guhathakurta, Amena Mohsin and Ellen Bal, and the participants in the Conference on 'Bangladesh at 25' (Columbia University, New York, 5–7 December 1996), for their comments and suggestions.

Notes

1 Muhammad Anisur Rahman, *The Lost Moment: Dreams with a Nation Born Through Fire – Papers on Political Economy of Bangladesh* (Dhaka: University Press Limited, 1993).

2 This annual day of remembrance refers to 21 February 1952, a turning-point in the Bengali language movement which culminated in the demand for an independent Bangladesh. Badruddin Umar, 'Language Movement', in Sirajul Islam, ed., *History of Bangladesh, 1704–1971* (Dhaka: Asiatic Society of Bangladesh, 1992), vol 1, pp. 422–61. Cf. Shyamali Ghosh, 'Bangladeshi Cultural Symbols and the Bangladesh State', in Sekhar Bandyopadhyay, Abhijit Dasgupta and Willem van Schendel, *Bengal: Communities, Development and States* (Delhi: Manohar Publications, 1994), pp. 194–208.

3 This day marks the genocidal attack by the Pakistan army in March 1971, the declaration of independence, and the beginning of the war of independence.

4 On this day in 1971, the Bangladesh war of independence ended and the state of Bangladesh came into existence.

5 The 'nation' in Bangladesh shares its language, Bengali, with some 80 million people in India, with whom it also shared much of its territory and history till 1947. There is no agreement, however, as to whether the 'nation' refers to Bengalis or Bangladeshis. Those who think in terms of 'Bengaliness' consider language, cultural style, long-term history and the territory of Bengal as crucial markers of nationhood, and Bangladeshi statehood as the felicitous outcome of unpredictable historical forces. Those who think in terms of 'Bangladeshiness', however, lay more stress on regional identity (i.e. East vs. West Bengal), separate development since 1947 (East Pakistan/Bangladesh vs. West Bengal), and the relative size of religious communities (Muslims dominating in Bangladesh and Hindus in West Bengal). These views have become part of fierce party politics. In its attempts to gain a monopoly over nationalism, the state elite in Bangladesh has increasingly relied on what has been called the 'Bismillah factor' in government politics, as well as state patronage for a curious cultural mix deemed to be Muslim Bengali which remains nebulous and appears to satisfy no one. 'Renewal nationalists' see it as a sell-out to the Islamists (see below), and the Islamists suspect only a wishy-washy commitment to their tenets. For an exploration of the various meanings of 'Bangladeshi nationalism' as propagated by the ruling elite in the late 1970s, see Golam Hossain, *General Ziaur Rahman and the BNP: Political Transformation of a Military Regime* (Dhaka: University Press Limited, 1988), pp. 60–64.

6 In the 1990s renewal nationalists of many hues gathered around the

Committee for Resisting Killers and Collaborators of the Bangladesh Liberation War of 1971 (the Nirmul Committee), till 1994 headed by Jahanara Imam. The Nirmul Committee 'stand[s] in defence of the secular tradition inherent in our Bangladeshi nationhood', as do other non-governmental organizations, notably the Muktijuddha Smriti Trust and the Muktijuddha Museum. See Shahriar Kabir, ed., *Resist Fundamentalism: Focus on Bangladesh* (Dhaka: Nirmul Committee, 1995), p. 95.

7 The following of political Islam is much broader than direct support for its most vocal political organizations indicates. This was demonstrated during 1994, when the Jamaat-i-Islam and its active student wing, the Chhatra Shibir, were joined by many other voices demanding political action to punish Tasleema Nasrin for her reportedly anti-Islamic utterances.

8 The Bangladeshi nationalist project developed as a counter-ideology during the Pakistan years and, although the vast majority of Bangladeshis are Muslims, secularism became such a central tenet of nationalism that it was incorporated in the constitution after 1971. During the liberation struggle Islamists became strongly compromised by their support for Pakistan but they were able to reassert themselves gradually from the mid-1970s. But now a new generation tried to broaden the appeal of political Islam in Bangladesh by linking up with new Islamist movements outside the subcontinent. One of the more important features of this innovation was a much stronger emphasis on 'the West' as the principal enemy.

9 Cf. Shireen Hasan Osmany, *Bangladeshi Nationalism: History of Dialectics and Dimensions* (Dhaka: University Press Limited, 1992); Kabir, *Resist Fundamentalism.*

10 The concept of pluralism has various connotations. Many political theorists use it to refer to the degree and type of unity which actually exist, or ought to exist, in particular states (David Nicholls, *Three Varieties of Pluralism* (London: Macmillan, 1974), p. 1.) Here the term is not used to highlight the state's dilemma of how much uniformity should be imposed on society in order to keep it manageable. Rather, it refers to the thinking of those who adhere to concepts of nationalism and state which allow for and encourage diversity without challenging the state itself. In other words, they reject the idea that monocultural 'nation-states' are possible, or desirable, and argue that state-societies should 'recognise cultural pluralism, the dignified co-existence of different cultural collectivities within their territories' T. K. Oommen, Gravers (238) calls this 'civic pluralism'. Cf. Nicholls, *Three Varieties of Pluralism*; T. K. Oommen, *Alien Concepts and South Asian Reality: Responses and Reformulations* (Delhi: Sage Publications, 1995); Mikael Gravers, 'The Karen Making of a Nation', in Stein Tønnesson and

Hans Antläv, eds, *Asian Forms of the Nation* (London: Curzon Press, 1996), pp. 237–69.

11 Cf. Swaraj Basu, 'The Colonial State and the Indigenous Society: The Creation of the Rajbansi Identity in Bengal', in Sekhar Bandyopadhyay *et al.*, pp. 43–64. For competing 'regional' and 'national' identities in the case of people from Sylhet, see Rod Chalmers, *Sylheti: A Regional Language of Bangladesh* (Bath: European Network of Bangladesh Studies, ENBS/EC Research Paper no. 5/6–96, 1996).

12 Ben Whitaker, *The Biharis in Bangladesh* (London: Minority Rights Group, 1972); Md. Habibur Rahman, 'The Shandar-Beday Community of Bangladesh: A Study of Social Change of a Quasi-Nomadic People' (PhD thesis, Department of Sociology, University of Dhaka, 1990); Jahanara Huq Choudhury, 'The Effect of Sedentarization on a Nomadic People', *Journal of the Asiatic Society of Bangladesh*, vol. 41, no. 1 (June 1996), pp. 69–83.

13 The official figure for the 'tribal population' of Bangladesh, provided by the Population Census of 1991, stands at 1.2 million. Government of Bangladesh, *Statistical Pocketbook of Bangladesh 94* (Dhaka: Bangladesh Bureau of Statistics, 1995), pp. 108–9. Among the 'non-Bengali' groups which are not enumerated separately are the Biharis (whose citizenship, whether Bangladeshi, or Pakistani, is disputed) and the Bede, already mentioned, but also, for example, Anglo-Asians, Chinese, Urdu/Hindi-speaking non-Biharis, and tea-plantation communities. On under-enumeration, see Michael B. Malo, 'Aboriginals Struggling to Join the Mainstream', *Aranyak* (Dhaka, 7 September 1984), pp. 3–11; *Manderang-ni Chiti* (Dhaka, Easter Issue, 1996), p. 2; and Ellen Bal, '"Born a Garo, Always a Garo": Ethnic Awareness Among the Garo People of Bangladesh' (paper, 14th European Conference on Modern South Asian Studies, Copenhagen, August 1996).

14 This viewpoint is also put forward by some Bengali intellectuals, notably Anu Muhammad, who argued: 'Bangladesh is not just the homeland of the Bengalis. There are people in this country who are not Bengalis, whose mother tongue is not Bengali, and who have lived here for innumerable years, in some areas longer than Bengalis. They have created their own societies, organisations and cultures, and above all they consider Bangladesh to be their homeland. There are many groups like these who are not less deeply rooted here than Bengalis. Like Bengalis, they are citizens of Bangladesh, but it is absolutely essential to keep in mind that they are not Bengalis... Their histories are different, their societies are different, their languages are different, but we all share one undivided state identity' (Anu Muhammad, 'Banglades Sudhu Bangalir Basbhumi Nay,' [Bangladesh is Not Only the Homeland of Bengalis] *1993 Adibasi Barsa – 1993 Year of the Indigenous People: A New Partner-*

ship (Dhaka: Smaranika O Prakasana Upa-Kamiti, Antarjatik Bisva Adibasi Barsa 1993, Udjapan Komiti, 1993), pp. 29–30; my translation). For similar views, see especially Imtiaz Ahmed, 'Modern Bangladesh and the Hill People: The Politics of the Bhadrasantans,' in: S. R. Chakravarty, ed., *Society, Polity and Economy of Bangladesh* (Delhi: Har-Anand, 1994), p. 133; Amena Mohsin, 'The Politics of Nationalism: The Case of the Chittagong Hill Tracts, Bangladesh' (unpublished Ph.D. thesis, Cambridge University, 1995); Amena Mohsin, 'Military, Hegemony and the Chittagong Hill Tracts,' *The Journal of Social Studies*, 72 (April 1996), pp. 1–26; Amena Mohsin and Imtiaz Ahmed, 'Modernity, Alienation and the Environment: The Experience of the Hill People' (paper presented at the Asiatic Society of Bangladesh, Dhaka, 27 April 1996).

15 The connections between peasant, bourgeois and elite politics in the movement for Pakistan were explored by, for example, Bose, Das and Hashmi. Similar studies are still lacking for the movement for Bangladesh. Sugata Bose, *Agrarian Bengal: Economy, Social Structure and Politics, 1919–1947* (Cambridge: Cambridge University Press, 1986); Suranjan Das, *Communal Riots in Bengal 1905–1947* (Delhi: Oxford University Press, 1991; Taj ul-Islam Hashmi, *Pakistan as a Peasant Utopia: The Communalization of Class Politics in East Bengal 1920–1947* (Boulder, CO: Westview Press, 1992).

16 There are in fact remarkable similarities in the identity politics of the Awami League during the Pakistan period and the JSS (Parbatya Chattagram Jana Sanghati Samiti – United Peoples Party of the Chittagong Hill Tracts) after 1972, as well as in the political lines taken by the Pakistan and Bangladesh governments to counter, isolate, divide, discredit and belittle these oppositional movements – but this essay does not extent to a treatment of these similarities.

17 In December 1997, a peace agreement was signed between the government of Bangladesh and the Chittagong Hill Tracts People's United Party (*Jana Sanghati Samiti (JSS)*). The JSS ceased its insurgence and the Bangladesh armed forces their counter-insurgency. Violence continued between supporters of the agreement and others who wanted to continue fighting. The conflict has not yet been resolved but for the time being it has been contained. Much depends on the speed with which the agreement is going to be implemented, and on the rethinking in powerful circles which is to accompany that process.

18 For example, an otherwise interesting analysis of the role of 'the various subaltern social groups' in democratic politics in Bangladesh in the 1980s and 1990s is typical of a whole genre in not even acknowledging the intense struggle in the Chittagong Hill Tracts and its possible effects on national politics, and in presenting a view of national politics which is so Dhaka-centred as completely to obscure political processes outside the

capital: S. M. Shamsul Alam, 'Democratic Politics and the Fall of the Military Regime in Bangladesh', *Bulletin of Concerned Asian Scholars*, vol. 27, no. 3 (July–September 1995), pp. 28–42.

19 'At this,' A. B. Chakma adds, 'the tribal people left the meeting': A. B. Chakma, 'Look Back From Exile: A Chakma Experience', in Wolfgang Mey, ed., *They Are Now Burning Village After Village: Genocide in the Chittagong Hill Tracts, Bangladesh* (Copenhagen: IWGIA, 1984), p. 58. Cf. Mohiuddin Ahmad, 'The Ethnic Minorities of CHT: Root Causes of their Alienation,' *Holiday* (29 March 1991), pp. 4–5; S. Mahmud Ali, *The Fearful State: Power, People and Internal War in South Asia* (London and New Jersey: Zed Books, 1993), p. 184.

20 'Banglar Hindu, Banglar Khristan, Banglar Bauddha, Banglar Musalman, Amra Sabai Bangali.' For a reproduction, see M. A. Bari, *Muktijuddher Raktim Smriti – Memoirs of a Blood Birth* (Dhaka: Banimahal Prakashani, n.d.), p. 260. Most Buddhists, many Christians, some Hindus and some Muslims in Bangladesh do not consider themselves to be Bengalis.

21 In a recent paper on twenty-five years of economic performance in Bangladesh, Azizur Rahman Khan speaks of a general failure of governance as the greatest of all failures: 'In Bangladesh successive governments have failed all [tests to stay autonomous of the economic elite, make entrepreneurial groups submit to non-arbitrary rules, and create a broad social compact that allows a wide sharing of the benefits of economic development]. Most of them even failed to provide an acceptable level of law and order and the delivery of public services': Azizur Rahman Khan, 'A Quarter Century of Development in Bangladesh' (Paper for the 31st Annual Meeting of the Bengal Studies Association, Washington, DC, 3–5 May 1996), p. 16, cf. p. 17.

22 'The beneficiaries of the highly centralised state ... have repeatedly obstructed the dismantling of the present administrative system which is callous to the public interests and cannot respond to the needs of the time ... All such attempts were frustrated by the top brass of the civil bureaucracy, who are the principal beneficiaries of an age-old system that has proved anachronistic long ago. In the eyes of the ordinary man, the government is something that is always inaccessible to them ... incompetent, unaccountable, nontransparent and corrupt': 'Editorial: Centralised State', *Holiday – The National Weekend Newspaper* (Dhaka), 31 May 1996, p. 2.

23 The earliest known map of the Chittagong region, published by João Baptista Lavanha around 1550, shows a settlement named 'Chacomas' upstream from the coastal town of 'Chatigam' (Chittagong), exactly in the area now inhabited by Chakmas. See João de Barros, *Ásia. Dos feitos que os Portugueses fizeram no descobrimento e conquista dos mares e terras do Oriente* (Lisbon: ed. Hernani, 1945–6), 4 vols.

24 Here they joined small communities of Chakmas who had already settled there well before Partition. On Partition emigration, see Siddhartha Chakma, *Prasanga: Parbatya Chattagram* [Topic: Chittagong Hill Tracts] (Calcutta: Nath Brothers, 1392 BE (1985)).

25 See Harikishore Chakma *et al.*, *Bara Parang: The Tale of the Developmental Refugees of the Chittagong Hill Tracts* (Dhaka: Centre for Sustainable Development, 1995).

26 Siddhartha Chakma, *Prasanga.*

27 P. K. Debbarma and Sudhir Jacob George, *The Chakma Refugees in Tripura* (New Delhi: South Asian Publishers, 1993); *'Life Is Not Ours : Land and Human Rights in the Chittagong Hill Tracts, Bangladesh – Update 2* (Copenhagen/Amsterdam: The Chittagong Hill Tracts Commission, 1994), pp. 11–15 ('Refugees'). It is important to emphasize that other non-Bengali groups (e.g., the Marmas and Tripuras) were also involved in these upheavals and had to leave Bangladesh, but this essay concentrates on the Chakmas, who formed the largest contingent in each consecutive wave of migration.

28 See Willem van Schendel, 'The Invention of the "Jummas": State Formation and Ethnicity in Southeastern Bangladesh', *Modern Asian Studies*, vol. 26, no. 1 (1992), pp. 95–128; reprinted in R. H. Barnes *et al.*, eds., *Indigenous Peoples of Asia* (Ann Arbor: Association for Asian Studies, 1995), pp. 121–44.

29 These groups are, in order of diminishing size: Chakma, Marma, Tripura, Tangchangya, Mru, Riang/Mrung, Bawm, Khumi, Sak, Pangkho, Khyang and Lushai. The divisions between these groups are sometimes fluid, as with Tripura and Riang.

30 Short for 'Parbatya Chattagram Jana Sanghati Samiti' (United Peoples Party of the Chittagong Hill Tracts).

31 For details, see Van Schendel, 'The Invention'.

32 There is nothing novel about the use of the term *jati.* See, for example Satis Chandra Ghosh, *Chakma Jati: Jatiya Chitra o Itibritta* [The Chakma People: A Description and History of the Nation] (Calcutta: Bangiya Sahitya Parisat Granthabali, vol. 24, 1316 BE [1909]). On the other hand, the emphatic use of '*jati*' and 'nation' is used side by side with '*adibasi*', '*upajati*', '*sampraday*', 'community' and 'indigenous people' in the contributions of various authors to recent publications, for example, Hafiz Rasid Khan ed., *Bangladeser Upajati O Adibasi: Angsidaritver Natun Diganta* [The Tribals and Original Inhabitants of Bangladesh: A New Horizon of Partnership] (Bandarban: Banglades Upajati O Adibasi Aitihya Parsad, 1993); Philip Gain, ed., *Bangladesh: Land, Forest and Forest People* (Dhaka: Society for Environmental and Human Development, 1995); and *The Rakhaing Review* (Cox's Bazar), 2 (1995).

33 Mohiuddin Ahmad, 'Minority Communities Are on the Verge of Extinction', *Hotline Newsletter*, 88 (December 1995–January 1996), p. 1.

34 See Siddhartha Chakma, *Prasanga*.

35 *Outcome on the Emergency General Meeting of All India Leading Chakma Personalities at Pecharthal: Tripura, Organised by All India Chakma Cultural Conference (AICCC), Machmara, Tripura, on November 11–12, 1995* (n.p. [Shillong]: AICCC, 1996). The meeting also resolved to form the 'All India Chakma National Movement', whose aims are to achieve: '1. Fundamental rights of the Chakmas in India, 2. Justice for the Right Causes of Chakmas, 3. To stop Human Rights abuses upon Chakmas, etc.' Cf. the use of 'Chakma' and 'Jumma' in Bikach Kumar Choudhury, *Genesis of Chakma Movement [1772–1989]: Historic Background* (Agartala: Tripura Darpan Prakashani, 1991).

36 Although Bangladesh has some reservations' policies (notably in education and government service), these are less comprehensive than in India, and little is known about their actual implementation.

37 For example, the tens of thousands of Chakma refugees who arrived in India in the early 1960s, after the building of the Kaptai dam in the Chittagong Hill Tracts, were relocated in far-off Arunachal Pradesh. They never received full citizenship, nor were they identified as international refugees. They lingered on in limbo till the mid-1990s, when local residents mounted a campaign to drive them out. During this struggle the Chakmas appealed to the Indian High Court to get citizenship, and the Court ruled that they should have got it long ago. Cf. Ruben Banerjee, 'Chakma: Living Under Notice of Death,' *India Today* (15 October 1994), 42–43.

38 By contrast, Chakmas outside India have tended to use the regional 'Jumma' label. For example, in the 1980s Chakmas in Western countries set up a network called the *Jumma Peoples Network*. In 1996, the *Jumma Peoples Network of the Asia Pacific Australia* (JUMNAPA) presented itself by means of a Homepage on the Internet.

39 An overview is given in Nandalal Sharma, *Parbatya Chattagrame Shangabadpatra O Shangbadikata* [Newspapers and Journalism in the Chittagong Hill Tracts] (Rangamati: Rangamati Prakasani, 1983). From 1996 a new type of journal came into being with the first issue of *JumPada*. This journal, published by the Jumma Peoples Resource Centre Australia, uses the local languages of the Chittagong Hill Tracts and English, rather than Bengali. Moreover, it employs the Roman alphabet in preference to the Bengali, and aims at reviving the nearly-extinct Chakma alphabet ('We are printing Jumma scripts, and writing in our languages in JumPada in order to protect and practice our scripts and promote our literature'. JUMNAPA Homepage). Clearly, this journal no longer addresses a Bengali audience; instead, it is directed towards a

Jumma audience, no longer just in the Chittagong Hill Tracts, but worldwide.

40 For example, in his editorial to the first issue of *Girinirjhar* [Mountain Torrent], Sugata Chakma wrote: 'The great Mongoloid culture from the East and the rich Hindu-Aryan culture from the West have in continual interaction built a bridge here [= the Chittagong Hill Tracts]. Therefore this district's culture has become extraordinarily rich and attractive. But for a long time now the outside world has been ignorant and contemptuous of tribal life and culture, and that life and culture have been further weakened and subdued by a continual lack of proper presentation and development. ... I hope that this journal will provide an intimate introduction of this district's people to the other people of the country.' 'Sampadakiya', *Girinirjhar* (Rangamati), 1:1 (February 1982), i–ii (my translation). The same sentiments with regard to the Garos are expressed rather more covertly by Subhas Jengcham in his *Bangladeser Garo Sampraday* (Dhaka: Bangla Academy, 1994), viii.

41 This sentiment can be found in the publications of other groups as well. In a recent issue of the Garo periodical *Mande-rang-ni Chiti* (Dhaka, Easter Issue 1996, p. 4) it was expressed as follows: 'Why, is the question, do we have to abandon our ethnic identity to become part of this society? ... what [we] hope to see in the future, is a people which is modern without rejecting its past, fully taking part in the society on all levels, contributing and profiting like all others, but, with quiet pride, well conscious of its unique origin and identity.' Other groups are also beginning to express such views in an organised manner, e.g. the Manipuris who recently founded an information and study centre aimed at 'promoting and popularising the Manipuri culture and its rich heritage among the Bengali speaking people of the country.' (*Holiday* (July 5, 1996), 6)

42 S. Mahmud Ali, *The Fearful State*, p. 176.

43 For relatively disinterested and detailed discussions of the confused events of the last days of British India and the first days of Pakistan in the Chittagong Hill Tracts, see Nicholas Mansergh (Ed.-in-Chief), *The Transfer of Power 1942–7*, Volume XII (London: H.M. Stationery Office, 1983) and Norman Hermant, *The Partition of India and the Chittagong Hill Tracts* (Seminar Paper, University of British Columbia [1986]). The most extensive Chakma account can be found in Siddhartha Chakma, *Prasanga*, pp. 3–16.

44 Most crudely so in Khaled Belal (ed.), *Falconry in the Hills* (Chittagong, 1992) and Alimuzzaman Harun, *Sangbadiker Chokhe Parbatya Chattagram O 'Santi Bahini* [The Chittagong Hill Tracts and the 'Peace Troops' As Seen By A Journalist] (Dhaka: Zakiya Zaman, 1992).

45 Islamists present 'Muslims' as an essential, primordial, timeless category

and their version of history emphasises how this category struggled against the equally ahistorical categories of 'Hindus' and 'Europeans' to come into its own. Islamists see the history of Bangladesh as the gradual awakening of Bengali Muslims to their true Islamic selves. Their view highlights the struggles which enabled Muslims to emancipate themselves from their subordinated position in Bengali society, and to purify their religious practices from Hindu 'contaminations'. Political Islam has a long pedigree in Bangladesh. Older incarnations developed in a continual dialogue with colonial racial stereotypes of Bengalis as weak, non-martial and cowardly; and with dominant strains of colonial Bengali nationalism which based themselves on a myth of Aryan racial and cultural superiority which excluded non-Hindus. Resistance against such ideas coalesced in the movement for Pakistan in the middle of the twentieth century. For contemporary Islamists, the emancipation of Bengali Muslims cannot be concluded until they can establish an Islamic state in Bangladesh. In its most simplified form, this interpretation presents the essence of Islam as the prime mover in the history of Bangladesh.

46 Nationalists present the modern history of Bangladesh as that of a nation coming into its own through enormous sacrifice. There can be no doubt at all about the immensity of the sacrifices and suffering of many, culminating in the genocide unleashed upon the population of Bangladesh in 1971; these are evoked in an undiminishing stream of memoirs, historical studies, novels and poetry. In these works, the nation is generally presented as coterminous with the state, and Bangladesh is viewed as a nation-state. Nationalist histories emphasise that Bangladeshi nationhood is the outcome of the inexorable progress of modernity, the awakening of Bangladeshis to their true essence, that of members of a nation characterised by a single language and a well-defined territory. The future sovereignty of the national territory, and the state administering it, is of paramount importance to the preservation of the nation. In its most outspoken form, this account presents the 'Bengali nation' as the prime mover in the history of the region.

47 Admittedly, a good deal of Chakma history writing is 'foundational' in that it aims at establishing 'Chakma' as a firm identity which resists further decomposition into heterogeneity. But the critique of Bengali nationalism is no less valid. Moreover, these writings can be read as 'post-foundational' history of quite another type than the ones indicated by Gyan Prakash. These are 'subaltern' history in the sense that they represent historical interpretation, not by professional historians exploring the limitations of nationalist discourse, but by literate members of 'subaltern' groups who are directly subject to state repression but who find no place in the hegemonic (or even the 'subaltern') narratives of either the academy or the state. Gyan Prakash, 'Writing

Post-Orientalist Histories of the Third World: Indian Historiography Is Good to Think,' in: Nicholas B. Dirks (ed.) *Colonialism and Culture* (Ann Arbor: University of Michigan Press, 1992), pp. 353–388.

48 Many of these struggles are always going on at the same time. The intensity of one of the most massive of these, the struggle for the restoration of democracy after 1982, is beautifully documented in Yusuf Muhammed (ed.), *Ayalbam: Gana Andolan, 1982–90/Album: Mass Movement 1982–90*, Volume I (Chittagong: Tolpaar, 1993).

49 The term has become current in United Nations circles. For example, a large number of policy documents on 'indigenous peoples' is presently being produced by various United Nations bodies, national governments, and non-governmental organisations, notably around the 'Draft Declaration on the Rights of Indigenous Peoples.' See e.g. *doCip Update No. 13* (Geneva: Indigenous Peoples' Center for Documentation, Research and Information, March/April 1996). The term has also become widely used in scholarly discourse. See R.H. Barnes et al. (eds.), *Indigenous Peoples of Asia* (Ann Arbor: Association for Asian Studies, 1995); Nguyen Thi Dieu, 'The State Versus Indigenous Peoples: The Impact of Hydraulic Projects on Indigenous Peoples of Asia', *Journal of World History*, 7:1 (1996), 101–130.

For recent uses of 'indigenous people' in Bangladesh, see Raja Devasish Roy, 'Land Rights, Land Use and Indigenous Peoples of the Chittagong Hill Tracts', and Kabita Chakma and Glen Hill, 'Thwarting the Indigenous Custodians of Bio-Diversity', both in Philip Gain (ed.), *Bangladesh: Land, Forest and Forest People* (49–100 and 123–137); Sanchay Chakma, 'Bangladesh: Indigenous People's Legal Rights and Relationship with the State and the Non-Indigenous Population', *Indigenous Affairs*, 4 (Oct-Dec. 1995), 38–39; and Raja Devasish Roy, 'Forests, Forestry and Indigenous People in the Chittagong Hill Tracts, Bangladesh' (paper for the Workshop on The Rights of Tribal and Indigenous Peoples, London, 23–25 February, 1996).

50 'These Regulations still form the basis of the civil, revenue and judicial administration of the CHT, although there have been several amendments to the rules and several new laws have been made applicable to the CHT between 1900 and up to the present ... Until today the legal system in the CHT has significant differences with that prevailing in the rest of the country. Laws passed for the rest of the country do not automatically apply to the CHT unless they are specifically extended to the CHT in the manner laid down in the CHT Manual". Raja Devasish Roy, 'Land Rights', 54. For a distinction between provincial autonomy, regional autonomy and administrative autonomy, see Mizanur Rahman Shelley (ed.) *The Chittagong Hill Tracts of Bangladesh: The Untold Story* (Dhaka: Centre for Development Research, 1992), 86.

51 The local system of land rights in the Chittagong Hills was recognised to be fundamentally different right from the inception of colonial rule, and it was codified, with certain adaptations, in the Regulation of 1900. One of the major bones of contention in the present crisis is the tacit expansion of the very different system of land rights with which Bengalis have lived for generations. This system of private property in land, codified in the Permanent Settlement of 1790 and its permutations, was designed to regulate and tax lowland agriculture. The inhabitants of the Chittagong hills demand that their own concept of land rights is respected, i.e. they demand that the legal pluralism which Bangladesh inherited is recognised and continued. Cf. Roy, 'Land Rights'; Chandra K. Roy, *Land Rights of the Indigenous Peoples of the Chittagong Hill Tracts, Bangladesh* (n.p.: Jumma People's Network in Europe (JUPNET), 1996).

52 Even after the birth of Bangladesh, the state has in fact acknowledged the separate status of the Chittagong Hill Tracts by providing separate legislation, notably the special District Council Act of 1989. These councils have failed completely to live up to their stated goals because the central government refused to hand over the powers assigned to them. *'Life Is Not Ours : Land and Human Rights in the Chittagong Hill Tracts, Bangladesh* (Copenhagen/Amsterdam: The Chittagong Hill Tracts Commission, 1991), 31–38; *'Life Is Not Ours : Land and Human Rights in the Chittagong Hill Tracts, Bangladesh – An Update of the May 1991 Report* (Copenhagen/ Amsterdam: The Chittagong Hill Tracts Commission, 1992), 6–7; *'Life Is Not Ours : Land and Human Rights in the Chittagong Hill Tracts, Bangladesh – Update 2* (Copenhagen/ Amsterdam: The Chittagong Hill Tracts Commission, 1994), 2–4.

53 *Agreement Between the National Committee on CHT Affairs formed by the Government of the People s Republic of Bangladesh and the Parbattya Chattagram Jana Samhati Samiti* (Dhaka, 2 December 1997), Paragraph C.11. For an assessment by the Jana Samhati Samiti of the implementation of the peace agreement, see Goutam Kumar Dewan, 'The Chittagong Hill Tracts Problem and the CHT Agreement' (paper for the Meeting on Post-Conflict Development, The Hague, December 8-9, 1998).

54 The United Peoples Democratic Front (UPDF). For protests during the surrender ceremony on 10 February 1998, see e.g. Rashed Chowdhury, 'Chakma Faction Opposes Surrender,' *Dhaka Courier* (27 February 1998), 11; 'Shantibahini Men Surrender Arms,' *The Independendent* (Dhaka), 11 February 1998.

55 *Shanti Bahini Surrender Ceremony: A Humiliation – Jummas Demand Apology from Bangladesh Government for Genocide*; Press Release, Jumma Peoples Network, South Asia Coordination Section (New Delhi, 9 February 1998).

56 *Rangamati Declaration.* This declaration was adopted unanimously by the 100-odd participants at the broad-based Conference on Development in the Chittagong Hill Tracts, held in Rangamati on 18–19 December 1998.

57 Amena Mohsin, 'The Chittagong Hill Tracts Peace Accord and the Hill People' (unpublished paper), 9.

58 In November and December 1997, 'Begum Zia [the leader of the BNP-led Seven Party Opposition Alliance] had been crisscrossing the country telling people that the puppet government of Sheikh Hasina [the Prime Minister and leader of the Awami League which was elected in 1996] had been put in power to implement long-term Indian designs and as part of it the Hill Tracts would be delivered to New Delhi as soon as the peace accord was signed. "We won't let it happen and we're going to protect the integrity and sovereignty of our country at any cost," Begum Zia thundered at public meetings.' *Dhaka Courier* (12 December 1997), 15.

59 Before the agreement, coverage of the Chittagong Hill Tracts in the Bangladesh press had been minimal and was restricted largely to reports on violent acts by Jumma rebels, counter-insurgency propaganda and cautious commentary by Dhaka-based journalists. Jummas themselves had practically no access to the Bangladesh media and could make themselves be heard only through foreign media and their own publications. After December 1997, coverage of the conflict in the Bangladesh press increased enormously and Jumma voices suddenly burst into print. See e.g. the interviews with various Jumma people in the special issue "Parbatya Santi Chuktir 1m Barsapurti' (First Anniversary of the Hill Peace Agreement) in the national daily *Bhorer Kagaj* (2 December 1998).

60 '[M]uch of the world today faces what might be termed the *matrioshka* syndrome (after the famous Russian dolls-within-dolls) – as soon as one ethnic minority achieves independence, a minority within the new state promptly commences its own struggle for liberation.' Roshwald, 'Untangling,' 303.

61 Mahmood Mamdani, *Citizen and Subject: Contemporary Africa and the Legacy of Late Colonialism* (Princeton: Princeton University Press, 1996).

62 Rafiuddin Ahmed makes the important point that the question of whether religion or linguistic-cultural identity should form the basis of nationalism in Bangladesh is actually of peripheral interest to most people. 'The political elite as well as the military-bureaucratic regime want to keep alive the controversy over these issues in the absence of any constructive programme aimed at the well-being of the ordinary people.' Rafiuddin Ahmed, 'Introduction,' in Rafiuddin Ahmed (ed.), *Religion, Nationalism and Politics in Bangladesh* (New Delhi: South Asian Publishers, 1990), 30.

63 Charles Tilly, *Big Structures, Large Processes, Huge Comparisons* (New York: Russell Sage Foundation, 1984), 11. In this book, Tilly reviews eight 'pernicious postulates' burdening the social sciences which emerged from a mistaken reading of nineteenth-century social changes.

64 For a recent critique of convential categories of anthropological thought, notably 'peasant', see Michael Kearney, *Reconceptualizing the Peasantry: Anthropology in Global Perspective* (Boulder, Col.: Westview Press, 1996).

65 Cf. Partha Chatterjee, *The Nation and its Fragments: Colonial and Postcolonial Histories* (Delhi: Oxford University Press, 1994).

66 For example, Chakma writers may be said to employ '*Jumma Time*' in which, as we have seen, particular historical turning points are privileged. The years 1860 and 1900 have no particular significance in Indian, Pakistani or Bengali nationalism, but they serve as crucial markers of Jumma Time. Conversely, Jumma Time is not concerned with 'nationalist' turning points such as 1905 (the first Partition of Bengal), 1940 (the Pakistan Resolution) or 1952 (the upsurge of the Bengali language movement). The ways in which time is conceptualised and ordered in Chakma (and other pluralist) narratives remains a completely uncharted area for historians of Bangladesh. Similarly, we have seen that '*Jumma Space*' differs from the historical geography of nationalists, not just in terms of the geographical vantage points from which history is observed, but also in terms of boundaries – between hills and plains, between ethnic groups, between rulers and ruled, between male and female space – and possibly in the very concept of space employed. In other words, historians searching for postnationalist visions of Bangladesh need to provide us with historical analyses which allow for a plurality of time and space.

67 Geoff Eley and Ronald Grigor Suny, 'Introduction: From the Moment of Social History to the Work of Cultural Representation', in Geoff Eley and Ronald Grigor Suny (eds.), *Becoming National: A Reader* (New York/Oxford: Oxford University Press, 1996), 12.

68 Anthony D. Smith, 'Culture, Community and Territory: The Politics of Ethnicity and Nationalism', *International Affairs*, vol. 72, no. 3 (1996), pp. 445–458.

69 This is essential but often painful work, as Guhathakurta demonstrates in her paper on the language and symbols of Pakistani domination during the war of 1971. Meghna Guhathakurta, 'The Bangladesh Liberation War: A Summon to Memory', *Samaj Nirikkhan*, Nr. 61 (1996).

6· The Struggle for the Afghan State: Centralization, Nationalism and their Discontents

Gabriele Rasuly-Paleczek

Analogous to developments in other neighbouring states – similarly characterized by ethno-linguistic, religious and socio-cultural multiplicity and political decentralization – the establishment of firm state control and the formation of a uniform Afghan nation-state have been the primary goals of Afghanistan's rulers since the end of the nineteenth century. However, despite numerous attempts to integrate the various socio-political entities into one cohesive state machinery and to create a common collective identity for the country's extremely heterogeneous society, the envisaged aims could not be achieved.

On the contrary, both the enforcement of administration and jurisdiction by the state and the latter's efforts to promote national identity led to further cleavages and controversies between state and society as a whole, as well as between the various socio-political entities constituting Afghan society.[1] This occurred especially in periods when the rulers abandoned the delicate *modus vivendi* of sharing power with the various sociopolitically influential groups (such as the ulema, the chiefs of the Pashtun tribes, or other locally prominent personalities) in favour of attaining more direct control and authority, or when they introduced models of governance and nation-building that were alien to Afghan society (such as the modernization programme under Amir Amanullah Khan in the 1920s or the import of the Soviet system by the communist regime from 1978 to 1992).

Furthermore, the manner in which the Afghan state implemented this centralization of power and advocated its nation-building process was characterized by contradictory and uneven measures affecting the various segments of Afghan society in different ways and to diverse degrees. In total, these processes prepared the ground for further conflicts within Afghan society, which became increasingly visible after the establishment of the Islamic State of Afghanistan in 1992 and the subsequent civil war.

Using the Uzbeks of Afghanistan – one of the country's larger minority groups – and their relations with the Afghan state as a case study, I shall in the following, outline some of the problems of centralization and nation-building in Afghanistan. Moreover, I shall analyse the Uzbeks' reactions and political strategies in this process of increasing encapsulation by the Afghan state.[2]

Three aspects of the process are of major concern here. First, an assessment of Afghan state policies to achieve effective state control and national unity. Second, an analysis of concrete political actions and strategies developed by the Uzbeks to resist this total control and discipline by the Afghan state. And third, an evaluation of Uzbek self-perception and identity construction in the light of a Pashtun-dominated power and value system. I shall therefore focus on the mobilization of counterforces and the manner in which minority groups in Afghanistan expressed their discontent with the ongoing encroachment process and tried to develop a viable strategy in terms of political actions as well as perceptions of identity. What is striking in this respect is the fact that, in contrast to recent developments in the Balkans or in the newly independent states of the former Soviet Union, where the creation of independent nation-states became 'the option' per se for the various ethno-linguistic minorities, 'opting out of the nation-state' does not seem to represent an attractive goal for the minorities of Afghanistan. The reasons for this will also be tackled in this essay.

The Nation-building Policies of the Afghan State

Lack of space means that a detailed analysis of the Afghan state, its nature and its relations with Afghan society must be omitted here.[3] I shall restrict myself to a brief description of the political interaction between state and society and the various ideologies employed by the country's rulers since the end of the nineteenth century to establish a strong central power and to create national unity.

To begin with, some general remarks on Afghan society seem to be important for achieving a better understanding of the problems the country's rulers were confronted with in this venture. For Afghanistan is marked by an enormous heterogeneity of population in terms of ethno-linguistic and religious affiliation and socio-political organization. This multiplicity is reflected in the existence of around fifty-seven different ethnic groups, some forty to fifty languages and dialects belonging to several distinct language families, and two official languages: Pashtu and Farsi-Dari.[4] Some of these ethno-linguistic groups are quite large, totalling several millions, as in the case of the Pashtuns, Tajiks, Uzbeks and Hazaras, whereas others are quite small, such as the Ormur, who at present number only a few hundred.[5] Moreover, the regional distribution of the various groups is again disproportionate. Some regions, such as northern and western Afghanistan, show a fairly multi-ethnic composition of their population, whereas others, such as the central highlands or the eastern and southern parts of the country, are ethno-linguistically more or less homogeneous.[6] Similarly complex is the adherence to religious sects. Although the majority of the Afghans are Muslims, and Islam is therefore one of the essential unifying forces evoked to promote national unity, the country's religious structure is not at all homogeneous.[7] On the contrary, Hanafite Islam, which is the official rite of the country, contrasts sharply with Imami and Ismaili Islam, whose adherents are often discriminated against.[8]

However, the peoples of Afghanistan are distinguishable not only in terms of their ethnicity, language or religion, but also in terms of their socio-political structure. Within some groups, such as the Pashtuns, Turkmens and part of the Uzbeks, tribal structures still play an important role.[9] In these societies – though to a varying degree – cohesion is primarily achieved by referring to a common ancestor and by underlining genealogical links which both – together with a specific value system and world view – create unity among individuals and constitute individual and collective identities, thus allowing the creating of large, cohesive socio-political entities. Among tribal groups it is especially among the Pashtuns that tribal structures are still strongly present. This becomes evident from the Pashtuns' emphasis on genealogically defined relations and their reference to the Pashtunwali.[10] In other groups, such as the Tajiks, the Hazaras and some of the Uzbeks, larger kinship-based forms of social organization have either lost their significance or never existed. Here it is primarily residence in a specific community that creates a certain sentiment of unity and helps to organize socio-political interactions. Compared to societies based on tribal structures, these groups possess much less social cohesion and often lack a mechanism to mobilize people on a larger sale than at the level of the immediate local community. Furthermore, owing to the impact of market economy that gained momentum after World War II, patron–client relationships have increasingly begun to replace formerly prevailing genealogically defined relations. Last but not least, various forms of alignments of people from different linguistic backgrounds under the tutelage of religious authority (saints, sufi pirs, and so on) have had an effect on the socio-political structure.[11]

Frequently, this briefly described ethnic; cultural, linguistic, and religious diversity, as well as the geographical conditions, primarily Afghanistan's mountainous terrain and its lack of modern infrastructure, have been held responsible for the country's deficiencies in nation-building. Although I do not completely reject the significance of these factors, I agree with M. N. Shahrani in his criticism of this line of argument. Geographical characteristics and ethnic, religious, linguistic diversity cannot be considered the sole reasons for not achieving political centralization and national unity. Following Shahrani it is also the nature of the state and its historical manifestations in the country (such as its political ideology, its political economy, the basis of its support structure) and the particular attitudes, policies and practices of the state-building agents in the nation-building process which are essential in this respect.[12] In the following I shall therefore summarize these aspects.

Substantial centralization and nation-building efforts started rather late in Afghanistan and were to a large extent instigated by external pressures, primarily by British and Russian political interests in Central Asia. It was only after Amir Abdurrahman Khan ascended the Afghan throne in 1880 that increased measures were taken – supported by British subsidies – to establish an austere, organized central state. The formation of an efficient and loyal army under the direct control of the amir, and the introduction of an extensive administrative and taxation system as well as attempts to deprive the leaders of the various ethnic and tribal groups of their political power, or at least to weaken their political influence, were the central elements of Amir Abdurrahman Khan's endeavour to establish firm state control over the country.[13]

However, in his attempt to enforce supremacy and to destroy the formerly prevalent model of power balance between the ruling dynasty and the leaders of the various segments of Afghan society, the Amir followed an uneven strategy. Whereas the non-Pashtun groups, like the Uzbeks, Hazaras and Kafirs (later called Nuristani), against whom he had carried out several military expeditions, were more or less completely subdued, the Pashtuns were faced with less suppressive measures and even played a major role in his centralization policy. Equipped with numerous privileges (such as exemption from tax payments, and distribution of land) Pashtun tribesmen were settled in various parts of Afghanistan, primarily in the north, and acted as representatives of the central state.[14] While Amir Abdurrahman Khan was able to neutralize political contestants for power and to enlarge the state's resource base and its authority, he was – despite referring strongly to Islam as an encompassing ideology – less successful in creating national unity.[15] On the contrary, the suppression of the various segments of Afghan society and the practised patronage of the Pashtuns produced, as Shahrani comments, 'alienation and resignation among large segments of the tribal and ethnic populations, giving rise to the development of smaller, community-based, parallel power structures, which enabled them to avoid costly contacts with state authorities. ... Tribal stratification among Pushtuns, as well as ethnic inequalities favouring the Pushtuns over non-Pushtuns, was formally instituted.'[16]

Abdurrahman Khan's centralization policy – later on often called 'internal imperialism', 'interior colonization', or 'Pashtunization of Afghanistan' – thus not only led to profound changes in the make-up of the population of various regions (for example, northern and central Afghanistan), but likewise provoked a grading of ethnic groups within the newly emerging political system.[17] This development had major consequences for the future, as it sowed the seed of ethnically motivated conflicts and power struggles which became focal points of politics in the 1990s and contributed to the current plight of Afghan society.

Following Abdurrahman Khan's efforts to augment state supremacy, the search for a common national identity gained increasing momentum. Whereas Abdurrahman Khan's successor, Habibullah I, concentrated on the consolidation of his father's achievements in terms of enlarging the institutional and infrastructural framework of the Afghan state, it was Amir Amanullah Khan (1919–28) who again took up the goal of transforming Afghanistan into a uniform state. In line with the then popular Islamic modernists – Al Afghani, Abduh and Mahmud Tarzi – whose ideas had a profound influence on the Amir's perception of the world, Amanullah Khan opted for modernism as the means to achieve the formation of a uniform Afghan nation-state. By transforming Afghanistan into a modern state in the European sense, and by extinguishing all forms of discrimination as well as by forming a society based on the principles of equality, brotherhood and justice, Amanullah Khan intended to create national unity and to enforce loyalty to the Afghan state.[18]

Yet, although initially supported by the vast majority of the population, Amanullah Khan failed to realize his plans. His policy of direct state interference in the socio-cultural life of the peoples (for example, his attempt to ban the veiling of women, and to reduce the payments of bride wealth), through which he had aimed at a rapid modernization of the country, provoked widespread revolts and eventually forced the Amir to resign. In the subsequent turmoil Habibullah Kalakani (1928–29), a Tajik from Kohistan (a region north of Kabul) seized power and established himself as the new Afghan king. However, the existence of a non-Pashtun ruler in Kabul mobilized the Pashtun tribes, who – in spite their opposition to the state – considered themselves the *staatstragende* ethnic group, the only one entitled to rule the country.[19] Forming a coalition, the Pashtuns overthrew Habibullah Kalakani and appointed Nadir Khan, a member of the former ruling family, king. Thereby Pashtun rulership, which had existed since Ahmad Shah, a tribal leader of the Abdali Pashtuns, had been proclaimed king of Afghanistan in 1747, was re-established.

It was during the reigns of Nadir Khan and his successors, the so-called Musahiban dynasty (Nadir Khan 1929–33, Zahir Shah 1933–73 and Daud Khan 1973–78), that new efforts were made to increase centralization and nation-building. Influenced by former experiences the Afghan state under the Musahibans put up with a minimal realization of its sovereign demands (taxes, rudimentary administration and judiciary, recruitment of soldiers for the national army) and a selective modernization of the country, mainly by extending the infrastructure of the country and by avoiding direct political involvement at local level.[20] Instead of depriving the local elite (the Pashtun tribal chiefs, ulemas and leaders of the various non-tribal groups) of all their power, the Musahibans integrated them into the administration by assigning them the role of middlemen between the local society and the central state, without, however, allowing them any direct influence on state policies.[21] Yet, once again, the Pashtuns kept more influence and privileges than the non-Pashtuns.

Another important focus of the policy of the Musahiban dynasty lay in fostering national unity and in promoting a common national identity. Their predecessors had relied on encompassing ideologies, such as Islam (at least, Hanafi Sunnism), as in the case of Amir Abdurrahman Khan, or modernism and development of a national ideology 'based on traits common to all citizens of Afghanistan', as in the case of Amir Amanullah Khan, and had developed no interest in altering the multi-cultural and multi-ethno-linguistic character of the country. The Musahiban introduced nationalism as a driving force for their nation-building process. In their attempt to establish a uniform Afghan nation and a common national identity, the Musahibans, without explicitly mentioning Pashtunism as the underlying framework of the Afghan nation-state, referred heavily to a nationalistic concept, which was essentially built on the values and the culture of Pashtun society in Afghanistan.[22]

This effort by the Musahibans to find a new basis for the creation of a modern Afghan state coincided with the emergence of a strong intellectual and political movement among the Pashtuns, which aimed at promoting Pashtun literature and culture vis-à-vis the Farsi-dominated Afghan intelligentsia.[23] However, this Pashtun-biased nationalism was not only informed by the demands of these newly emerging Pashtun intellectual circles. To a certain extent it was also influenced by German National Socialist ideology, which gained momentum in Afghanistan during the 1930s and the early 1940s, leading to, among other things, the promotion of 'Pan-Afghanism' in the Afghan press. Accordingly, the Afghans were signified as 'Aryans of the East', as 'the sole civilized nation' amidst a 'sea of barbarian people'.[24]

This emphasis on Pashtunism as the basis of Afghan national identity became particularly obvious in the government's education system. By making Pashtu compulsory for all Afghan pupils, and by forcing all government officials to apply it in their communications, the government intended to disseminate the use of Pashtu.[25] These efforts to promote Pashtu not only focused on strengthening the role of that language in Afghan society, but aimed at replacing the hitherto dominant Farsi, the main lingua franca, with Pashtu, which would eventually emerge as the sole national language of Afghanistan.[26]

Pashtunism as the basis of nation-building was also accentuated in textbooks and historiographies, where the foundation of the Afghan central state and its subsequent developments were depicted solely as the product of the efforts of the Pashtuns. By contrast, the contributions of other ethnic groups to the country's history and the culture were ignored or played down.[27]

In the political arena, this emphasis on Pashtunism was reflected in the government's economic, educational and social policies. Non-Pashtun groups were excluded from leading positions in the state bureaucracy and army, which were reserved for the Pashtuns, particularly for members of the Mohammadzai, the tribal segment to which the royal family also belonged.[28] Moreover, non Pashtuns were likewise disadvantaged in the development policy of the state, which directed most of its infrastructual investment and services (for example, construction of irrigation schemes, introduction of educational and health facilities) towards the Pashtun settlement areas.[29]

Major shifts in this favouritism of the Pashtuns occurred only in the early 1960s, when the Musahiban dynasty adopted a new constitution and tried to introduce a more democratic political system.[30]

In total, however, the nation-building attempts, especially with regard to creating a sentiment of national unity, proved not very successful. On the contrary, the grading of ethnic groups, which had begun under Abdurrahman Khan, was further institutionalized and Pashtun nationalism gained increasing momentum in the nation-building process. From time to time – in particular during the period when Mohammad Daud Khan ruled the country (1953–63 as prime minister and 1973–78 as president) – Pashtun nationalism and the 'Pashtunistan issue', that is, the attempt to reunite all Pashtuns currently living in Afghanistan and Pakistan within a common territory, became major preoccupations of the Afghan state.[31]

Dissociation from this Pashtun-biased nationalism occurred only when the Musahiban dynasty was finally overthrown in the communist coup d'état of 1978. Unlike the preceding regime, the Communist Party of Afghanistan (the PDPA) – although itself dominated by Pashtuns – tried to implement a policy of equal rights for all ethno-linguistic groups living within Afghanistan. In this the PDPA copied Soviet nationality policy.[32] By granting official status to some of the minority languages (such as Uzbeki, Turkmeni, Baluchi and Pashai), by propagating education in these newly defined national languages and putting out radio programmes and publications in them, and by nominating members of the country's minorities into top positions within the government and the PDPA's ruling circles, the new regime tried to win the support and the sympathy of the non-Pashtun ethnic groups.[33] However, in spite of all their attempts, which were extensively supported by the Soviet Union, they had only limited success.

In opposition to the communist regime, the various Muhajedin factions – in spite of drawing their support from specific ethnic, linguistic, religious and regional groups – remained for the most part reluctant to stress ethnicity. They rather emphasized the unity of the Islamic community (Umma), at times even trying to bridge the gap between Sunni and Shia Muslims, and only gradually started to use anything but the two official languages – Farsi-Dari and Pashtu – as means for their written and oral communications.[34]

Similarly, the government of the Islamic State of Afghanistan that replaced the communist regime in April 1992 – at least in its beginnings – promoted the concept of the unity of the Islamic community.[35] At the same time, an end of all forms of discrimination in terms of ethno-linguistic or religious adherence was postulated. Both goals were highlighted in a speech by Professor Burhanuddin Rabbani when he took office as president on 30 June 1992: 'The Government is no longer the property or possession of a party, a particular ethnic group, or a limited number of people. It belongs, instead, to all the valiant, brave and heroic Afghan nation. Islam considers political, social, economic and cultural self-determination the legitimate right of the people. It rejects any type of oppression and despotism under any name and title. The Islamic State is the government of equity and justice of God. It repudiates any kind of privilege or discrimination based on racial, ethnic, tribal, or linguistic considerations. No factor but piety and God-consciousness can be the criterion for priorities among the people. In the Islamic State, all ethnic groups will enjoy fully political, economic, social and cultural rights. Monopolies and the hoarding of power are categorically rejected.'[36] In spite of this emphasis on national unity and the proclamation of equality, it was only a short while until the various contenders for power started a war against each other which at the time of writing is still going on. In this civil war, characterized by constantly shifting coalitions among the major political factions – Rabbani Gulbuddin Hekmatyar and the Taleban, and General Dostum and the Hezb-e Wahdat – ethnicity gained increasingly momentum as a political tool.[37] Each war faction legitimates its involvement in the fightings and its uncompromising attitudes in the various peace talks that have taken place since 1994, with the necessity to defend the rights of a specific segment of Afghan society it claims to represent. In this context ethnicity and the demand for an acknowledged status of the various ethnic groups in the political establishment are often used as rhetorical devices by the political players to achieve their own personal goals. For ordinary Afghan citizens, the issue of ethnically based political representation is also gaining importance, though to a lesser degree. For them the struggle to survive and the yearning for peace after twenty years of war and civil war have priority over other political goals.

From all this it follows, that – in spite of all efforts to popularize the idea of a common national identity – state-sponsored nationalism did not win much support from the peoples of the country, whether Pashtuns or non-Pashtuns. The Pashtuns, especially the tribes, although politically and militarily weakened, still viewed any interference by the state as a threat to their political autonomy and therefore remained hostile towards state policies as a whole. For the Pashtun nationalists the nation-building process was not far-reaching enough to allow a transformation from Farsi urban culture to genuine Pashtun culture.

However, the majority of the non-Pashtun Afghans rejected this Pashtun-biased concept of identity, not only on the grounds of its contents, but also because of their own experiences with the Afghan state. Not only were they disadvantaged by the economic, educational and social policies, which favoured Pashtun groups (in the infrastructural developments, and the like), but they were similarly excluded from leading positions in the state bureaucracy, which were more or less exclusively reserved for Pashtuns.[38]

It is therefore not surprising that the peoples of Afghanistan did not associate the term 'Afghan' with Afghan citizenship, as was the common official usage, but rather considered it to be synonymous with 'Pashtuns'.[39] Furthermore, in popular understanding 'Afghan' referred – as Orywal has pointed out – to the historical fact of Afghan–Pashtun interior colonization and the refusal to grant equal opportunities to all citizens of the country.[40]

To sum up, it was the low degree of penetration of society by the state and its institutions, which derived from the prevailing relations of power, as well as the emphasis on Pashtunism and the simultaneous discrimination against non-Pashtuns, that prevented the development of a sentiment of national unity and caused the rejection of the state-sponsored model of Afghan nationhood by Afghanistan's citizens.

But, if the Afghan state did not provide the framework of identity and allegiance of the individual and the various social groups in the country, what else was there to create unity and to shape the construction of individual and collective identities?

Identity Construction within Afghan Society

As to the creation of identity and communal unity Afghans refer to a large number of aspects. The latter are not only – as Barth, Tapper, Orywal, Canfield and many others have illustrated – highly flexible (that is, situational and contextual), but also influenced by the policies of the Afghan state.[41]

Referring to the collective identities of the Afghan population, Canfield underlines that these are 'associated with several kinds of ideal groupings: with territorial groupings suggested in the word for homeland, watan; with kinship groupings of varying scales suggested in the word for partilineal kinship group, qawm; with Islamic sect affiliation suggested in the word for doctrinal tradition, mazhab; and with the followers of a "saint" who call themselves hampir in some contexts or tariqat members in others.'[42] In particular the terms 'Qaum', 'Watan' and 'Mazhab' are used as bases of identity in Afghan popular discourse. 'All three are ambiguous, or rather polysemic, but to varying degrees.'[43] The term 'mazhab' (sect groups) suggests the relationship among members of one of the Islamic sects in Afghanistan of which there are three, Sunnis . . . , Twelver Shi'ites . . . , and Ismail'ili Shi'ites.[44] Unlike 'mazhab', which is rather definite, 'watan' (homeland), sometimes simply called 'ja' (place), is highly ambiguous 'as to both scope (village, valley, district, province, region, nation . . .) and time (place of origin, or place of residence). Identity based on watan is very strong for most people. Even nomads identify themselves with their watan (usually winter quarters) and the varied population there, as against fellow-tribespeople or nomads from other regions.'[45]

However, the term most often used among Afghans (and researchers) for the definition of social groups and identity is 'qaum'.[46] Within Afghan popular discourse it has many meanings and is used to denominate various social groups. 'Among its connotations are "ethnic group" and "tribe", but it can be both broader and narrower than these: not merely "nation" but also descent groups and their subdivisions down to the family, and linguistic, regional and occupational, groups, sects, castes. ... Perhaps most often it implies linguistic and/or tribal identity.'[47] According to Canfield it 'may be used to include, not only those persons reckoning themselves agnates through a common ancestor, but also the persons who mutually assist each other and share goods with each other, not all of whom are always close kinsmen. It may apply to affinal as well as agnatic kinsmen, and even to unrelated persons who become assimilated into a group by marriage. And it may refer to friendly families who may eventually form kinship ties through reciprocal marriages. Conversely, the word can be contracted so as to exclude certain actual kinsmen who no longer co-operate with the rest of one's in-group.'[48] In essence, the 'qaum' refers to a 'solidarity unit'. As Canfield puts it, 'The central intent of the word 'qawm' is that the members are united by agnatic kinship, have a common home territory, and enjoy warm social fellowship. A qawm in its conception is a social solidary group. The members of a qawm, in local usage, are qawmi to each other. Qawmi are in-group persons; non-qawmi are in some sense out-group persons. Qawmi should dwell in the same territory. They should cooperate in work when needed; they should be politically united, operating as wholes for political purposes; and they should be religiously united, celebrating the Muslim holidays together and gathering at appointed times to pray and listen to sermons or the reading of religious literature. The local members of a qawm, therefore, are ideally a territorially and socially integrated group, joined together through ties of kinship, political action, and religious belief and ritual.'[49] Or as Centlivres remarks, the term 'implies common origins and basic cultural unity and identity: the most used markers of qaum-membership are stereotypes of language, dress, customs, comportment and somatology.'[50]

Next to a common ancestry that binds individuals together and a common shared territory, it is above all behaving as one solidarity unit that constitutes membership in the qaum, as Roy points out in his definition: 'Qawm is the term used to designate any segment of the society bound by solidarity ties. It could be an extended family, a clan, an occupational group, a village etc. Qawm is based on kinship and client/patron relationships; before being an ethnic group it is a solidarity group which protects its members from encroachments from the state and other qawm, but which also is the scene of inside competition between contenders for local supremacy.'[51]

This rather broad conceptualization of the qaum makes it possible in a concrete situation to include individuals of diverse ethnic and linguistic origin as members of the same group so as to allow inhabitants of multi-ethnic villages to consider themselves as one qaum, that is, as one solidarity unit. According to context and situation, qaum may involve a varying number of individuals, close kinsmen, a village, an ethnic group, a religious sect or a linguistic group. It is therefore 'a highly ambiguous and flexible concept allowing scope for strategic manipulations of identity'.[52] Or, as Canfield says: 'Actually, the word "qawm", rather than describing an empirical social pattern, is a term for a locally conceived structural category. It therefore may be adjusted to suit various actual social situations. It may be invoked, when appropriate, for various ranges and degrees of kinship reality, and denied when not appropriate.'[53]

Despite all centralization and nation-building efforts of Afghan rulers, groups defining themselves as qaums are still the most essential constituents of socio-political organization in Afghanistan. The relevance of the qaum as a unit of solidarity, and as a socio-political framework that structures the interaction between individuals, groups and the state, emerges particularly in situations of political crisis. As the country's recent political history illustrates, political ideologies and entities will tend to be of minor significance in the formation of alliances.[54] This became especially obvious after the coup d'état of 1978. The Communist Party of Afghanistan (PDPA) as well as the various Mujahedin factions recruited their adherents primarily from their own qaums.[55]

However, since the 1970s when national politics began to have a stronger impact at the local level and the socio-political and economic situation was increasingly interpreted in terms of ethnic affiliation, leading to a certain awareness among the Turkic peoples and the Hazara of being oppressed and excluded by a Pashtun-dominated state, the qaum concept also underwent some modification, primarily towards enlarged entities, transcending the local level and thus stressing ethnic and/or religious affiliations. As Roy points out, 'Qawm affiliations, at the very local level, play a bigger role than ethnic ones. But participation in a nationwide political game induces the local qawm to express themselves in terms of broader ethnic affiliations.'[56] With regard to this development, specific events and situations (such as the decisive participation of General Dostum and his Uzbek militia in the defeat of the communist regime in April 1992) may act as a catalyst for increased ethnic consciousness and even lead to the development of nationalist movements.

In what follows I shall use the interaction of the Uzbeks of northeastern Afghanistan with the Afghan state and their framework of identity construction and self-perception as a case study to illustrate some of the problems of the nation-building process and the reaction of the Afghans to it.

The Uzbeks of Afghanistan

Before describing the relationship between the Uzbeks and successive Afghan governments, I shall give a brief outline of the Uzbeks living in Afghanistan.

Within the vast number of ethno-linguistic groups that make up the population of Afghanistan the Uzbeks form a major segment. With an estimated number of 0.75 million to 1.649 million the Uzbeks accounted for roughly 10 per cent of the country's 10 to 20 million inhabitants in the late 1970s.[57] The other major groups were the Pashtuns (some 39 per cent), the Tajiks (26 per cent) and the Hazaras (10 per cent).[58] The Uzbeks were therefore not only the largest Turkic-speaking group in Afghanistan, but represented the third largest ethno-linguistic group after the Pashtu- and Farsi-speaking groups.[59] However, because of the war-induced mass exodus and displacement of large numbers of the Afghan population, the percentage rates of the various ethnic groups in total, as well as the distribution of specific ethnic groups in various regions of the country, may have changed substantially since the early 1980s.[60] Although no concrete information is available it is generally assumed that the Uzbeks account for about 14 per cent of the total Afghan population (the Pashtuns being 22 per cent, the Tajiks 34 per cent and the Hazara 14 per cent).[61]

Like the majority of Afghans, the Uzbeks are Sunni Muslims of the Hanafi branch. Their main settlement area lies in northern Afghanistan, more precisely in the provinces of Fariyab, Jozjan, Balkh, Samangan, Kunduz and Baghlan, where they constitute the majority or plurality of the population, living in close proximity to other ethno-linguistic groups such as the Tajik, Pashtun, Turkmen and Arabs, to mention just the most important ones.[62] Smaller groups of Uzbeks are located in cities like Kabul, Kandahar, Herat and Laskargah, where they came either as a consequence of Amir Abdurrahman's deportation policies following the defeat of their rebellion in 1888, or due to labour migration in more recent times.[63]

The Uzbeks of Afghanistan although regarded by the other citizens of Afghanistan as one uniform group – the main criterion being their Turkic language – are not a homogeneous group. Due to historic events within the last few centuries, which led to major population shifts in the region, the Uzbek community in Afghanistan is made up of a number of distinct groups, which have not developed a profound sense of unity and have not merged into an Uzbek nation. On the contrary, they exhibit great differences in terms of their socio-political organization and their political alignment structure.

According to Shalinsky the Afghan Uzbeks comprise the following three groups.[64] The first consists of those Uzbeks whose ancestors migrated to Afghanistan at the beginning of the sixteenth century as a consequence of Shaibani Khan's conquest of northern Afghanistan. Until the nineteenth century, when the various chiefdoms they had formed there were annexed by the Afghan state, these Uzbeks represented the politically dominant force.[65]

The second group comprises those who came, during the period from the late nineteenth century until the 1917 Russian Revolution because of increased political and economic pressures after the tsarist conquest of the Central Asian amirates. The third group is made up of those whose forebears fled to Afghanistan between 1917 and the 1930s as a result of the collapse of the Central Asian resistance movement (the so-called Basmachis) and the sovietization of Central Asia. Again, this group of refugees was not homogeneous, but included people of various socio-economic and linguistic origins. On the one hand, there were rural people, predominantly Uzbeki-speakers, with tribal affiliations, often similar to those of the Uzbek tribes already present in Afghanistan, and with a nomadic or semi-nomadic or farming background, who upon their arrival in Afghanistan joined existing Uzbek villages or established their own settlements.[66] On the other hand, this group included bilingual people (Uzbeki- and Tajiki-speakers) with urban origins, primarily from the cities in the Ferghana valley, who settled in Afghan towns near the border, such as Imam Saheb, Kunduz and Khanabad, where, according to their regional origin, they established their own urban neighbourhoods (mahalles), such as the Kasani-Mahalle in Kunduz studied by Audrey Shalinsky.[67]

Yet the picture we get from this subdivision into three groups is not so neat as it appears at first sight. First of all, it is overshadowed by a distinction between those Uzbeks known as Watani ('local people') or Asli ('original' or 'old-established') and those known as Mohajirin ('refugees'), Narg-e Bet (literally: 'from the other side') or Yengi Geldi ('newcomers'), though the distinction is relevant only in the inner Uzbek discourse on identity and socio-political affiliation.[68] This holds especially good for the category Mohajirin, which is rather ambiguous in comparison to Watani. Generally speaking, 'Watani' and 'Asli' are used of those Uzbeks descended from sixteenth-century immigrants, whereas 'Mohajirin', 'Narge-e Bet' and 'Yengi Geldi' are used of those who are descended from nineteenth- and twentieth-century immigrants and who therefore comprise the second and third of Shalinsky's three groups.

Despite their long residence in Afghanistan the Watani Uzbeks are not a united group in terms of identity, self-perception or language.[69] Some of them, especially those (like the Qataghan Uzbeks) inhabiting the north-eastern part of the country, still draw their identity primarily from their tribal affiliation, whereas those living in the north-west have to a large extent replaced their tribal links with a regional identity.[70] Furthermore, the Watani include not only those Uzbeks in Shalinsky's first group but also the descendants of a substantial number of more recent refugees: people who, after the conquest of northern Afghanistan by Amir Abdurrahman Khan in 1888, initially fled north of the Amu Darya, but returned to Afghanistan during the first three decades of the twentieth century.[71] However, unlike the other refugees known as Mohajirin, these returnees (among them many of their former tribal leaders who had tried to escape oppression by Amir Abdurrahman Khan) were reintegrated into the local society without major problems.[72]

In contrast to the use of 'Watani' the application of the categories 'Mohajirin' and 'Narg-e Bet' is ambiguous and is much debated within those two groups.[73] Whereas the Watani, as well as other non-Uzbeks in northern Afghanistan, describe as Mohajirin all groups (Uzbeki- as well as Tajiki-speakers) immigrating to Afghanistan since the late nineteenth century, thus including Shalinsky's second and third groups, the Mohajirin themselves employ the word in a more limited sense.[74] For them it applies only to those immigrants who came after 1928 – that is, after the crackdown on Islam in Soviet Central Asia – thereby emphasizing that they immigrated to Afghanistan for the sake of maintaining their religious identity.[75] It is solely this group of refugees that calls itself Mohajirin and distinguishes itself from all the other émigrés – Basmachi sympathizers, disposed peasants and victims of famine from the countryside – who had earlier (that is, between 1917 and 1928) sought refuge in Afghanistan.[76]

Besides the emphasis they put on the maintenance of their Islamic traditions as an identity-marker, it is also their town origins (for example, from Kasan in the Ferghana Valley) and their cultural background, as well as their settlement pattern in Afghan towns, which distinguish them from the other refugees.[77] Furthermore, whereas the Watani Uzbeks and other émigés from Central Asia distinguish themselves from others by drawing clear-cut ethno-linguistic boundaries (for example, between Uzbeki- and Tajiki-speakers), the Mohajirin do not make this distinction. Despite linguistic differences and differing town origins, the Uzbek and Tajik Mohajirin view themselves as an endogamous group in Afghanistan, distinct from other Uzbeki- and Tajiki-speaking groups, either local or refugee groups.[78] Likewise, they have not developed a strong attachment to Afghanistan. For most of them Central Asia remains their watan ('homeland').[79] Only a few members of the Mohajirin community, mostly young men born in Afghanistan, who have attended higher educational institutions, consider Afghanistan their watan and identify with a larger grouping, giving 'Uzbek' as their ethnic group.[80] This lack of feeling at home in Afghanistan may also have influenced the Mohajirin's decision to leave Afghanistan after 1978 and to become refugees once again.[81] This renewed flight had a major impact on the Mohajirin's identity and self-esteem. Now the concept of emigration for the sake of religion has become even more crucial to the Mohajirin and has resulted, as Shalinsky has pointed out, in their self-esteem as 'double Mohajirin'.[82]

In contrast to the Mohajirin, who have crossed ethno-linguistic boundaries and used adherence to Islamic values as a major identity-marker, the other Uzbek refugees, although also called Mohajirin by the Watani Uzbeks and the other inhabitants of northern Afghanistan, by and large retained their tribal affiliations and ethno-linguistic identity, and did not call themselves Mohajirin.[83] Furthermore, owing to their rural existence and partly similar tribal affiliations they came into closer contact with the Watani Uzbek population.[84]

In conclusion, it may be stated that although some links developed between the Mohajirin and the Watani Uzbeks, especially in view of the increasing encroachment by the politically and economically dominant Pashtun settlers, both groups of Uzbeks continued to exist as more or less separate entities. Consequently, up to the early 1990s no profound sense of unity had developed among the various Uzbek groups in Afghanistan and the distinction between Watani or Asli Uzbeks and Mohajirin, Narg-e Bet or Yengi Geldi Uzbeks remained a major element in the internal Uzbek discourse in Afghanistan. However, this lack of a sense of unity among the Afghan Uzbeks does not only result from their diversity in terms of cultural and historic background. It is also closely related to the Afghan nation-building process and the role the Uzbeks and other minorities assumed in it.

The Uzbeks and the Afghan State

Until their integration into the Afghan state under Amir Abdurrahman Khan in the late nineteenth century, the Uzbeks were the politically dominant ethnic group north of the Hindu Kush, where they had established various petty chiefdoms (amirates) that were entangled in constant struggles for power among themselves.[85] Although these Uzbek amirates had been annexed by the Afghan kings in the second half of the eighteenth century, the amirs had been able to retain much of their independence. Despite their function as local representatives of the Afghan kings, who were their nominal suzerains, and for whom they collected taxes and levied troops, the Uzbek tribal elite (amirs, begs and moyzafids) had followed their own political ends, and remained powerful contestants of the kings' influence. At times the amirs and begs were even able to expand their own sphere of influence, for example when in the 1830s Sultan Murad Beg, the amir of Kunduz, brought large parts of north-eastern Afghanistan under his control and raided territories to the south of his own.[86]

It was only when Amir Abdurrahman Khan had defeated their last revolt against the Afghan state in 1888 that the political relationship between the Uzbeks and the Afghan government changed dramatically.[87] As a consequence of their subjection the formerly powerful Uzbek political elite lost much of their independence and were confronted with increasing control and dominance by governors, army personnel and other officials, mainly Pashtuns, who were sent from Kabul to administer the region. The remaining political influence of the Uzbek elite was now more or less completely restricted to local affairs (at village level) and each beg and moyzafid was forced to play the role of middleman between his own group (village, tribal group, and so on) and the Afghan state.[88]

Even more crucial than the political deprivation were the effects of the colonization and settlement policy, another major strategy employed by the Afghan state to increase its control in the region. In contrast to the period before 1888, when Pashtuns – with the exception of a few civil servants and soldiers – had seldom settled down permanently in the region, large numbers of Pashtuns were now transferred north of the Hindu Kush, primarily in two waves (after 1888 and in the 1930s). Provided with numerous privileges and support measures (such as allotment of land – especially irrigated plots and pastures – that had been taken away from their former owners, usually indigenous Uzbeks; preferential treatment in all land-distribution programmes and infrastructural improvements) these Pashtuns, mainly tribal groups from southern and south-eastern Afghanistan, were now settled in the north of the country.[89] This settlement policy not only led to far-reaching changes in the composition of the population (for example, a numerical dominance by the Pashtuns in certain areas, such as Dasht-i Archi in the province of Takhar), but also caused alterations in the interethnic relations and in local politics. The influx of Pashtun settlers put the indigenous population under severe economic pressure as the most profitable land was given to the newcomers.[90] Furthermore, northern Afghanistan, especially the fertile plains of north-eastern Afghanistan and the city of Kunduz, was closely drawn into the market economy and became a major centre of agrarian and industrial production. In total, the region provided a substantial amount of the government's tax income and about 70 per cent of Afghanistan's foreign income (pre-war period) through the export of natural gas, lamb skins (especially karakul furs), cotton, melons and so on.[91] However, in spite of its importance to the Afghan economy, public investment as well as foreign development aid projects remained low and focused mainly on measures for further Pashtun settlements in the region.[92] In comparison to other parts of the country, modern educational and medical facilities were provided to a limited extent and were implemented late – not until the late 1950s[93] – and it was often Pashtun villages that got access to these facilities first.[94]

The Uzbeks were not only neglected in the Afghan government's improvements to the country's infrastructure, but were also disadvantaged in public employment, a sector dominated by the Pashtuns and the Tajiks.[95] Largely deprived of access to state employment, most Uzbeks gained a living as farmers, artisans, tradesmen and workers in cotton mills and the gas industry. Thus they, like many other ethnolinguistic groups, remained a marginal group in terms of education, socio-economic standing and political position, and their opportunities for upward mobility were limited.

It was not until the collapse of the communist regime in 1992 that the Uzbeks – owing to the decisive contribution of General Dostum to the victory of the Mujahedin and his military strength and cunning policies – re-emerged as a major factor in Afghan national politics and started to demand their equality within Afghan society and their proper share in the national power structure.[96]

Uzbek Reactions to the Afghan Nation-building Process

Against this background of discrimination and deprivation, how did the Afghan Uzbeks respond to their underprivileged status within Afghan society in terms of political action and self-perception? And why did they take so long to react to the socio-economic and political discrimination against them?[97]

To begin with, some general remarks on the political system of Afghanistan may be useful. Until the communist coup d'état and the Soviet invasion of Afghanistan, no large-scale political mobilization of the peoples of Afghanistan – especially not in the rural areas, where most Afghans lived – had taken place. Till then national politics had been of little concern to the ordinary Afghan citizen, as is reflected in the low participation rate in the national polls.[98] With the exception of a few intellectual circles in Kabul and other major cities, who focused on political issues such as democracy, political participation and the freedom of the press, and were engaged in increasingly polarized debates (for example, the PDPA versus the Islamists at Kabul University), the majority of Afghans were not interested in the state itself or its political character. The crucial concern for them was to keep state influence at local (village, tribe, etc.) level as low as possible and to secure the power balance that had developed over the last decades between the state and the local socio-political entities.[99]

It was finally due to the war against the communist regime and the

Soviet forces that a major socio-political transformation process took place, one which, for the first time in Afghan history, involved all strata of society and led to a profound mobilization of that society from below.[100] This not only included the emergence of a kind of 'national consciousness' among all Afghan citizens, but simultaneously initiated a general emancipation of formerly disadvantaged ethnic and religious groups (such as the Uzbeks and the Hazara), and led to an accentuation of identities, based either on ethnicity or religious affiliation. Legitimized by their participation in the resistance fight, these formerly suppressed groups now demanded their political rights within the Islamic State of Afghanistan set up in April 1992.[101]

Leaving these more recent developments aside, Uzbek reaction to the centralization and nation-building process focused on two aims: first, on neutralizing state influence as far as possible, and, second, on developing viable strategies against the increasing number of Pashtun settlers who were pouring into their settlement area and who – being granted extensive usufruct rights in agricultural and grazing lands – were endangering the resource basis of the local population. In this the Uzbeks were strongly influenced by their historical experiences with the Afghan state. As military resistance had proved counterproductive, leading to even more Pashtuns being settled in the region (as in the early 1930s), the only remaining alternative was to seek peaceful co-operation with the Afghan state and to attempt to manipulate the state's institutions at local level for their own interests. This corresponded with the state's own policies. In the past, any large-scale penetration of society had led to revolt (as during the reign of Amir Amanullah Khan, 1918–28), so the Afghan state contented itself (until 1978) with a minimal realization of its suzerainty and avoided direct political involvement at local level (especially in the Pashtun tribal areas).[102] Administration and the implementation of state regulations were left to the representatives of villages, tribes and other local bodies, that is, to the leaders such as begs and moyzafids). In the case of the Uzbeks of north-eastern Afghanistan those leaders corresponded with the former politically dominant families, who had disposed of their former regional political importance, and had become middlemen between their own group and the Afghan state as well as between their own group and other ethno-linguistic entities (such as the Pashtun settlers).

Their political activities focused on defending their tribal and local interests and on acting as mediators in conflicts between the regional representatives of the Afghan government, such as the governor or military commander, or as go-betweens in disputes with other ethnic groups. Likewise, in using their close ties with the government's representatives – who were assigned to the region for only short periods and so were dependent on them for information and support – the moyzafids and begs tried to neutralize the Afghan state's local influence and to negotiate favourable conditions for their own group and for themselves.[103]

Furthermore, by skilfully using kinship ties (for example, by putting their own family members in local administrative positions), and by establishing a vast network of patron–client relationships (for example, with indebted co-tribesmen, or with affiliated refugee groups from Central Asia) they tried to enhance their political prominence and influence. Another major task of the Uzbek elite was related to efforts to create strong alliances with other ethno-linguistic groups, such as the Tajiks, the Qarluqs and Arabs, against the Pashtun settlers.[104] In this, interethnic marriages played a prominent role.[105]

These politically vital alliances also had their impact on the formulation of local identities. Although the various Uzbek communities considered themselves distinct groups in terms of language, customary practices, costume and so on, they developed a sense of closeness with their non-Uzbek allies against the Pashtuns, who were considered as 'intruders'.[106] Consequently, in confrontations with the Pashtuns, the local Uzbeks and Tajiks, and others belonging to the same alliance network, saw themselves as forming one temporary social entity (that is, a Qaum).[107] In interactions with the Pashtuns, the existing linguistic and other differences, which were usually employed to create boundaries between the various ethno-linguistic groups – thus representing key elements for defining ethnic identity – were played down, and a common identity as 'locals' versus the 'intruders' was formulated. As most Uzbeks are bi-lingual (especially the males, who dominate the political discourses), language was not a problem in these alliances. Furthermore, owing to their long co-existence in the region the various ethno-linguistic groups (above all the Uzbeks, Qarluqs and Tajiks) had mutually influenced each other.[108]

Although the Uzbeks of north-eastern Afghanistan generally realized their underprivileged position within Afghan society, the political discourse at local level did not focus on demands for national rights (such as public acknowledgement of their culture and language). The alliances they established were primarily aimed at neutralizing state influence and counteracting too much encroachment by the Pashtun settlers, thereby uniting Uzbeks, Tajiks, Qarluqs and Arabs. In line with this, the traditional Uzbek elite as main proponents of these alliances concentrated on successfully fulfilling these aims and did not promote Uzbek identity or demands for socio-political and cultural rights at national level.

However, with the communist coup d'état in 1978 these traditional Uzbek leaders, exposed to severe suppression by the new government, lost their function as middlemen between the state and the local Uzbek communities. Furthermore, as most of the former begs and moyzafids either had been executed by the communist regime or else had fled abroad, the traditional Uzbek elite – with few exceptions – could not play a major role in the resistance movement. Among the Mujahedin it was mainly young, educated men, often of modest origins, who became leading figures.[109] Similarly, the former alliances that had united the Uzbeks with other ethno-linguistic groups against the Pashtun settlers were transformed into new political formations aimed at organizing the resistance fight. In this, it was initially – that is, before ethnicity gained momentum among the ex-Mujahedin in the 1990s – allegiance to a particular commander or membership in a specific Muhajedin party that united the Mujahedin. Yet in the course of time, especially after 1992, these alliances regrouped, giving increasing importance to the ethnic background of their members.

With regard to general calls for socio-economic, cultural and political rights for the Uzbeks, it took a long time till these demands were put forward. Not until the late 1960s did a modern Uzbek elite emerge.[110] It consisted mainly of students who attended higher educational institutions in Kabul. Inspired by the debate on civil rights, which was going on in intellectual circles in Kabul at the time, they began to criticize the low position of the Uzbeks in Afghan society. In the late 1960s and 1970s, the new elite directed its efforts primarily towards promoting Uzbek culture and literature. At that time, however, they had no impact outside their own intellectual milieu.[111]

Eventually, in the early 1990s a large majority of the Uzbeks developed an interest in their own cultural heritage. Until then many of them had denied their origins and concealed their ethnic affiliation.[112] In public, especially when outside their own settlement area, Farsi-Dari was most often used, even among Uzbeks, as a means of communication. Outside of their home region, they generally avoided representing themselves as Uzbeks and introduced themselves simply as as 'people from the north'. Moreover, many Uzbeks considered their mother-tongue, despite its importance for their identity construction, inferior to Farsi-Dari. This probably had to do with the fact that the Uzbek language was not officially acknowledged until 1978 by the Afghan state.[113] Furthermore, with the exception of those who had been educated in some of the traditional madrasas in northern Afghanistan where the Chagatay language was part of the curriculum, most Uzbeks did not have access to their written traditions.[114] As Uzbeki was not taught in the state education system, the few Uzbeks who had attended modern public schools had to rely on Farsi-Dari and Pashtu in their written communications.[115] This perceived low status of the Uzbek language led many Uzbek parents, especially those living in urban areas, to speak only Farsi-Dari with their children and to avoid giving them Uzbek names. Likewise Farsi-Dari was dominant in Uzbek–Tajik mixed families and prevailed in interethnic communication between the Uzbeks and the Tajiks.[116]

Here, too, the resistance fight that produced changes in the perception of Uzbeki language and culture by the Uzbeks themselves. From this followed a growing accentuation of 'Uzbekishness' that was reflected in other things, an increased use of Uzbeki in public discourses. To speak Uzbeki instead of Farsi-Dari was now intended as a political statement to demonstrate the Uzbeks' participation in the resistance.[117] Moreover, the use of Uzbeki became a tool to emphasize the Uzbeks' claim to their share in the newly emerging political structure of the country.

Opting Out of the Afghan State or Opting In?

Assessing the reactions of the Uzbeks of Afghanistan to the centralization and nation-building process that has taken place during the last decades it becomes clear that the Uzbeks in their reactions initially focused more on local than on national affairs. Led by members of their traditional elite, they concentrated on keeping state influence at the local level as low as possible and on developing viable strategies (such as the formation of cross-ethno-linguistic alliances with the Tajiks, Qarluqs, Arabs and others) to oppose further discrimination and marginalization by the state supported Pashtun settlers. Like other minority groups who had been exposed to suppression and deprivation in the course of the Afghan state's centralization and nation-building process, the Uzbeks responded late at national level to their minority status. This was for several reasons. First, the Uzbeks had not developed a common identity (such as that of the Pashtuns with their collective genealogy and the Pashtunwali) which embraced the various Uzbek groups nor did they have a political elite that could demand equal socio-economic and cultural rights: the only exception was a group of university students, who had no impact on the ordinary Uzbek population. The lack of a collective identity and of a modern political elite was closely connected to the state's nation-building process, which favoured the Pashtuns.

It was only after the establishment of the Islamic State of Afghanistan in 1992 that Uzbek ethnicity became a driving force of politics. For the collapse of the communist regime and the subsequent civil war led not only to further polarization within Afghan society but also – until the Taleban reunified some 80–90 per cent of the Afghan country under one rule – to a fragmentation of the country into more or less independent warlord dominions.[118] It also provoked violent confrontations between the various ethnic groups and – because of the constantly shifting coalitions of the various Mujahedin factions – intensified the Islamic State's political instability.

In this constant battle for power and influence, formerly marginal groups, such as the Uzbeks and the Hazaras, became increasingly politicized and gained political and military importance. For the Uzbeks, these developments led to alterations in their self-representation and identity construction and strengthened the ethnic consciousness of the Uzbeks of Afghanistan. Unlike in former times, when the Uzbeks denied their origin and tried to conceal their ethnic affiliation and language, especially when outside their home region, they no longer refer to themselves as 'people from the north', but proudly call themselves Uzbeks; and a new interest in the Uzbek language is developing. The growing importance of 'Uzbekishness' is also visible in the emergence of a collective feeling of unity among Uzbeks, who until the early 1990s, partly for the above-mentioned reasons, did not perceive themselves as a united ethnic group. Currently, most Uzbek groups in Afghanistan are developing a new identity which, as in the case of the Qataghan Uzbeks of the north-east, goes beyond their narrowly defined group and increasingly includes other Uzbek groups as well. Consequently, in the nation-wide political context and in the discourse with other ethnic groups the term 'qaum', which, as pointed out above, allows for strategic manipulations, is acquiring a more encompassing significance. Besides meaning a person's kin group, subtribe or tribe, it is coming more and more to denote all Uzbeks of Afghanistan. This enlarged concept of membership in the 'qaum' is also clear in responses by the Qataghan Uzbeks to questions about membership in specific tribal groups or subtribal groups. Many of my informants were of the opinion that membership of a particular tribe or subtribe is irrelevant, as 'We are all one' ('Hamamiz bir'). In contrast to this growing sense of unity and the connected reconceptualization of membership of the 'qaum', which now stresses Uzbek ethnicity, the formerly prevalent inclusion of non-Uzbeks in the local 'qaum' is declining sharply, and is creating strong local antagonisms between formerly allied ethno-linguistic groups.

However, in spite of all this, and in spite of the splitting of the various Mujahedin factions along ethnic lines, a movement promoting Uzbek nationalism and irredentism has not yet emerged.[119] Political mobilization and enforced ethnic consciousness have so far led solely to a strong call for acknowledgement of their political and cultural rights and for them to be granted a fair share in the field of national politics. In this the existing Uzbek movements, the Shura-e Qaumi (Council of the Population) and the Jonbesh-e Milli Islami Afghanistan (National Islamic Movement of Afghanistan), however, do not highlight Uzbek identity. Although the majority of their members are Uzbeks, both movements view themselves as advocates of the political and cultural rights of the disadvantaged Turkic peoples of Afghanistan.

The Shura-e Qaumi was founded in 1991–2 by a number of ulema, traditional political leaders and university graduates, living in Pakistan, who were of the opinion that the Afghan Turkic peoples were not well represented by the existing Mujahedin groups. They therefore concentrated on informing Afghan refugees and the international media about the part played by the Turkic peoples in the resistance and on securing the involvement of Turkic representatives in the UN-sponsored peace negotiations.[120] The Shura-e Qaumi pleaded for a pluralistic democratic system within the framework of an Islamic state in which all political discrimination would be abolished and the Turkic peoples of Afghanistan would be able to participate in the field of politics at all levels. Still more important to the Shura was the introduction of the Turkic languages as a means of instruction in all schools of Northern Afghanistan.[121] Yet the Shura-e Qaumi had neither a political nor a military impact on the resistance movement in Afghanistan.[122]

It was the Jonbesh-e Milli Islami Afghanistan (JMIA), founded by General Rashid Dostum shortly after the formation of the Islamic State of Afghanistan, that became the first really influential movement of the Turkic minorities of Afghanistan. Initially, it consisted of a group of Uzbek generals, who had left the former government's army together with General Dostum, as well as some Mujahedin commanders and a few ulema.[123] However, owing to the increasing antagonism within the newly emerging power structure of the Islamic State of Afghanistan, in particular the conflict between the Massoud–Rabbani faction and General Dostum about representation in the government, which was viewed as Tajik-dominated, the JMIA became a reservoir for disappointed Uzbek, Turkmen and other Mujahedin, ulema and intellectuals.[124] They turned away from the Jamiat-e Islami, where they had initially been organized, and joined the JMIA, which became a platform for the increasingly self-aware Turkic peoples of Afghanistan, especially the Uzbeks, who numerically dominate the movement.[125] In particular, General Dostum, without whose support the Mujahedin would have been unable to capture Kabul in April 1992, became an inspiration to the hitherto deprived Turkic communities.[126] With regard to its political goals, the JMIA votes for a confederated, democratic political system based on Islam, in which all the different groups should have an equal share in political domain.[127] Furthermore, as General Dostum emphasized in an interview with Rasuly, the JMIA supports the establishment of a secularly oriented polity and the emancipation of Afghan women.[128] As a party regarding itself as an advocate of the interests of all ethnic groups living in Northern Afghanistan the JMIA strives to achieve equal rights for all ethnolinguistic groups and to secure their political participation at all levels of the Islamic State of Afghanistan. However, in spite of these aims and General Dostum's attempt to avoid any impression of favouring Uzbek separatism, of promoting Uzbek nationalism or of renewing Uzbek dominance in the region, the JMIA may be viewed as the first Afghan Uzbek political movement focusing on supporting Uzbek interests within the country's new power structure.[129]

To sum up, so far the Afghan state has been unsuccessful in its attempts to realize centralization and to create a common national identity. Moreover, as both efforts were closely linked with a policy of promoting Pashtun interests at the expense of the other ethnolinguistic groups, the nation-building process was rejected by the non-Pashtun citizens, as the case study of the Uzbeks of north-eastern

Afghanistan has illustrated. However, not having developed a profound sense of unity and a collective identity, and lacking a modern elite that would demand their socio-economic, political and cultural rights, the reaction of the non-Pashtuns to the state's nation-building efforts was initially restricted to local level. It focused on neutralizing state influence and on developing strategies against the increasing dominance by the Pashtuns. This led to, among other things, the formation of alignments that crossed ethno-linguistic boundaries and united people of different origins in alliances which operated at local or regional level and did not involve them in national politics. It was only the war of resistance against the Soviet-backed communist regime, and the subsequent civil war among the various Mujahedin factions, that brought about a large-scale politicization of the Afghan peoples, especially the formerly disadvantaged ethnic minority groups such as the Uzbeks and Hazaras. Legitimized by their participation in the resistance war these groups now demand equality within Afghan society and their proper share in the field of politics. Likewise, both the self-representation and the self-esteem of these groups have changed. Now they proudly declare their ethnic adherence and stress their origin, language and culture. Furthermore, as with the Uzbeks, a collective feeling of unity is developing. This increased ethnic consciousness is similarly accompanied by the emergence of political movements such as the Jonbesh-e Milli Afghanistan which focus on promoting the rights of the various groups within the framework of the Afghan state. It is thus not opting out of the nation but rather opting in that is the current political goal of the various ethno-linguistic and religious groups of Afghanistan.

Notes

1 In this essay, the term 'Afghan' refers to a citizen of the former state of Afghanistan and not to the prevailing connotation of the term within Afghan society, where it is most often employed as a synonym for the 'Pashtun'.

2 The following statements on the Uzbeks of Afghanistan are primarily based on my own field research among Uzbek refugees (winter/spring 1991 and 1992 in Pakistan and September 1991 in Turkey) as well as on private communications since then. As no accurate information was available to me on the current situation of the Uzbek communities in

Afghanistan I shall use the past tense in my text for most of the argumentation refers to the period up to mid-1990s.

3 For details, see M. N. Shahrani, 'State Building and Social Fragmentation in Afghanistan: A Historical Perspective', in A. Banuazizi and M. Weiner, eds., *The State, Religion and Ethnic Politics: Pakistan, Iran, and Afghanistan* (Karachi, 1987), pp. 23–75; Shahrani, 'Afghanistan: State and Society in Retrospect', in E. W. Anderson and N. Hatch Dupree, eds., *The Cultural Basis of Afghan Nationalism* (London and New York, 1990), pp. 41–50; S. Rasuly, *Politischer Strukturwandel in Afghanistan* (Frankfurt am Main, 1993); Rasuly, *Die politischen Eliten Afghanistans* (Frankfuirt am Main, 1997).

4 E. Orywal 'Erläuterung zur Verbreitungskarte' and 'Die ethnischen Gruppen: Kurzcharakterisierung und ausgewählte Literatur zur Verbreitung', in Orywal, ed., *Die ethnischen Gruppen Afghanistans: Fallstudien zur Gruppenidentität und Intergruppenbeziehungen* (Wiesbaden, 1986), pp. 12, 18–73; J. Pstrusinska, *Afghanistan 1989 in Sociolinguistic Perspective* (Incidental papers Series, no. 7, *Central Asian Survey*, 1990), pp. 3–17. Except for a short period in the 1970s, when radio programmes were permitted in some Turkic languages (Uzbeki and Turkmeni), other languages spoken in Afghanistan were only recognized in 1978 when the communist regime, following Soviet nationalities policy, bestowed official status on a number of languages such as Uzbeki, Turkmeni, Baluchi and Pashai. The Persian language spoken in Afghanistan is usually called Farsi or Farsi-Dari; Farsi-speakers are sometimes called 'Farsiwan'. The term 'Tajiki' for the Tajiks' Persian mother-tongue is never used.

5 With regard to demographic figures, it should be pointed out that as yet no comprehensive census has been undertaken. Therefore all published figures are merely based on more or less reasonable estimates and may vary considerably.

6 E. Orywal 'Verbreitungskarte der ethnischen Gruppen Afghanistans', *TAVO-Blatt A*, vol. 8, no. 6 (1983); and Pstrusinska, *Afghanistan 1989*, pp. 3–17. Both these authors refer to the situation before 1978. The war, however, has altered the ethnic distribution in various regions, for example north-eastern and central Afghanistan, where most of the Pashtuns are reported to have fled; see M. Sliwinski, *Afghanistan 1978–87: War, Demography and Society* (Incidental Papers Series, no. 6, *Central Asian Survey*, 1988); ad Pstrusinka, *Afghanistan 1989*, p. 45.

7 W. Steul, 'Afghanistan – mit dem Islam zur Nation', in A. Bucholz and M. Geiling, eds., *Im Namen Allahs: Der Islam – eine Religion im Aufbruch?* (Frankfurt am Main, Berlin and Vienna, 1980), p. 114; R. L. Canfield, 'Afghanistan's Social Identities in Crisis', in J.-P. Digard, ed., *Le Fait ethnique en Iran et en Afghanistan* (Paris, 1988), pp. 189, 194; A. Olesen, *islam and Politics in Afghanistan* (Richmond, 1995).

8 O. Roy, *Islam and Resistance in Afghanistan* (Cambridge, 1986), pp. 30–54; Canfield, 'Afghanistan's Social Identities', p. 87; Rasuly, *Politischer Strukturwandel*, pp. 165–97; E. Grötzbach, *Afghanistan: Eine geographische Landeskunde* (Darmstadt, 1990), p. 66.

9 In spite of recent critique on the terms 'tribe', 'tribal' and 'tribesmen' which calls for their rejection I use them here, thereby referring to the current debate in the social anthropology of the Middle East which – although accepting some of the critique – regards these terms as undeniable categories for analysing Middle Eastern societies; see R. Tapper, 'Introduction', in R. Tapper, ed., *The Conflict of Tribe and State in Iran and Afghanistan* (London and Canberra, 1983); R. Tapper, 'Anthropologists, Historians and Tribespeople', in P. S. Khoury and J. Kostiner, eds., *Tribe and State Formation in the Middle East* (London and New York, 1991); E. Gellner, 'The Tribal Society and its Enemies', in R. Tapper, *The Conflict of Tribe and State*; Gellner, 'Tribalism and the State in the Middle East', in Khoury and Kostiner, *Tribe and State Formation*; W. Kraus, 'Islamische Stammesgesellschaft' (mimeo, Vienna, 19980; D. F. Eickelman, *The Middle East: An Anthropological Approach*, 2nd edn. (Englewood Cliffs, NJ, 1981). In Afghanistan and elsewhere in the Middle East, many groups define themselves as tribes, and from this follows, first, that tribe is an important emic concept, which should not be tossed aside. Secondly, because of the importance of that concept and the emphasis on genealogical ties and a specific world view (e.g. the Pashtunwali of the Pashtuns), tribal societies possess a much higher degree of social cohesion, and a greater capacity to mobilize people for political action, than societies bound together by common residence in a specific village or region.

10 In the Pashtunwali, the value system, the code of decent behaviour and the customary law of Pashtun society is laid down; for details, see Steul, *Afghanistan*. For a case study on tribal structures among the Uzbeks of Afghanistan, see Rasuly-Paleczek, 'Ethnic Identity versus Nationalism: The Uzbeks of Northeastern Afghanistan and the Afghan State', in T. Atabaki and J. O'Kane, eds., *Post-Soviet Central Asia* (London, Leiden and Amsterdam, 1998).

11 J.-H. Grevemeyer, *Afghanistan: Sozialer Wandel und Staat im 20. Jahrhundert* (Berlin, 1987), pp. 59–65. R. L. Canfield ('Ethnic, Regional and Sectarian Alignment in Afghanistan', in A. Banuazizi and M. Weiner, eds., *The State, Religion, and Ethnic Politics: Pakistan, Iran, and Afghanistan* (Karachi, 1987), pp. 77f) differentiates between three types of socio-political cooperation: tribal societies, peasant societies and those that unite people from different ethno-linguistic groups.

12 Shahrani, 'Afghanistan: State and Society', p. 42.

13 Ibid, pp. 42, 44f; Shahrani, 'State Building and Social Fragmentation',

pp. 39–53; Rasuly, *Politischer Strukturwandel*, pp. 44f; Mir Munshi Sultan Mohammed Khan, ed., *The Life of Abdur Rahman, Amir of Aghanistan*, vol. 1 (reprinted Karachi, 1980).

14 N. Tapper, 'Abd-al-Rahman's North-West Frontier: The Pashtun Colonisation of Afghan Turkestan', in R. Tapper, ed., *The Conflict of Tribe and State in Iran and Afghanistan* (London and Canberra, 1983); E. Grötzbach, *Kulturgeographischer Wandel in Nordost-Afghanistan seit dem 19. Jahrhundert* (Meisenheim an Glan, 1972), pp. 55f, 67f, 82, 94f.

15 See Shahrani, 'Afghanistan: State and Society', pp. 44f; Olesen, *Islam and Politics* , pp. 62f.

16 Shahrani, 'Afghanistan: State and Society', pp. 44f.

17 Grevemeyer, *Afghanistan: Sozialer Wandel*, p. 39; Grötzbach, *Kulturgeographischer Wandel*, pp. 65, 94f.

18 Among other things, Amanullah Khan supported the emancipation of Afghan women and proclaimed the equal treatment of all ethnic and religious groups. This granting of equal rights to minority groups was also laid down in his 1923 constitution, which was the first in the history of the Afghan state. See Rasuly, *Politischer Strukturwandel*, pp. 70f; Shahrani, 'Afghanistan: State and Society', p. 45. For details on the contents of the constitution, see Rasuly, *Politischer Strukturwandel*, pp. 165f; G. Vercellin, 'Le Fait ethnique dans les politiques des états Iranien et Afghan', in J.-P. Digard, *Le Fait ethnique en Iran et en Afghanistan* (Paris, 1988), p. 223.

19 This demand of Pashtun supremacy is also evident in Afghan historiography, where Habibullah Kalakani is not called by his proper name but rather mentioned as Bacha-e Saqao ('Son of the Water-carrier'). For details of his reign, see Rasuly, *Politischer Strukturwandel*, pp. 76–86.

20 Ibid, pp. 86–165.

21 Grevemeyer, *Afghanistan: Sozialer Wandel*, pp. 59–65, esp. 60, 64; G. Rasuly-Paleczek, 'Beg, Moyzafid and Arbab: Das politische System der Chechka-Uzbeken und der afghanische Zentralstaat', in A. Gingrich, S. Haas, G. Rasuly-Paleczek and T. Fillitz, eds., *Culture, History and Power: Studies in Oriental Society: Festschrift for Prof. Dr. Walter Dostal on the Occasion of his 65th Anniversary* (Frankfurt am Main, 1993).

22 Shahrani, 'Afghanistan: State and Society', p. 45.

23 Rasuly, *Die politischen Eliten*, pp. 136f. With regard to the importance of Farsi, it should be mentioned that, besides being a widespread and generally accepted lingua franca, Farsi was also the court and administrative language of the Pashtun rulers; see E. Orywal, 'Ethnische Identität: Konzept und Methode', in Orywal, ed., *Die ethnischen Gruppen Afghanistans. Fallstudien zur Gruppenidentität und Intergruppensbeziehungen* (Wiesbaden, 1986), pp. 73–86; M. A. Miran, 'The Function of National Languages in Afghanistan' (in Occasional Paper no. 11, Afghanistan Council of the Asia Society, New York, 1977).

24 Rasuly, *Die politischen Eliten*, pp. 136, 314; in this context, the term 'Afghan' refers to the Pashtuns.

25 V. Gregorian, *The Emergence of Modern Afghanistan* (Stanford, CA, 1969), pp. 351, 371; Shahrani, 'State Building', p. 56.

26 Orywal, *Ethnische Identität* (1986c:82), Shahrani, p. 82; Shahrani, 'Afghanistan: State and Society', p. 45; miran, *The Function of National Languages*, p. 5; O. Roy, 'Ethnies et appartenances politiques en Afghanistan', in J.-P. Digard, ed., *le Fait ethnique en Iran et en Afghanistan* (Paris, 1988), p. 203, Psustrinska, *Afghanistan 1989*, pp. 25f; N. A. Dvoryankov, 'The Development of Pushtu as the national and Literary Language of Afghanistan', *Central Asian Review*, vol. 14, no. 3 (1966), pp. 213f; Rasuly, *Die politischen Eliten*, p. 37.

27 M. N. Shahrani, 'Ethnic Relations and Access to Resources in Northeast Badakshan', in J. W. Anderson and R. F. Strand, eds., *Ethnic Processes and Intergroup Relations in Contemporary Afghanistan* (Occasional paper no. 14, Afghanistan Council of the Asia Society, New York, 1978), p. 21; Grevemeyer, *Afghanistan: Sozialer Wandel*, pp. 145f.

28 Shahrani, 'Afghanistan: State and Society', p. 45; D. C. Montgomery, 'The Uzbeks in Two States: Soviet and Afghan Policies towards an Ethnic Minority', in W. O. McCagg and B. D. Silver, eds., *Soviet Asian Ethnic Frontiers* (New York, 19789), p. 161; L. W. Adamec, ed., *Historical and Political Gazetteer of Afghanistan* , vol. 1: *Badakshan Province and Northeastern Afghanistan* (Graz, 1972); L. W. Adamec, ed., *Historical and Political Who s Who of Aghanistan* (Graz, 1975).

29 Thus, all three major development projects (Helmand, Nangarhar and Paktia) undertaken with international development aid were located in Pashtun settlement areas; R. S. Newell, 'The Prospect for State Building in Afghanistan', in A. Banuazizi and M. Weiner, eds., *The State, Religion, and Ethnic Politics: Pakistan, Iran, and Afghanistan* (Karachi, 1987), p. 112.

30 This development is among others reflected in the nomination of Dr Mohammad Yussuf Khan, a Tajik university graduate, as Afghan prime minister in 1964; see Rasuly, *Die politischen Eliten*, pp. 47f.

31 R. Tapper, 'Ethnicity, Order and Meaning in the Anthropology of Iran and Afghanistan', in J.-P. Digard, ed., *Le Fait ethnique en Iran et en Afghanistan* (Paris, 1988), pp. 25f; Shahrani, 'State Building and Social Fragmentation', pp. 58f, 63f.

32 E. Naby, 'The Ethnic Factor in Soviet–Afghan Relations', *Asian Survey*, vol. 20, no. 3 (March 1980); E. Naby, 'The Uzbeks in Afghanistan', *Central Asian Survey*, vol. 3, no. 1 (1984).

33 Roy, 'Ethnies et appartenances', pp. 207f; Naby, 'The Ethnic Factor', pp. 237, 241f, 244–9; Naby, 'The Uzbeks in Afghanistan', pp. 3, 14, 17; Montgomery, 'The Uzbeks in Two States', p. 162; Pstrusinska,

Afghanistan 1989, pp. 51f; Grötzbach, *Afghanistan: Eine geographische Landeskunde*, p. 67.

34 Roy, 'Ethnies et appartenances', pp. 206f; O. Roy, 'Ethnic Identity and Political Expression in Northern Afghanistan', in J.-A. Gross, ed., *Muslims in Central Asia: Expressions of Identity and Change* (Durham and London, 1992), pp. 83f. With regard to the use of Turkic languages by the Mujahedin Naby ('The Ethnic Factor', p. 246) mentions that since summer 1979 some resistance groups have broadcast radio programmes in Turkic languages. Roy ('Ethnic Identity', p. 84) points out that the Jamiat-i- Islami is encouraging Uzbeks mullahs to preach in Uzbek. Some Muhajedin publications by the Jamiat-i Islami and the Hezb-e Islami, which are mainly published in Farsi-Dari, provide articles in Uzbek, written in Arabic script; observation during my field studies in Pakistan in 1991–2.

35 Rasuly, *Die politischen Eliten*, pp. 276, 281.

36 B. Rabbani, 'Address to the nation by Prof. Burhanuddin Rabbani, President of the Islamic State of Afghanistan', radio and TV speech, 30 June 1992, cited in Rasuly, *Die politischen Eliten*, pp. 281f.

37 A. Fänge, 'Afghanistan after April 1992: A Struggle for State and Ethnicity', *Central Asian Survey*, vol. 14, no. 1 (1995); Roy, 'Ethnic Identity'; K. Berg Harpviken, 'Political Mobilization among the Hazara of Afghanistan, 1978–1992' (doctoral thesis, Department of Sociology, University of Oslo, 1995).

38 Shahrani, 'Afghanistan: State and Society', p. 45; Adamec, *Historical and Political Gazetteer and Historical and Political Who s Who*.

39 Re the use of 'Afghan' and 'Pashtun' as synonymous terms, see R. Tapper, 'Ethnicity, Order and Meaning', p. 239; Vercellin 'Le Fait ethnique', pp. 222, 224; Psustrinska, *Afghanistan 1989*, p. 27. On the official meaning of the term 'Afghan', Montgomery ('The Uzbeks in Two States', p. 161) says: 'The 1965 constitution ... places no ethnic qualification on citizenship, stating, "that the Afghan nation is composed of all those individuals who possess the citizenship of the state in accordance with the provisions of the law and that the word Afghan shall apply to each such individual" '; see also Vercellin, 'Le Fait ethnique', p. 223.

40 Orywal, 'Ethnische Identität', p. 81.

41 See F. Barth, 'Introduction', in Barth, ed., *Ethnic Groups and Boundaries: The Social Organisation of Cultural Difference* (Bergen, Oslo and London, 1969); F. Barth, 'Enduring and Emerging Issues in the Analysis of Ethnicity', in H. Vermeulen and C. Govers, eds., *The Anthropology of Ethnicity: Beyond 'Ethnic Groups and Boundaries'* (Amsterdam, 1994); R. Tapper, 'Ethnicity, Order and Meaning'; Orywal, 'Ethnische Identität'; Canfield, 'Afghanistan's Social Identities'.

This will be illustrated in detail below, in the case study on the Uzbeks of Afghanistan.

42 Canfield, 'Afghanistan's Social Identities', p. 186.
43 R. Tapper, 'Ethnicity, Order and Meaning', p. 26.
44 Canfield, 'Afghanistan's Social Identities', p. 187.
45 R. Tapper, 'Ethnicity, Order and Meaning', p. 27.
46 Ibid.
47 Ibid. For further discussion of Qaum, see Roy, 'Ethnies et appartenances', pp. 201f; Roy, 'Ethnic Identity', pp. 75f; R. L. Canfield, 'Faction and conversion in a Plural Society: Religious Alignment in the Hindu Kush', in *Anthropological Papers*, vol. 50 (Ann Arbor, MI: Museum of Anthropology, University of Michigan, 1973), pp. 34f; Canfield, 'Afghanistan's Social Identities', pp. 185f; R. Tapper 'Ethnicity, Order and Meaning', pp. 25f; Orywal, 'Ethnische Identität', pp. 78f; P. Centlivres and M. Centlivres-Demond, 'Pratiques quotidiennes et usages politiques des termes ethniques dans l'Afghanistan du nord-est', in J.-P. Digand, ed., *le Fait ethnique en Iran et en Afghanistan* (Paris, 1988), pp. 239f.
48 Canfield, 'Faction and Conversion', pp. 34f.
49 Ibid, p. 34.
50 P. Centlivres, cited in R. Tapper, 'Ethnicity, Order and Meaning', p. 27.
51 Roy, 'Ethnic Identity', pp. 75f.
52 R. Tapper, 'Ethnicity, Order and Meaning', p. 27.
53 Canfield, 'Faction and Conversion', p. 34; for details, see Canfield, 'Afghanistan's Social Identity', pp. 185, 194; Rasuly-Paleczek, 'Ethnic Identity versus Nationalism', pp. 213f.
54 See Roy, *Islam and Resistance* and 'Ethnic Identity'.
55 Roy, 'Ethnic Identity'.
56 Ibid, p. 76.
57 As with many other ethno-linguistic groups, the figures for the Uzbeks vary considerably. See Orywal, 'Die ethnischen Gruppen', p. 23 and Table A, p. 70; Montgomery, 'The Uzbeks in Two States', pp. 145, 170 n. 1; Grötzbach, *Afghanistan: Eine geographische Landeskunde*, Table 1, p. 375, Table 5, p. 381; Sliwinski, *Afghanistan 1978–87*, cited in M. N. Shahrani, 'Afghanistan's Muhajirin (Muslim 'Refugee-warriors') in Pakistan: Politics of Mistrust and Distrust of Politics' (mimeo of paper prepared for UNU/WIDER. Workshop on 'Trust and the Refugee Experience', Bergen, 11–13 June 1992), p. 21 n. 13. According to figures from the PDPA regime, there were approximately 3 million Uzbeks living in Afghanistan; Pstrusinka, *Afghanistan 1989*, p. 51.
58 Sliwinski, *Afghanistan 1978–87*, cited in Shahrani, 'Afghanistan's Muhajirin', p. 21 n. 13.
59 Grötzbach, *Afghanistan: Eine geographische Landeskunde*, p. 73;

Pstrusinska, *Afghanistan 1989*, pp. 3–17; Naby, 'The Ethnic Factor', p. 242, and 'The Uzbeks in Afghanistan', pp. 1f.

60 The Pashtuns are supposed to have constituted the largest refugee group outside Afghanistan, accounting for 80–85 per cent of all Afghan refugees in Pakistan, whereas only 6 per cent were Tajiks and 1 per cent were Turkmen. Uzbeks and Hazaras each accounted for less than 1 per cent. See Sliwinski *Afghanistan 1978–1987*, cited in Shahrani, 'Afghanistan's Muhajirin, p. 21 n. 13.

61 Ibid, p. 21. No data are available on the current situation.

62 Psustrinska, *Afghanistan 1989*, pp. 3–17; Orywal, 'Die ethnischen Gruppen', pp. 23f; Grötzbach, *Afghanistan: Eine geographische Landeskunde*, pp. 68, 74; Montgomery, 'The Uzbeks in Two States', pp. 159f; Naby, 'The Uzbeks in Afghanistan', p. 3; G. Jarring, 'On the Distribution of Turk Tribes in Afghanistan; An Attempt at a Preliminary Classification', *Lunds Universistets Arsskrift NF Avd a*, vol. 35, no. 4 (Lund and Leipzig, 1939).

63 D. Ballard, in E. Grötzbach, ed., *Aktuelle Probleme der Regionalentwicklung und Stadtgeographie Afghanistans* (Meisenheim am Glan, 1976), pp. 211, 200f; Naby, 'The Uzbeks in Afghanistan', p. 3 n. 11; R. Tapper, 'Ethnicity and Class: Dimensions of Intergroup Conflict in North-Central Afghanistan', in M. N. Shahrani and R. L. Canfield, eds., *Revolutions and Rebellions in Afghanistan: Anthropological Perspectives* (Berkeley, CA, 1984), p. 237; Orywal, 'Die ethnischen Gruppen', pp. 23f.

64 See A. C. Shalinsky, 'History as Self-Image: The Case of Central Asian Emigreés in Afghanistan', *Journal of South Asian and Middle Eastern Studies*, vol. 3, no. 2 (1979), pp. 9–14.

65 See J. L. Lee, *The 'Ancient Supremacy : Bukhara, Afghanistan and the Battle for Balkh, 1731–1901* (Leiden, Cologne and New York, 1996); Montgomery, 'The Uzbeks of Afghanistan', p. 100.

66 For example, the founders of Ibrahim Beg, a prominent leader of the Basmachi movement, founded their own village in northern Afghanistan. See Shalinsky, 'History as Self-Image', p. 13; Naby, 'The Uzbeks in Afghanistan', p. 10.

67 See Shalinsky, 'History as Self-Image', pp. 9, 13, 16f; A. C. Shalinsky, *Central Asian Emigreés in Afghanistan: Problems of Religious and Ethnic Unity* (Afghanistan Council, Occasional Papers, no. 19), p. 3; A. C. Shalinsky, 'Uzbek Ethnicity in Northern Afghanistan', in E. Orywal, ed., *Die ethnischen Gruppen Afghanistans. Fallstudien zur Gruppenidentiät und Intergruppensbeziehungen* (Wiesbaden, 1986), p. 290.

68 Roy, 'Ethnic Identity', pp. 75, 95; Shalinsky, 'History as Self-Image', pp. 9, 14; Shalinsky, *Central Asian Emigreés*, pp. 3, 7; A. C. Shalinsky, 'Group Prestige in Northern Afghanistan: The Case of an Interethnic

Wedding', *Ethnic Groups*, vol. 2 (1980), p. 270; Balland (1976), pp. 211f; D. Balland, 'La Diaspora des Turcs de Basse-Asie central soviétique au XXe siècle', *Bulletin de la Section de Géographie*, vol. 82 (1975–7), p. 24.

69 Jarring, 'On the Distribution', esp. pp. 10, 18; Roy, 'Ethnic Identity', Pstrusinska, *Afghanistan 1989*, p. 15.

70 R. Tapper, 'Ethnicity and Class', p. 223; Rasuly-Paleczek, 'Ethnic Identity versus Nationalism', pp. 214, 218; Montgomery, 'The Uzbeks in Two States', p. 160.

71 See Balland, 'La Diaspora des Turcs', pp. 24, 26f; L. W. Adamec, ed., *Historical and Political Gazetteer of Afghanistan*, vol. 4: *Mazar-i-Sharif and North-Central Afghanistan* (Graz, 1979), pp. 587f; Montgomery, 'The Uzbeks in Two States', pp. 149, 164; Shahrani, 'Ethnic Relations and Access to Resources', p. 181; Naby, 'The Ethnic Factor', pp. 7f; P. Centlivres, 'L'Histoire récente de l'Afghanistan et la configuration ethnique des provinces du nord-est', *Studia Iranica*, vol. 5, no. 2 (1976), p. 265.

72 Centlivres, 'L'Histoire récente', p. 265; Rasuly-Paleczek, 'Ethnic Identity versus Nationalism', p. 216.

73 'Mohajirin' is an Arabic word used in the Qur'an to refer to those who migrated with the prophet Mohammad from the town of persecution, Mecca, to the town of refuge, Medina; see Shalinsky, 'History as Self-Image', p. 14. 'Narg-e bet' refers to the 'other side' of the Amu Darya river, see Shalinsky, *Central Asian Emigrés*, p. 7.

74 A. C. Shalinsky, 'Islam and Ethnicity: The Northern Afghanistan Perspective', *Central Asian Survey*, vol. 1, nos. 2–3 (1982–3), pp. 72f.

75 The term 'Mohajirin' refers to one of the two options available to Muslims in the case of conquest by non-Muslim forces. Muslims can either make jihad or take refuge in the domain of a Muslim ruler, who is obliged to protect them.

76 Shalinsky, 'History as Self-Image', pp. 13f, and 'Islam and Ethnicity', pp. 74f.

77 Shalinsky, 'History as Self-Image', pp. 13, 16, 'Uzbek Ethnicity', p. 290, 'Islam and Ethnicity', p. 71; Naby, 'The Uzbeks in Afghanistan', p. 10; Balland, 'La Diaspora des Turcs', p. 213.

78 A. C. Shalinsky, 'Ethnic Reactions to the Current Regime in Afghanistan: A Case Study', *Central Asian Survey*, vol. 3, no. 4 (1984), p. 51, and *Central Asian Emigrés*, p. 4.

79 See Shalinsky, *Central Asian Emigrés*, pp. 7f, 'Islam and Ethnicity', pp. 77f, 'Ethnic Reactions', p. 56, 'Group Prestige', p. 270.

80 See Shalinsky, *Central Asian Emigrés*, p. 8, 'Islam and Ethnicity', p. 78.

81 Among the Uzbek and Tajik refugees in Pakistan, the Mohajirin are a major group; see Shalinsky, 'Ethnic Reactions', pp. 57, 59; Shahrani, 'Afghanistan's Muhajirin, p. 23.

82 Shalinsky ('Ethnic Reactions', p. 57) mentions a Mohajirin informant who pointed out that the Mohajerin are 'double Mohajirin' ... [the] only ones who have been driven from their homes by the Russians twice'.

83 Shalinsky, 'History as Self-Image', p. 13.

84 This holds good for north-eastern Afghanistan. To the best of my knowledge, no concrete information is available about the Uzbek communities in the north-western part of the country.

85 See Lee, *The 'Ancient Supremacy'*.

86 See J. Wood, *A Journey to the Square of the River Oxus* (reprinted London, 1872), pp. 138f, 155; P. B. Lord, 'A Memoir on the Uzbek State of Kundooz, and the Power of its Present Ruler, Mahomed Murad Beg', in Sir A. Burnes, Lieutenant Leech, Dr Lord and Lieutenant Lord, *Reports and Papers, Political, Geographical and Commercial, Submitted to Government, Employed on Missions in the Years 1835–36–37 to Scinde, Afghanistan and Adjacent Countries* (Calcutta, 1839); M. B. Koshkaki, *Qataghan et Badakshân. Description du pays d après l inspection d un ministre afghan en 1922*, trans. M. Reut (3 vols., Paris, 1979), esp. pp. ivf, 8–15; Adamec, *Historical and Political Gazetteer*, vol. 1, pp. 9f, vol. 4, pp. 18–36.

87 In 1888 Ishaq Khan, a relative of Amir Abdurrahman Khan whom the amir had nominated governor of northern Afghanistan, allied himself with the local political elite – among them the Amir of Kunduz and the begs of the Qataghan Uzbeks – and instigated a rebellion again Abdurrahman Khan. After initial successes Ishaq Khan and his local supporters were finally defeated and sought refuge in the amirate of Bukhara; see J.-H. Grevemeyer, 'The Revolt of Eschaq Khan in Afghan-Turkestan 1888: Peasant Mobilisation and Re-formation of Patron–Client Relationships', in J. M. Bak and G. Benecke, eds., *Religion and Rural Revolt: Papers Presented to the Fourth Interdisciplinary Workshop on Peasant Studies, University of British Columbia 1982* (Manchester, 1984).

88 Grevemeyer, *Sozialer Wandel*, pp. 59–65, esp. 60, 64; Rasuly-Paleczek, 'Beg, Moyzafid und Arbab'.

89 See Centlivres, 'L'Histoire récente', pp. 257f, 261, 263f; M. Centlivres-Demont, 'Types d'occupation et relations interethniques dans le nord-est de l'Afghanistan', *Studia Iranica*, vol. 5, no. 2 (1976), pp. 272f; Grötzbach, *Kulturgeographischer Wandel*, pp. 56, 67f, 82, 94f; Adamec, *Historical and Political Gazetteer*, vol. 1, pp. 7, 96; N. Tapper, 'Abd-al-Rahman's North-West Frontier'; Roy, 'Ethnic identity', p. 74. Re support for Pashtun settlers, see Grötzbach, *Kulturgeographischer Wandel*, pp. 65, 97f; Centlivres-Demont, 'Types d'occupation', p. 273.

90 Naby, 'The Uzbeks in Afghanistan', p. 8; Montgomery, 'The Uzbeks in Two States', Table 28, p. 299; Roy, 'Ethnic Identity', pp. 74f.

91 Grötzbach, *Kulturgeographischer Wandel* and *Afghanistan: Eine geographische Landeskunde*.

92 M. N. Shahrani, 'Ethnic Relations under Closed Frontier Conditions', W. O. McCagg and B. D. Silver, eds., *Soviet Asian Ethnic Frontiers* (New York, 1979), pp. 183f; Newell, 'The Prospect for State Building', p. 112.

93 See Shahrani, 'Ethnic Relations under Closed Frontier Conditions', 183f; Montgomery, 'The Uzbeks in Two States', pp. 162f.

94 The first public elementary school in the Dasht-e Archi area in north-eastern Afghanistan was opened in a Pashtun village; personal communication of the arbab of the Chechka Uzbeks, February 1989.

95 Shahrani, 'Ethnic Relations under Closed Frontier Conditions', p. 181; Montgomery, 'The Uzbeks in Two States', p. 161. As to public employment, the Pashtuns dominated the army and high-level bureaucracy, whereas the majority- and low-level administrative staff were Tajiks.

96 Roy, 'Ethnic Identity'; Rasuly, *Die politischen Eliten*; Fänge, 'Afghanistan after April 1992'. Regarding General Dostum, it should be pointed out that because of the conquest of his stronghold Mazar-e Sharif, by the Taleban, he has lost much of his political influence and military strength.

97 The following statements refer primarily to my own case study on the Uzbeks of north-eastern Afghanistan. For more general details on the reaction of the Afghan Uzbeks, see Roy, 'Ethnic Identity'.

98 The first national elections took place in 1964. For details, see Rasuly, *Die politischen Eliten*, p. 48.

99 Rasuly, *Politischer Strukturwandel* and *Die politischen Eliten*.

100 J.-H. Grevemeyer, *Afghanistan nach über zehn Jahren Krieg: Perspektiven gesellschaftlichen Wandels* (Berlin, 1989).

101 J.-H. Grevemeyer, 'Ethnicity and National Liberation: The Afghan Hazara between Resistance and Civil War', in J.-P. Digard, ed., *Le Fait ethnique en Iran et en Afghanistan* (Paris, 1988); Roy, 'Ethnic Identity'; Fänge, 'Afghanistan after April 1992'; Harpviken, 'Political Mobilization among the Hazara'.

102 Rasuly, *Politischer Strukturwandel*, pp. 86–165.

103 G. Rasuly-Paleczek, 'Kinship and Politics among the Uzbeks of north-eastern Afghanistan', in I. Baldauf and M. Friederich, eds., *Bamberger Zentralasienstudien, Konferenzaken* ESCAS *VI, Bamberg, 8–12 Oktober 1991 (Islamkundliche Untersuchungen, Band 185* (Berlin, 1994).

104 Rasuly-Paleczek, 'Ethnic Identity versus Nationalism', p. 216, and 'Kinship and Politics'; see Roy, 'Ethnic Identity', pp. 73f.

105 G. Rasuly-Paleczek, 'Verwandtschaft und Heirat als Mittel zur Festigung von Macht und Enfluß: Ein Fallbeispiel aus Nordost-Afghanistan', in B. G. Fragner and B. Hoffmann, eds., *Bamberger Mittelasien Studien,*

Konferenzakten Bamberg, 15–16, ????, 1990 (Islamkundliche Untersuchungen, Band 149) (Berlin, 1994).

106 Locally the Pashtun settlers were called 'Naqil', which means 'Displaced'; see Roy, 'Ethnic Identity', p. 73.

107 For details on the Qaum, see above and see Rasuly-Paleczek, 'Ethnic Identity versus Nationalism'.

108 This mutual influence is reflected in, among other things, a number of loan words in both languages, and also a marked similarity in customary practices.

109 See Grevemeyer, *Afghanistan nach über zehn Jahren Krieg.*

110 According to Montgomery ('The Uzbeks in Two States, pp. 162f), the low literacy rate and the lack of educational opportunities contributed to the low upward mobility of the Uzbeks and the emergence of a modern elite. For years the Madrasa Assadiya, a secondary level religious school operated by the municipality of the city of Mazar-e Sharif, was the principal educational facility in the region.

111 See Naby, 'The Uzbeks in Afghanistan'.

112 Shahrani, 'Ethnic Relations under Closed Frontier Conditions', p. 191, p. 20; Shalinsky, *Central Asian Emigrés*, pp. 8f.

113 Montgomery, 'The Uzbeks in Two States', pp. 161, 169; Vercellin, 'Le Fait ethnique', p. 225; Pstrusinska, *Afghanistan 1989*, pp. 3–17.

114 See Naby, 'The Ethnic Factor', p. 247; Montgomery, 'The Uzbeks in Two States', p. 155; Shahrani, 'Ethnic Relations under Closed Frontier Conditions', p. 182.

115 Miran, *The Function of National Languages*, pp. 3f; Shalinsky, *Central Asian Emigrés*, p. 9; Montgomery, 'The Uzbeks in Two States', p. 162; Shahrani, 'Ethnic Relations under Closed Frontier Conditions', p. 183.

116 My own observations; see also Pstrusinska, *Afghanistan 1989*, pp. 30f.

117 In a video made by the Jamiat-e Islami on the conquest of Khwojaghar (north-eastern Afghanistan) in summer 1991, Qari Amir, one of the Uzbek resistance commanders, speaks in Uzbeki, although he is bilingual. A Farsi-Dari translation of his words is given in subtitles.

118 Despite numerous military successes since their advent in 1994, the Taleban have not yet been able to defeat all their opponents. At the time of writing, there is renewed fighting in central Afghanistan, and in some western and north-eastern parts of the country. See international media reports, for instance, Reuters and the BBC on developments in Afghanistan, April–June 1999.

119 With the exception of the strong support given of General Dostum by the government of Uzbekistan, there are no close political or cultural links between the Afghan Uzbeks and the Uzbek population of Uzbekistan.

120 See Rasuly, *Die politischen Eliten*, pp. 193f. At that time the UN was

very active in trying to establish a new government that could replace the Najibullah regime.

121 Rasuly, *Die politischen Eliten*, p. 194.

122 Ibid, p. 193.

123 Ibid, p. 195.

124 For details on the conflict between Massoud–Rabbani and General Dostum, see ibid, pp. 88f, 282f.

125 Ibid, 195f.

126 Re Dostum's contribution to the Mujahedin's victory, see ibid, pp. 194f.

127 See, for example, Dostum's 1992 statement, published in Jonbesh-e Milli Islami-e Afghanistan, cited in Rasuly, *Die politischen Eliten*, pp. 194f.

128 Rasuly, interview with General Dostum, Mazar-e Sharif, October 1994, cited in *Die politischen Eliten*, pp. 196, 333 n. 135.

129 Rasujly, *Die politischen Eliten*, p. 196.

7· Does Class Ever Opt Out of the Nation? Nationalist Modernization and Labour in Iran

Asef Bayat

There is an apparent contradiction between class consciousness and national identity. Class consciousness implies identity and the unity of action of members of a class – in this discussion, the working class – from any distinct national origin or religion, often against other classes (in particular, the exploiters), be they native or foreigners. Nationalist identity signifies the unity of citizens, including the exploited and exploiters, in distinction from members of other nationals, including their exploited segments. This seems in line with the Communist Manifesto, in which Marx and Engels present workers as having 'no country', and being free from 'every trace of national character' and 'bourgeois prejudices'.

While evidence abounds on nations standing against one another, there is little historical indication pointing to the unity of action or combined struggles of workers from different nations against the international bourgeoisie.[1] Despite the attempts of the European labour internationalists in the late nineteenth century and later, the experience of the Second International during World War I clearly showed that workers chose to rally behind their exploiters to defend their 'fatherlands'. It seems, then, evidence points to the primacy of national sentiments and identities over class. Why is that?

A functionalist social scientist would deny the existence and the effectivity of class action. For him/her, this contradiction is irrelevant, since workers and employers are seen as fulfilling complementary functions in the social structure. A Marxist, on the other hand, may argue that workers who follow their exploiters in defence of their nation, perhaps lack sufficient class consciousness. The participation of Iranian workers in the war against the Iraqi invasion in 1980 somehow surprised many Iranian Marxists. The Ettihad-i Mobarezan-i Komonist, a Marxist–Leninist organization, for instance, argued that 'the nationalist and religious beliefs among workers and toilers' are implanted by the 'bourgeoisie and the ruling minority'. If workers and masses, it concluded, become 'conscious of their true interests . . . these ideas will rapidly melt away'.[2]

This scenario does not seem to be limited to Iran. Writing about the European working class, Eric Hobsbawm suggests that workers often enjoyed a high degree of class identity, at least of the primary kind – that is, a trade-union consciousness where they expressed organized opposition to their bourgeoisie in normal conditions. He, nevertheless, argues that 'working-class consciousness, however inevitable and essential, is probably politically secondary to other kinds of consciousness', including national consciousness. While Hobsbawm reveals this historical tendency, there is unfortunately little theoretical discussion around the issue. How can we explain this phenomenon?

Peter Waterman, who over the past decade or so has advocated a 'new' labour and social movement internationalism, concludes that 'class and national consciousness amongst workers are mutually supportive rather than contradictory' and that 'socialists did not understand this'.[3] Like Waterman, many other Marxists have acknowledged the failure of Marxism to give due analysis and weight to nationalism[4] and to understand the logic and material conditions of the 'old' proletarian internationalism as discussed in the Communist Manifesto. Whatever the argument of the Communist Manifesto, which Waterman finds 'class-reductionist', 'evolutionist' and 'stageist', he argues that the socio-political conditions (such as the weakness of early national cultures and identities, few or no citizen rights, leadership by self-educated artisans with internationalist ideals, and so on) that gave rise to the 'old' proletarian internationalism have now been transformed.[5] The stage, instead, is set for the advent of 'new' labour and social-movement internationalism – that of shop-floor workers of the multinational companies, of women, human rights, peace, environment and solidarity movements. While there is evidence for this new type of internationalism, the complex relationship between class and national consciousness has remained largely unexplored. Ethnic identities may lead, as has happened in recent years, to opting out of the nation, but working-class consciousness and struggles have not – in fact they never have.

Workers do struggle to extend their share of power and profit. In this way they may indeed subvert the national project when it is felt not to benefit them. However, they tend to articulate this not against their nation, nor often even the state, but against their employers, politicians and bureaucrats. For, in the last analysis, it is within a national boundary that they can realize their gains and engage in struggles at all. Even internationalism of the working class has never meant struggles of workers against their own states; it has meant struggles against international capital from within the confines of nation-states. This is so because, as Haworth and Ramsey argue, there is a profound asymmetry between capital and labour; while internationalism is necessary for capital, it is not so for labour. Whereas multinational capital has to take decisions on a global level, the struggle and strength of labour is necessarily local, at workplace, community or national level. Whereas workers' struggles for wages and conditions occur in a plant or company, management or global capital is concerned with financial matters that are not necessarily related to a plant, a company or a production process.[6] It is indeed for this reason that many internationalists have advocated transcending economism and asking the labour movement to take political stands. However, how to do this has remained unresolved.[7]

In this essay, by looking at the experience of Iran after the Islamic Revolution of 1979, I would like to show the complexity of the relationship between (working-) class and national identity and struggles. I would argue that class and national identity are not necessarily contradictory. Indeed, working-class consciousness can be realized in conjunction with the concepts of nation, state and citizenship. Class consciousness is articulated only in terms of the language of rights and citizenship. I shall conclude, on the other hand, that the concept of nation has the flexibility to allow for different imaginings, the kind of imagining that allows (working-) class struggles to be accommodated within it.

I shall show that workers in Iran did develop a distinct identity, waged struggle against the employers and the government, did impact on the national development projects that the government was trying to implement but in which it wanted the workers' cooperation of labourers. Workers also did try to subvert the discourse of Islam and national development as tools of mobilization, by providing alternative discourses and perception. Nevertheless, they remained patriots – many volunteered for the front in the war against Iraq or made donations to war efforts, and attempted to do their share by increasing production. Yet, once they felt a sense of injustice in the behaviour of the employers or the government, they resisted and tension emerged: some refused to pay for the war efforts, others refused to work harder for the sake of the revolution and 'Islamic nation'. In the end many complained against the war. Indeed, the very novel sense of a strong nationhood emerging out of the fervour of the Revolution created a strong language of rights which in turn contributed to labour militancy.

Strategies and Discourse of Economic Development

Unlike the nationalist strategy of modernization, economic strategy under the Islamic Republic was not clear-cut. The Islamic Revolution brought a significant shift in the discourse and ideology of economic policies. Under the Pahlavis, during the 1930s Reza Shah sought to rebuild Iran in the image of the West by means of secularism, anti-tribalism, nationalism, educational development and state capitalism. The state laid the infrastructure for economic, especially industrial, development by the construction of transnational railways and roads and by modernizing the state bureaucracy. The state itself carried out direct industrial investment. By the end of the 1930s, it had established 64 factories and was allocating some 20 per cent of its budget to industrial development. It also succeeded in creating new classes including close-knit groups of state bureaucrats, landowners, and merchants. Upon these stood the Shah as the embodiment of the will of the nation – one resting on Persian chauvinism.

Mohammad Reza Shah, who replaced his father during World War II, followed his path in earnest. After the coup of 1953, which toppled the secular nationalist prime minister Mohammad Mosaddeq, Iran became the closest ally of the US in the region. It signed military, political and economic treaties with Western countries, becoming an integral element in the Western orbit. In a big stride to enhance modernization, the Shah inaugurated in 1963 the 'White Revolution' in which land reform, women's enfranchisement, and the Literary Corps, were the most important elements with far-reaching social consequences. In the meantime, thanks to rising oil prices and through a series of five-year development plans, a remarkable 11 per cent-plus annual growth rate was sustained for the entire 1963–72 period. The rate jumped to a staggering 30 per cent during 1974 and 1975. Oil income was able to finance impressive programmes of industrialization and national education. Between 1963 and 1978, industrial output rose almost twelvefold, with an average growth rate of 72 per cent per year. This meant the growth of a sizable industrial working class with factory and workshop workers constituting one-third of the total workforce in 1977.

Compared to the secular nationalist modernization strategy of the Pahlavis, 'ambiguity, *ad hoc* decision making, and scant planning' marked the major features of the economic policies under the Islamic Republic.[8] The initial desire for the establishment of an 'Islamic economic order' – formulated by Bani Sadr, Baquer Sadr, and Bazargan – proved no more than 'a disputed utopia'.[9] Despite the language of the First Five Year Plan – 'The ultimate objective of the Islamic Society is Man's development'[10] – the post-revolution reality rendered planning little more than a day-to-day management of the national economy. Until the beginning of the postwar reconstruction in the late 1980s, development thinking vacillated between two principal views. The 'moderates', grouped round Prime Minister Bazargan, preferred a moderate continuation of the past policies, industrialization and modernization. The 'populist etatists', on the other hand, opted for state domination of the economy, limiting the activities of big capital, privileging agriculture and small-scale industry, and activities of the mobilization of the Islamic grassroots.[11] The differing views, nevertheless, converged in the notion of Islamic nationalism. The child of the conditions of war with Iraq, and of the crisis of productivity resulting from the revolutionary chaos, the notion of Islamic nationalism was employed to cement a rather divided people (along ethnicity, class, and ideological orientations) in order to pursue the monumental task of war efforts and of development within an Islamic nation (*mihan-i Eslami*). Seen as soldiers behind the front lines, the labouring classes, notably factory workers, became a major target of these mobilization efforts.

Mode of Labour Mobilization

Confronted with unprecedented labour unrest and the growing influence of socialist groups among the industrial workers, the new Islamic government utilized a series of spectacular campaigns to win the support of labour (along with the urban poor in general) for the war effort and economic reconstruction. Discursive campaigns were as significant as disciplinary measures. In a great stride to encourage people to raise productivity, the Islamist ideologues constructed an Islamic ideology of work. As a reaction to the socialist and radical views on labour, the regime granted great dignity and religious piety to labour and the labourer. The case is exemplified in the widely expressed *hadith* (the Prophet's sayings and doings) that the 'Prophet Mohammed kisses the hands of a labourer', and Ayatollah Khomeini's saying that 'Labour is the manifestation of God.' At the same time, however, work was advocated as a religious duty – an attempt which only reminds one of Calvin's doctrine and arguably its well-known contribution to capital accumulation in Europe. In a departure from classical Islamic thinking,[12] President Khamaneii declared on May Day 1981:

> The hours of work are the moments of [*ibadat*] worshipping of God, paying debt to martyrs, the deprived people and the down-trodden of society. Wasting even one moment is equivalent to violating the rights of the deprived, and to disrespecting the blood of the martyrs.[13]

Based upon a *hadith* from the Prophet Mohammed which states that 'to work is like *jihad* in the service of God', the religious conception of work was widely employed by the ruling clergy to secure the cooperation of the workers in raising production. It advocated that the performance of work brings rewards which are not material but spiritual, granted not in this world but in the next. However, the penalty for misconduct is a matter for worldly punishment, as well as God's wrath in the world to come. This view was widely propagated by the special factory clergy, who were dispatched by the ruling Islamic Republican Party in the early 1980s to spread the government's brand of Islam in the workplace.

With this neo-Protestant work ethic came a novel image of the working class – one which had elements of the canonization of labour practised in the USSR. It was postulated that 'all human beings are the *bandeh* [slave] of God; all are *kargars* [workers]; and every one works for the other. In this way, they set in motion the machinery of life and human evolution. In short, this is the divine conception.'[14]

Every person in society, then, is a *kargar*, a worker, in one form or another; they are all the 'slaves' of God. What distinguishes between them is not the fact of property ownership, prestige or market capacity, but the degree to which each has incorporated 'justice' in his work and life, that is, the extent to which he is close to God. According to this view, class distinction, in any system, emerges when those who hold power and property get involved in an 'unjust' accumulation of wealth (or *ifraat* and *takathor*). Capitalism, as such, is not an un-Islamic and illegitimate economic system. It becomes so only when accumulation is carried out through such un-Islamic methods as '*riba* [usury], lying, betraying, fraud' and reluctance to pay a fair wage.[15] Once these evils are removed from the society, and when everyone, in whatever 'useful' occupation, works justly, then 'the conflict between the worker and employer would wither away from the world'.[16]

For the early ideologues of the Islamic regime, therefore, 'justice', was the basis for social demarcation and stratification. The relations of injustice divide society into two broad social groupings: *mustakbarin* and *mustaz afin*. The term *mustakbarin* described all those who have acquired power and property through 'illegitimate' and 'unjust' channels. They were the enemies of Islam and Islamic *ummat*. The *mustaz afin*, on the other hand, included all those who were 'oppressed' by the injustice of the *mustakbarin*. These included the rural and urban poor, the unemployed, shanty-town dwellers, as well as 'decent' business people, who make up the backbone of the Islamic *umma*.

In this concept of social stratification, the 'working class' was dissolved within, and represented by, the broader category of *mustaz afin*, the downtrodden. In this image, not only did the working class lose its position as a 'special' class and its 'revolutionary potential', as understood by the Marxists, but it also lost its 'classness' in terms of its position in relation to the economic resources. On May Day 1981, President Khamaneii declared in an address to the workers:

> The workers must approach labour questions through the Islamic view. The differences in interests and trades must not divide the various layers of population, must not damage the Islamic brotherhood. The *ilhadi* [atheist] ideologies attempt to use these means to define the workers as a class, so separating them from the Islamic *ummat* [people] and crushing its unity.

Indeed, official attempts to change the representation of the working class in contemporary Iran are not new. The authorities in the previous regimes also indulged at times in such practices. In any period, when labour asserted some independence and militancy, attempts were made to obliterate its identity. During the twentieth century the definition of the words *kargar* and *karfarma* (boss or capitalist) has been the cause of a long struggle. During Reza Shah's rule (1925–44) and as a reaction to the activity of the newborn labour movement, a Majlis deputy totally denied the existence of workers (*kargaran*) in Iran. 'We do not yet have workers in Iran,' he declared. 'Everyone is an employer.'[17] In the early 1940s, during the re-emergence of a militant trade-union movement under the Tudeh Party, the use of the term *kargar*, 'worker', was banned.[18] It continued, however, to be used. Later, in the 1970s, during the heyday of economic development as well as the anti-Shah armed struggles, the state ideologues declared that the term 'proletariat' (then used widely in Iranian Marxist literature) was no longer appropriate to Iranian workers; it was only the Western working class which had launched a 'class war'. Similarly, it was suggested that the 'boss' was no longer a '*karfarma* which is reminiscent of class privileges', but a '*karamaa* which is appropriate to the hearty cooperation of all groups in the new system of production ... in the era of [White] Revolution'.

From Discursive Campaigns to Discipline

These forms of discursive campaigns went hand in hand, under both pre- and post-revolutionary regimes, with draconian labour discipline against those who did not conform. During the early 1980s, the discourse of the factory was one of 'barricades against *koffar*' (infidels) wherever 'the divine duty of production' takes place. Clergymen were dispatched in huge numbers to factories not only to counter nonconformist workers, but also to construct a new religious-inspired workplace. The new identity was to be constructed by organizing Islamic sermons, putting up revolutionary posters, inscribing grafitti, slogans and the like. Loud broadcasting of religious recitation and official speeches during the prayer and lunch break were to ensure the state's presence in the industrial sites.

The Islamic Associations (IA) became the agent of disciplining nonconformist workers. Established by the pro-regime zealots and supported by the ruling Islamic Republican Party, the IAs conveyed the ideas of the ruling clergy to Islamize industrial plants. They sabotaged the independent workers' councils (elected directly by workers), and undermined the '*non-maktabi*', or liberal managers, who in their functions relied on professional managerial rationale rather than ideological considerations associated with the ruling clergy. More importantly, the IAs policed workplaces by identifying and reporting on oppositional workers, and recruited workers for the purpose of mobilization in pro-regime rallies. Where the activities of the Islamic Associations were not sufficient, groups of Pasdaran (or Revolutionary Guards) were stationed in industrial sites on a long-term basis to keep firm control over labourers' activities.

Draconian labour control was not new in Iran. The Shah's nationalist modernization had also employed harsh measures. The post-coup regime in Iran banned strikes, forbade workers to form independent unions or to join their chosen political organizations. Instead, the state launched its own corporatist and factory-based workers' syndicates – ones which were infiltrated by the SaVAK secret police, as well as by paid informers who reported on workers' activities on the shop floor. Many of these activities were coordinated by special Idare-ye Hifazat (Security Offices) set up inside the plants.

Labour control under the two regimes differed in that, while the Islamic state relied on religious rhetoric and obligations, and on selectively mobilizing the pro-regime workers (often using heavy language equating nonconformist workers' activities to 'imperialist conspiracy'), the Shah's idea of modernization and labour control was based upon a tacit social contract whereby workers were to cooperate in the modernization process in exchange for the gains they would receive from it. Thus, a profit-sharing scheme (a component of the White Revolution), by which the Shah was to 'eliminate class conflict' in society, was extended to workers in exchange for hard work and raising productivity. Interestingly enough, these reform measures were eliminated by the post-revolutionary government on the grounds that they were policies initiated by the defeated regime.

Labour's Response and Labour Identity

Although such heavy-handed labour discipline resulted in part from the fear of workers' industrial action, it contributed to furthering labour unrest. Thus, those who at the outset had accepted the idea of 'work as ideology', making a commitment to work 'for our revolution', began to get demoralized. 'Both at the time of *taugout* [the Shah] and now,' a worker complained, 'there are only words – all talk and no action. Both then and now; nothing has happened. It's just bloody show.'[19] Another, referring to the authorities' hostile attitude to elected workers' representatives stated, 'If they outlaw the *shura* [factory councils], from then on the workers will never let them [the managers] inside here. If they dissolve the *shura*, they themselves must go.'[20]

Response to the state and managerial discipline ranged from petitioning the authorities to go-slows, strikes, sit-ins, and the detention of managers. When state repression mounted, covert poor-quality production became an expression of discontent. In the post-revolutionary era, the year 1979–80 marked the climax of the working-class industrial actions: some 366 industrial actions were reported.[21] The number declined to 180 in 1980–81, and to 82 in 1981–2 as a result of mounting repression which forced the workers to resort to covert industrial action. The year 1984–5, however, marked the start of a widespread workers' struggle when 200 industrial incidents were reported. Of these 90 were illegal strikes, the most important being the strike of Isfahan steelmill workers against the redundancy programme.[22]

Labour unrest, together with disruption in management and administration, contributed substantially to the negative growth rate of industrial productivity in the post-revolutionary years. According to the official figures, production per worker declined at an annual rate of 10.6 per cent since 1978.[23] In 1981, the Minister of Labour admitted that the 'disturbances within the factories' had resulted in a production decline of 30 per cent.[24] There is no accurate figure for 1981–2, except that the state industries made a loss of Rls 60b ($800,000), and that industries overall were running at just over half their capacity (51.2 per cent).[25] It was not until 1982–3 that the adequate supply of raw materials resulted in positive growth in the rate of production per worker in relation to the loss of the previous years. Yet, after five years the net value was still 27 per cent below its pre-revolutionary peak value.[26]

Labour response of this sort was not simply a spontaneous reaction to workers' economic circumstances. It also reflected and in turn contributed to a growing working-class consciousness. The origin of a sense of classness goes back to earlier decades.

The term *kargar*, the equivalent of 'worker', that we use today in Iran to refer to the class of wage workers, originates from Avesta, the holy book of the Zoroastrians. It came to public language in a new historical context, towards the end of the Qajar period in the 1890s, when the first wave of modern manufacturing began in Iran. At that time, the category of 'urban wage-earners' – the casual, seasonal and unskilled construction labourers – was widely referred to as *amalajat*, not *kargars*. Thus, the *kargar* referred exclusively to a new historical category, workers in the 'modern' *manufacturing* industry, although later it described various other categories of wage-earners. Yet despite the attempts of the early-twentieth-century social democrats to present *kargaran* as a social category, the public discourse still described the 'workers' in terms of *amala* and *fa'ala*.[27] It was still the terminologies like *taa'ifa* (kin), not *tabaqa* (class), that were used to describe the workers in their collectivity. It was not until the 1940s that certain indications of a development of modern classness among Iranian workers became evident.

The decade of the 1940s followed a new wave of industrialization under Reza Shah, which increased the number of modern factory workers. At this juncture, three developments represented a sense of class identity among the workers in the modern sector. The first was trade-union organization, expressed in the United Central Council of the unified Trade Unions of Iranian Workers (CCFTU) which, strongly influenced by the Tudeh Communist party, became the largest and most militant labour organization in the Middle East. The second included affiliation to a 'party of labour', the Tudeh Party, as the strongest opposition party in the 1940s with its own representatives in the *Majlis*, the Iranian parliament, and an effective power in the streets and the factories.[28] And thirdly, voting behaviour – political differentiation and conflict between the workers and their employers (as a social group) manifesting itself at the electoral level.[29] These served as the institutional mechanisms through which the workers would articulate the identity of their economic and political interests.

During the two decades after the 1953 coup, however, this working-class identity was undermined. On the one hand, the coup eliminated the (already discussed) institutional manifestations of classness by suppressing the independent trade unions and oppositional political parties. Like other segments of the population, workers experienced an intense state surveillance. On the other hand, the new wave of economic development and industrialization diluted the working class.[30] The extensive industrialization during the late 1960s and early 1970s further diversified the industrial workforce in terms of its regional and cultural backgrounds. Yet, from the mid-1970s, things began to change. By this time, the new workers of the 1960s had begun to acquire a fair amount of experience in industrial work and urbanism. Thus, by the eve of the revolution of 1979, workers had developed an 'industrial consciousness' – one which derived its elements from an industrial setting, an urban lifestyle and industrial work. Not only was this evinced in a series of industrial actions during the mid-1970s, but, more interestingly, it was manifested in their discursive expressions.

Bourdieu has argued that a theoretical group or class becomes real (that is, assumes manifest identity) only when it is 'represented'.[31] Such 'representation' has assumed an interesting expression among Iranian workers. A way in which Iranian workers expressed their sense of classness in 'language' was through identifying themselves with the *singular* noun '*kargar*' (meaning 'worker') – as the following statement by a factory worker during 1981 in Iran shows: 'The employer attempted to divide the *kargar* into three parts ... He would keep one group at the top [economically], one group at the middle, and the rest were destitute and under his thumb.' This labourer perceived the individual workers as identical with one another, so that the name and characteristics of one represent those of all. In contrast, the usage of the plural form, *kargaran*, signifies diversity and particularity, pointing to a numerical ensemble of different, diversified and concrete workers.[32] Thus '*kargar*', in the language of workers has a connotation of collective identity and wholeness. It connotes totality, generality and abstraction, representing all those who have common interests and identity.[33]

Interests and identity notwithstanding, the language of class was, however, rather complex. It was a matrix of various discursive influences including common-sense knowledge, secular trade-unionist, socialist, and Islamic. Islamic language came to play a particularly significant part in articulating working-class subjectivity in the conjuncture after the Islamic Revolution of 1979. Interestingly, such discourse often helped workers appropriate, and utilize against the state/capital, those egalitarian Islamic concepts which the authorities attempted to use in order to win them over from rival socialist groups. Thus concepts such as *qisti-Islami*, *idalat* and *mustaz'afin* became part of the language of many workers. These workers often subverted the regime's reliance on religious concepts to encroach on what they considered as 'their rights'. Thus, their response to Ayatollah Khomeini's famous statement that 'we have made not revolution for cheap melons [that is, for economic improvement] but for Islam', became 'What does Islam mean, then?'

Class Consciousness and Nationalist Sentiments

Recognition of their particular interests and identity did not mean, however, that workers were indifferent to broader national interests. On the contrary, however paradoxical it may sound, workers advanced their struggles side by side with expressing strong nationalist sentiments, and a sense of firm belonging to a nation-state. Along with making demands and even going on strike, workers, nevertheless, expressed their support for 'our revolution', 'our country', and 'our Islam'. 'We accept the revolutionary [Islamic] government,' stated a worker at Pars Metal factory in Tehran in 1980: 'We would defend this revolution to our death; would sacrifice our lives for it. [But] this does not mean that we would support any corrupt person in the administration. After all, so many of them have recently been swept aside.' Another worker at the factory said: 'We want to work legally; don't want to force anybody [the state]. We would abide by the government laws. But we won't work with these capitalists; no way, we won't.'

Some workers felt ashamed of themselves when they saw so many of their compatriots being rendered homeless refugees by the war and having to live in miserable condition in war camps. They were deeply dismayed by the sacrifice of a great many for the sake of defending the nation. 'We feel that we can't complain too much now,' a worker at an Azmayesh factory confided to me. 'You see, a war is going on right now. Last year we got 12,000 tumnas for our New Year Bonus. This year they said, "We don't have it." And we said, "That's OK." We are even prepared to help out as much as we can.' Indeed, many workers did help. As part of the activities of the 'workers' mobilization' (*basij kargari*), they donated some 140 million tumans to the war effort in the first four years of the war. More importantly, some 700 gave their lives, 300 were injured, and 54 became prisoners of war during the same period. In addition, over 15,000 workers obtained military training to fight against the Iraqi forces.[34]

Undoubtedly, the war with Iraq had a crucial influence in heightening workers' patriotic feelings. However, this alone may not explain their sense of belonging to a nation and its defence. In contrast to ethnic identities and struggles whose ultimate success is to materialize in opting out of the nation, the short- and long-term objectives of class struggle can be realized only within the confines of the nation-state. Indeed, the new consciousness and militancy of Iranian labour in post-revolutionary years was not simply the consequence of the intense competition between the socialist groups and the ruling clergy to mobilize and gain the support of the working class. A significant element had to do with workers' strong identification with citizenship in a revolutionary nation-state which, in the workers' imagination, was to realize their expected rights. The post-revolutionary years therefore witnessed an upsurge in the language of rights, *haqq*. The more they became conscious of their rights, the more they developed the sense of belonging to a state from which they could derive the realization of those rights; and the more they identified with the state, the more they expected from it. The competition between the socialists and the ruling clergy to mobilize labour simply helped the workers to articulate and extend that expectation of rights. While many did contribute financially and by other means to the war effort, they still maintained their expectations from the state. At the Zamyad car factory in Tehran, most workers protested against the cutback on 'lunch money'. The Islamic Association of the factory, a pro-government organization, had, together with the management, proclaimed that 'Demanding lunch money is *haram* [anti-Islamic].' In response workers reasoned, 'What do they mean by *haram*? This is not *haram*, this is our right. We get only 800 tuman monthly wage and have to pay so much for the rent! What about the money that government got from us for the war?! Wasn't it *haram*?' One went on angrily: 'Swear to God, if they refuse our lunch money, I will ask back the money that I have donated for the war.'

Conclusion: Opting Out of the Nation?

How can we explain this seemingly contradictory behaviour – being class conscious and militant, and yet supporting the state, the nation and the war effort? Does it reflect what Gramsci regarded as the 'dual consciousness' of the working class, one part reflecting the ideas of the ruling elite and their ideologues, while the other is a common-sense knowledge derived from workers' everyday experience of work and life? On the other hand, to what extent, if at all, do these forms of labour's response represent some sort of 'opting out of the nation'? The history of labour–state relations in post-revolutionary Iran shows that the relationship between nation and class is complex. Does the national identity obliterate class awareness? Do, on the other hand, workers who have acquired a good deal of class identity necessarily undermine their national affiliation?

The nation is not an externality to class formation. Class is formed within the confines of the nation-state. Dipesh Chakrabarty has argued that 'The language of class is an integral part of the language of citizenship and thus of that of the nation and the state.'[35] When workers struggle to create their own organizations, party or trade unions, they are speaking the language of 'rights' and therefore of citizenship within the framework of a national state. Thus, while Marshal's famous thesis that in the twentieth century citizenship and capitalism/class inequality have been at war is perhaps far-fetched,[36] it is, however, true that the state and citizenship are instrumental in creating class identity. Indeed, the 'old Internationalism' of the nineteenth century was partly made possible not only because the formation of working-class communities preceded the consolidation and reinforcement of national languages and cultures, but also because workers were denied citizen rights as nationals in the present-day sense, and thus excluded from the polity.[37]

While state formation seems essential for class formation, at the same time it is this very state that attempts to invent, promote, reconstruct nationhood, or reinforce an alternative sort of identity which may come to contradict the former type. National planning has been one important mechanism in this process. Planning is significant because, as Partha Chatterji has shown, it has come to serve as a national and rational apparatus which hides political allegiance by appearing to be supra-political; it embodies 'the single, universal and rational consciousness of the state in promoting the development of the nation as a whole'.[38]

As members of an imagined community created by such measures, workers, may adhere to both class and national identities. In this sense, then, there is no opting out of the nation. However, once the state's nationalist development strategies entail encroaching on the perceived rights of the citizens, when, for instance, national mobilization is translated into labour discipline, then conflicts are likely to arise. Since the very act of disciplining violates certain rights that workers feel get violated. This duality in people's approach to the nation-state in some ways reflects the tension between what Homi Bhabha identifies as 'pedagogical' vs 'performative' discourses of the nation. While the former describes the authoritative discourse based upon the pre-given or constituted historical origin, the latter derives from the 'scraps, patches and rags of daily life'.[39]

We saw how workers in Iran resisted the attendant disciplines of nationalist or 'Islamist' modernization. But these instances of resistance do not necessarily mean undermining national consciousness. Class-conscious workers may, at the same time, remain nationalist.

Class identity of nationalist workers reminds one of the gender consciousness of those women who seem to have accepted and internalized patriarchy – though they seem to accept the legitimacy of male power in discourse, in everyday practice they may resist it. In other words, these women are in fact against domination *per se*, not patriarchy in particular. A clear gender consciousness perhaps requires women to identify patriarchy with domination and articulate that identity. Yet, by their day-to-day contestation, the women in fact undermine patriarchy, with the end result that it becomes a negotiated patriarchy.

Similarly labour unrest in Iran contributed to some disruption in national projects and planning that the state undertook in the name of the 'national modernization' under the Shah or for the sake of 'our Islamic nation' under the Islamic Republic. However, they fell short of undermining the national myth. Yet, these very acts of resistance imply a different perception by the workers of the nation, one which excludes 'exploiters, oppressors, and corrupt people'.[40] For if the nation is imagined, it is probably imagined differently by different sections of society. Its perception is far from a unified projection. By asserting their particular identities, social groups – workers, for example – render the nation a negotiated entity.

Acknowledgementes

Acknowledgments: I would like to thank the organizers and participants of the workshop 'Opting Out of the Nation', held in Antalya, Turkey, for their constructive comments and criticisms. I am also grateful to Professor Shahnaz Rouse for her careful reading and fine suggestions. Obviously I alone am responsible for the conclusions of this paper.

Notes

1 There have been some instances of workers of different countries and of the same multinational company, such as Pepsi-Cola, who in the 1980s coordinated collective action against the company management. However, the number of such incidences is not considerable. Indeed, the incidence of dividing the workers on national lines by far exceeds that of their cooperation. For some examples, see various issues of monthly *International Labour Reports*, London, 1980s.

2 See *Kargar-i Komonist*, no. 6, Farvardin 1362/1983, p. 11.

3 Peter Waterman, 'The New Internationlisms: A More Real Thing Than Big, Big Coke', *Review*, vol. 11, no. 3 (summer 1988), p. 296.

4 Michela Lowy, 'Fatherland or Mother Earth? Nationalism and Internationalism', *Socialist Register 1989* (London: Merlin Press), pp. 213–4.

5 Peter Waterman, 'Understanding Socialist and Proletarian Internationalism: The Impossible Past and Possible Future of Emancipation on a World Scale' (The Hague: Institute of Social Studies, Working Paper no. 97, March 1991).

6 Nigel Haworth and Harvie Ramsey, 'Workers of the World United: International Capital and Some Dilemmas in Industrial Democracy', in Roger Southhall, ed., *Trade Unions and the New Industrialization of the Third World* (London, Zed Books, 1988).

7 Peter Waterman, 'Social Movement Unionism: A Brief Note', unpublished paper, The Hague, Institute of Social Studies, 1988.

8 Sohrab Behdad, 'The Political Economy of Islamic Planning in Iran', in H. Amirahmadi and M. Parvin, eds., *Post-Revolutionary Iran* (Boulder CO: Westview Press, 1988), p. 122.

9 Sohrab Behdad, 'A Disputed Utopia: Islamic Economics in Revolutionary Iran', *Comparative Studies in Society and History*, vol. 36, no. 4 (October 1994).

10 Cited in Kamran Mofid, *Development Planning in Iran: From Monarchy to Islamic Republic* (Cambridgeshire: Menas Press, 1987), p. 205.

11 Behdad, 'The Political Economy of Islamic Planning'.

12 I have discussed what I perceive as the classical Islamic thinking (work as moderate affair and as alternative to leisure] in Asef Bayat, 'Work Ethics in Islam: A Comparison with Protestantism', *Islamic Quarterly*, vol. 36, no. 1 (1992).

13 President Khamenii's message for May Day 1981.
14 Hojjat al-Islam Imami Kashani in *Jomhuri-e Islami*, 29 April 1982, Appendix, p. 2.
15 See ibid, p. 3.
16 Ibid.
17 See Habib Lajevardi, *Labor Unions and Autocracy in Iran* (Syracuse, NY: Syracuse University Press, 1985), p. 16.
18 Anwar Khameii, cited ibid, p. 34.
19 Azmayesh factory worker, interview with the author, February 1981.
20 A worker in Pars Metal plant, interview with the author, February 1981.
21 Asef Bayat, *Workers and Revolution in Iran* (London: Zed Books, 1978), p. 180. Table 10.3.
22 Ibid, chapter 7.
23 Ibid, p. 179.
24 *Jomhuri Eslami*, 20 May 1981.
25 Ministry of Planning and Budget.
26 *Bayat, Workers and Revolution*, p. 179.
27 See Fereydoun Adamyyat, *Ideologi-ye Nehzat-i Mashrutyyat-i Iran* (Tehran: Amir Kabir, 1976), p. 282.
28 See Ervand Abrahamian, *Iran Between Two Revolutions* (Princeton: Princeton University Press, 1982).
29 Ervand Abrahamian, 'Strengths and Weaknesses of the Labor Movement in Iran, 1941–1953', in M. E. Bonnie and N. Keddie, eds., *Continuity and Change in Modern Iran* (Albany: State University of New York Press, 1981), p. 191.
30 See Asef Bayat, 'Capital Accumulation, Political Control and Labour Organization in Iran, 1965–75', *Middle Eastern Studies*, vol. 25 (April 1989).
31 See Pierre Bourdieu, 'What Makes a Social Class? On the Theoretical and Practical Existence of Groups', *Berkeley Journal of Sociology*, no. 32 (1987).
32 For instance, note this statement: 'We, all the *kargaran*, demand a *shura* [council] in order to work resolutely for us, the *kargaran*.' Interview with the author, February 1981.
33 For a more detailed discussion on this issue see Asef Bayat, 'Historiography, Class and Iranian Workers', in Z. Lockman, ed., *Workers and Working Classes in the Middle East: Struggles, Histories, Historiographies* (Albany, NY: State University of New York Press, 1994).
34 Figures were released by the head of the Labour Mobilization regiment of the Revolutionary Guards (*sepah-i pasdaran*), cited in *Kayhan*, no. 17, 26 Mehr 1363 (printed in London).
35 Dipesh Chakrabarty, 'Labor History and the Politics of Theory: An Indian Angle on the Middle East', in Z. Lockman, ed., *Workers and*

Working Classes in the Middle East: Struggles, Histories, Historiographies, (Albany, NY: State University of new York Press, 1994), p. 329.

36 T. H. Marshall, 'Citizenship and Social Class', in *Sociology at the Crossroads* (London: Heinemann, 1963).

37 Peter Waterman, 'Understanding Socialist and Proletarian Internationalism: The Impossible Past and Possible Future of Emancipation on a World Scale', The Hague, Institute of Social Studies, Working paper no. 97, March 1991, p. 15.

38 Partha Chatterji, *Nationalist Thought and Colonial World* (London: Zed Books, 1986), p. 206.

39 Homi Bhabha, ed., *Nation and Narration* (London: Routledge, 1990), pp. 296–98.

40 This is how a worker at the Zamyad car factory in Tehran expressed himself when describing his perception of *mellat*, the nation.

8· 'Fundamentalism' as an Exclusionary Device in Kemalist Turkish Nationalism

Erik J. Zürcher

From Muslim Solidarity to Turkish Nationalism

Throughout the decade of war which preceded the establishment of the Turkish Republic in 1923 (Balkan war 1912–23, World War I 1914–18, War of Independence 1919–22), the Ottoman/Turkish governments dominated by members or former members of the Young Turks' 'Committee of Union and Progress' mobilized the population on the basis of Muslim solidarity. Whatever had been the views held by the different Young Turk factions on the communal identity underpinning their state in future, when faced with a struggle for survival they had no choice but to ally themselves to the one communal identity which held emotional appeal to the mass of the population in order to raise support for the war effort.

In this period 'national' (*millı*) became the dominant term in the Young Turk ideological vocabulary, but the context shows that the term at the time had strong religious overtones and that, in fact, the nationality it was intended to describe was that of Ottoman Muslims, not of Turks.[1]

By 1923, the Anatolian Muslim population had, against all odds, managed to secure the continued existence of a state of their own in Anatolia. Then, from 1923–4 onwards, the Kemalist leadership of the republic broke the bonds of solidarity that had been forged during the preceding ten years, when it opted for far-reaching secularization and for Turkish (as opposed to Ottoman–Muslim) nationalism.

More research remains to be done on the reasons underlying the change, but there can be no doubt that the decision to seek a new

Turkish national and secular corporate political identity to replace the Ottoman–Muslim one was deliberate. There was certainly nothing inevitable about it, and the switch was far too sudden to be explicable on the basis of any underlying socio-economic process. One can only assume that, of the two crucial questions that had faced the Young Turk reformers since 1908, the search for a corporate political identity underpinning the state lost some of its urgency now that continued independent survival had been secured and society had become relatively homogeneous in religious terms, and that the other question which had occupied the Young Turks since 1908, that of 'catching up with Europe' now again moved centre-stage. In the debate about Westernization, Kemal and his circle belonged to the radical wing of the Young Turk movement who believed implicitly in a popularized version of nineteenth-century European positivism. In their eyes, only scientific rationalism could form the basis for the modernization leap Turkey would have to make, and only a nation-state could give it the coherence needed to compete with the national states of Europe. Because of the emphasis on secularism in their thinking on modernization, a nationality in which religion was the dominant factor was not suitable as the basis for this nation-state. Now that the danger to independence had passed, they could afford to create what were in their eyes the ideal circumstances for successful modernization, so they opted for secular Turkish nationalism.

The assumptions underlying the Kemalist efforts at nation-building can be traced in a number of official texts: laws, government proclamations, and the statutes and programmes of the People's Party, founded in 1923 by Mustafa Kemal as the direct successor of and heir to the Defence of National Rights movement. Already in 1923 these do not talk about 'Muslims'. The third article of the 1923 statutes states that: 'Every Turk and every outsider who accepts Turkish nationality *and culture* [my emphasis] can join the People's Party.'[2]

Two years later, on 8 December 1925, the Ministry of Education announced in a proclamation on 'Currents trying to undermine Turkish unity' that the use of the terms describing minority communities and the areas they inhabited, such as *Kürt*, *Laz*, *Çerkez*, *Kürdistan*, and *Lazistan*, would be banned.[3]

Article 5 of the party programme of 1927 declared the spreading of the Turkish language and culture to be a guiding principle because 'among compatriots unity of language, of feelings and thoughts forms the strongest tie'.[4]

In 1931, at the second (officially: 'third') party congress, 'nationalism' was included among the *Altı Ok*, the 'Six Arrows', which together formed the basic principles of the People's Party and were included in the party programme. In the secondary-school history primer *Tarih* ('history'), the fourth and final volume of which appeared in the same year, the second 'arrow' is explained. In this context, a definition of 'Turk' is given: 'Any individual within the Republic of Turkey, whatever his faith, who speaks Turkish, grows up with Turkish culture and adopts the Turkish ideal, is a Turk.'[5]

The Kemalist concept of nationality was thus firmly based on language, culture and common purpose ('ideal'). This has often been remarked upon by authors who place the nationalism of the Turkish Republic fully within the traditions of the French revolution, with its emphasis on national self-determination and its legalist–voluntarist definition of 'nation'. They emphasize that Turkish nationalism is in no way based on racial or religious characteristics and that therefore anyone is free to join this nationality.[6]

It is not quite as simple as that, however. The problem lies in the way the central concept of 'culture' is defined.

When we go looking for texts from the Kemalist period which describe the national basis of the new state, we find that there are surprisingly few. Mustafa Kemal Pasha in his speeches constantly appealed to Turkish national pride, exhorting his people to show the world what Turks could accomplish. As a matter of fact, the inscription on the monument in Ankara's Güven Park, 'Türk, Çalış, Güven, Öğün!' ('Turk, Work, Trust [yourself], Be proud!') could well serve as a summary of many of his speeches. Neither in his six-day speech of 1927 nor in the speech he gave in 1933 on the occasion of the tenth anniversary of the republic (and from which the famous dictum 'Ne mutlu Türk'üm diyene!' ['How fortunate is the one who can say, "I am a Turk!"'] is taken) does he try to define or circumscribe the identity of the nation. In most of the speeches the modernizing ideal takes pride of place. '*Muasir*' (modern) and '*medenî*' (civilized) are the central terms. This seems to indicate that the Kemalists considered the issue of national identity settled and that, after a decade in which Young Turk leaders had been preoccupied with national survival, the modernizing of society had recovered the central position it had had before the decade of war began in 1912.[7]

Other texts from the early republic where one would expect a high ideological content also yield very little in the way of reflection on the problems of nationality and nationalism. *Ülkü* (Ideal), the journal of the Halk Evleri (People's Homes), which functioned as the educational arm of the People's Party from 1932 to 1951, concentrates almost entirely on spreading general knowledge. The booklet *İnkılâp Dersleri* (Revolutionary Lessons) by Recep Peker, the general secretary of the People's Party, who was also often described as the 'party ideologue', is equally barren in this respect. Obviously, Peker was an ardent nationalist and his book is a defence of the 'national state' and of a statist, one-party regime with a strong leader. It is a refutation of internationalism, Marxism, liberalism. Its author praised the 'national unity' of the Turks, but did not devote a single paragraph to the nature of modern Turkey's 'corporate political identity'. Peker also emphatically rejected expressions of minority identities, such as 'Kurdism' and 'Circassianism', using two arguments: first, these were 'false conceptions' resulting from historical oppression; and second, these groups were too small numerically to form a nation.[8]

One of the very few people to address the philosophical implications of the kind of nationalism adopted by the Kemalists after 1923 was the Kemalist ideologue Tekin Alp (Moïse Cohen), who, in his book *Le Kémalisme* published in 1937,[9] discussed the Kemalist concept of the nation. Tekin Alp first pointed out that the programme of the People's Party saw unity of language, culture and ideal as constituting the nation and said that they had replaced the older concepts of nationality based on race or religion. Seeing unity of ideal as a self-evident prerequisite for nation-building and language as part of culture, he described only the cultural element in detail. In his description he based himself on Ziya Gökalp's distinction between culture (*hars*) and civilisation (*medeniyet*).[10] According to Gökalp and Tekin Alp, culture consists of the sentiments and attitudes adopted from earliest childhood onwards from one's parents and immediate surroundings, while civilization is the high culture that is consciously learned at a later age. The latter international and can be changed at will.

Tekin Alp, who in this was the archetypal Kemalist, seemed unaware of the inconsistencies in his description of culture and its role in the nation. One could argue that the 'ideal' that was to bind together the Turkish nation, strengthening Turkey by achieving a modernization leap, made the changeover from Islamic civilization to modern European civilization inescapable and, while that would be difficult enough given the strength of Islamic high culture in Turkey, this was achievable on principle, since both 'ideal' and 'civilization' are inclusive categories – that is, one could opt for subscribing and supporting them. Changing one's culture (*hars*), however, is intrinsically impossible, since it is, in Tekin Alp's own words 'natural and so to speak biological'.[11] He quoted with approval Meyer's description of culture as 'a product of history, which one cannot create at will'. In other words, this vision of culture is an exclusive category as much as race. Hence, asking Kurds, Arabs or Circassians to adopt Turkish culture is an impossible demand, even in the eyes of the ideologues of Kemalism, and it can only logically mean asking them to acquiesce in the cultural monopoly of the Turks and to suppress their own culture as much as possible. Yet adoption of Turkish culture is a prerequisite for being a member of the Turkish nation, both in Tekin Alp's eyes and according to the statutes of the People's Party.

The cultural side of Kemalist nationalism and the problems it creates has received its fair share of attention from critics of Kemalism since the resurgence of militant Kurdish nationalism in the late 1970s and in particular during the bitter armed conflict between the Turkish state and the Kurdish Workers Party (PKK) between 1984 and 1999. The other element seen by the Kemalists as determining Turkish nationality, the 'Turkish ideal', or in other words 'the unity of thoughts and feelings', has received much less attention.

What was the 'Turkish ideal'? In the context of the mid-1920s the 'ideal' clearly meant the establishment of a strong Turkish nation-state, but in the later 1920s and 1930s, when the cultural transformation known as the 'Atatürk reforms/revolution' came into full swing, the meaning of 'ideal' changed to the radical modernization and Westernization of Turkish society. As full membership of the Turkish nation (according to the definitions given earlier) was possible only for those who subscribed to this ideal (as well as adopting the Turkish language and culture), the character of the groups *excluded* from the nation changed with it. Anyone opposed to the Kemalist concept, not only of nation-building but also of modernization, could now be considered as putting himself beyond the pale of the Turkish nation. It is this process of exclusion that forms the subject of the remaining part of this essay.

Fundamentalism as an Exclusionary Device

The elites of authoritarian modernizing regimes, such as that of Kemalist Turkey, which try to accomplish a modernization leap without broad grass-roots support, need to monopolize not only power but also political legitimacy. In order to push through the changes envisaged by the elite, power has to be concentrated in the hands of the dominant group, but at the same time this power monopoly must be shown to be for the good of the country and the nation. To a certain extent this is true of all governments, but a modernizing regime's claim to be acting in the nation's best interest depends on the claim that its vision of the future is correct – in other words, that it is uniquely able to identify the nation's problems and to show the way to progress and prosperity. Consultation is not necessary: the regime works for the people, even if and when it goes against its wishes (*halka rağmen halk için* ['for the people, in spite of the people'] was a Kemalist slogan). Competing ideological approaches and other social projects are then by definition invalid (they are not based on a correct interpretation of the present and the future) and illegitimate in that they endanger progress.

The two processes, monopolization of power and of political legitimacy, go hand in hand. Without political and military power, ideological programmes stand little chance of fulfilment; without an ideological agenda, political power is difficult to consolidate.

In the Republic of Turkey, both developments can be traced to the years after the founding of the republic, specifically to the spring of 1925.

Mustafa Kemal Atatürk and his circle of supporters had already made significant strides towards the monopolization of power in 1923. That year Kemal successively dissolved the national assembly and held elections under a new electoral law, launched a political programme which had to be underwritten by candidates in the election (candidates who were handpicked by the president), amended the High Treason Law to make campaigning on a monarchist platform impossible, and, last but not least, reconstituted the national liberation movement, the Society for the Defence of the National Rights of Anatolia and Rumelia (*Anadolu Rumeli Müdafaa-i Hukuk-u Milliye Cemiyeti*), as the People's Party (*Halk Fırkası*). This organization then laid claim to the heritage of the entire liberation movement, although in actual fact many people who had played key roles in the resistance movement were excluded from the new party. In October 1923, the seal was set on this creeping coup d'état by the proclamation of the republic with Mustafa Kemal as its first president.

It soon became clear, however, that even within the ranks of the new party there was dissent. In the winter and spring of 1923–4 an opposition group crystalized around the most senior leaders of the independence struggle, whom Kemal had been unable to exclude from the list of candidates because of their enormous prestige in the country. The group opposed the radical secularist tendencies of the first republican government, but most of all it opposed the concentration of all power in the hands of one man, Kemal.

Throughout the summer of 1924 tensions built up, and in November there occurred a split within the People's Party. The dissidents then left the party and founded the Progressive Republican Party (*Terakkiperver Cumhuriyet Fırkası*), which in the last months of 1924 and in early 1925 seemed to be attracting a lot of support, particularly in the east of the country and in the old capital, Istanbul.[12]

Then, in February 1925, an insurrection broke out among the Kurdish tribes in the south-east of the country. This insurrection, known in Turkish history as the 'Şeyh Sait rebellion' after its leader, the dervish sheykh Sait of Palu, gave the Kemalists the chance to do away with the political opposition and to delegitimize its opponents.

The rebellion was of a dual nature. It was organized by Kurdish officers, members of the nationalist organization Azadî (Freedom) who had become disenchanted with the government in Ankara when promises of autonomy, made during and even after the war of independence, were forgotten. But its appeal was also religious. It was led by a religious sheykh and among the rebels' demands were reinstatement of Islamic law and of the caliphate (which had been abolished a year earlier).[13]

The Ankara government's reaction to the rebellion was twofold. Large-scale military operations succeeded in suppressing the rebellion within a matter of weeks. At the same time, the Kemalist majority in the national assembly took legislative measures to neutralize the opposition. The measures consisted primarily of the proclamation of martial law in the eastern provinces, a change in the High Treason Law which included the political use of 'religion and sacred religious notions' (*dini ve mukaddesat-i diniye*) among the treasonable offences, and the adoption of the 'Law on the Maintenance of Order' (*Takrir-i Sükûn Kanunu*), which gave the government dictatorial powers. The two last-named measures were not restricted to the eastern provinces. They were implemented nation-wide and used to silence all dissident opinion. In May, the opposition Progressive Republican Party was officially closed down, because article six of its programme, expressing respect for religious feelings, was construed as an encouragement of 'reactionaries'.

That the Kemalists saw the struggle as one between progress (represented by them) and reaction (represented by religious organizations outside state control) was partly the effect of the trauma caused by the counter-revolution against the Young Turk constitutional regime of 1909. We should not forget that the Turkish national struggle and the establishment of the Republic of Turkey were the work of the same generation of officers and bureaucrats who, as members of the Committee of Union and Progress, had brought about the revolution of 23 July 1908 (10 July 1908 in the old-style calendar). For these people, the memory of April 1909, only sixteen years earlier, was vivid indeed.

On 12 April (31 March) 1909, Macedonian contingents in the garrison of Istanbul, together with students of religious colleges, took control of the capital, started a manhunt for leading Unionists, and presented the cabinet with a list of demands, including restoration of the *Şeriat* (holy law), but not the abolition of the constitution. The government and that part of parliament which had not gone underground gave in, but the rebellion did not spread outside the capital. After twelve days, the Unionist-controlled Action Army (*Hareket ordusu*), made up of army contingents from Macedonia and volunteer units, reconquered Istanbul.

There is evidence to show that the rebels were motivated by a number of different issues. The troops were incensed at the replacement of rankers (*alaylı*) with Young Turk graduates from the military schools (*mektepli*), who imposed a much stricter regime than the easy-going way of life in Abdülhamit's army. The theology students feared the loss of their privileges, notably their exemption from military service. Religious conservatives, mainly dervish sheikhs and lower-ranking ulema united in the Mohammadan Union (*İttihad-i Muhammedi*) resented the new and clearly more secular cultural climate after the revolution. The liberal opposition within the Young Turk movement, a leading member of which had recently been murdered by a Unionist gunman, tried to exploit the unrest in order to break the Unionists' hold on power.[14]

While the opposition thus came from a number of quarters, the Unionists, in their campaign to reconquer the capital and during the trials of the insurgents held (under martial law) after the rebellion had been suppressed, emphatically denounced the rebels as *erbab-i irtica* ('lords of reaction') in their media. The term '*irtica*' itself seems to have been a Young Turk neologism, perhaps coined on this occasion. There is no mention of the term in pre-constitutional dictionaries.

They clearly identified the whole episode as an attempt by the sultan, Abdülhamit II, to regain his former absolute power. In fact, there is very little evidence to support the idea that the sultan was behind the rebellion, but the accusation served to portray the Committee of Union and Progress as more than just a political actor – as the force of light, which defeated the forces of darkness.

That the memory of the traumatic events of 1909 played a role in the way the Kemalist government perceived the Kurdish insurrection in 1925 is evident from the statements made by Prime Minister Fethi Bey to the national assembly in Ankara. On 25 February, he said:

> I am going to talk about ... the 31 March incident. We must pay attention to the fact that the means and delusions used in those events have again surfaced in the insurrection of today. Gentlemen! Then, too, they incited the people, saying the Şeriat has been destroyed, the faith has been destroyed, this or that person is about to demolish the religion. O people, what are you waiting for? Stand up ... In this way they brought the people into action against the fatherland and, yes, even against the religion. Gentlemen! The government is prepared to take any measure to protect the Republic of Turkey from the heavy blows dealt to the fatherland by the 31 March incident and the Albanian insurrection.[15]

The emergency legislation of 1925, which gave the government almost unlimited power to deal with dissidents remained in force until 1929. By then, the single-party regime had been well and truly established. The penal code, adopted from Italy in 1926, made illegal the forming of associations on a religious basis. The political use of religion has remained an offence in Turkey to this day. What this means is not, of course, that the state is supposed to keep aloof from religious affairs. Official religion, as organized through the Directorate of Religious Affairs, has always been heavily politicized in the sense that it is supposed to function as a pillar of the state and to defend its interests. What it has meant, and still means, is that no social group is allowed to develop an alternative vision of Islam.

In the Kemalist republic religious activities outside the control of the government's Directorate of Religious Affairs were suppressed.

The repression affected not only those groups which meddled in politics but also those, like the Nurcu movement, which accepted the republican government, but wanted to base society on the morality of a revitalized Islam. In fact, the persecution of Sait Nursî and his followers, which was almost continuous during the 1930s and 1940s, is the clearest case of the Kemalist regime monopolizing legitimacy. Sait Nursî never constituted a direct threat to the Kemalists' power. Until the mid-1950s he did not encourage his followers to engage in politics. He openly supported the republican state and never argued in favour of a return of the Ottoman dynasty or the caliphate. What made him so dangerous was the fact that, from the 1920s onwards he developed an elaborate alternative formula for progress, which rejected imitation of the West and, instead, argued for a society which made full use of Western science and technology, but which was based on the moral codes of the community of believers. In Sait's view the state was very much the servant of the community – quite the opposite of the Young Turk and Kemalist view of the state as an autonomous body, bringing progress to the nation.[16]

After World War II, education and industrialization brought about a tremendous broadening of the elite in Turkey. The military–bureaucratic elite lost its hegemony in the 1950 elections which brought the Democratic Party to power and since the mid-1960s, people with a rural or provincial background and often a technical training have come to dominate civil politics. There was a broadening of the political debate, especially between the adoption of the new constitution in 1961 and the imposition of restrictions (at the army's behest) in 1971, but the old Kemalist bureaucratic–military elite always kept a watchful eye on things, determined that the basic tenets of the Kemalist state – national unity, a Western orientation and state control over religion – should be adhered to.

In September 1980, the Turkish army seized power when, in their eyes, the civilians seemed unable or unwilling to put a stop to political terrorism and economic mismanagement. Although they probably still saw the radical left as the greatest danger, there can be no doubt that the spectre of religious reaction also played a role. It was, after all, only a year and a half after the 'Islamic' revolution in neighbouring Iran.

The very first manifesto issued by the junta after they had grabbed power stated that the country was in danger of being split and on the brink of war because people had terrorized the educational, legal, administrative and political system 'while producing fundamentalist and other perverse ideologies in place of Ataturkism' (*Atatürkçülük yerine irticaî ve diğer sapık ideolojik fikirler üretilerek*).[17]

The army's concern was not with Islam as such. This was amply demonstrated when the junta decided to incorporate a strong Islamic element into its nationalist message in the guise of the 'Turkish–Islamic Synthesis', an ideology developed in the 1970s by İbrahim Kafesoğlu and already popular among rightist intellectuals, which held that Islam had found its true destination only when its message was adopted by the Turks, who by their temperament and world view were predestined to be the most faithful followers, the shocktroopers of Islam. This nationalist version of Islam was incorporated in the school curriculum, and lessons in 'religion and morality' were made compulsory.

The military thus consciously used a specific brand of Islam as an ideological antidote against those currents which they saw as threatening Turkey's Kemalist heritage, communism and religious 'fundamentalism' (that is, Islam outside state control).

In the aftermath of the 1980 coup the left was crushed so thoroughly that it never recovered. Its place as the state's enemy number one was taken by the one radical leftist organization to survive the crackdown (possibly because of its connections with the security apparatus), the PKK. For fifteen years from 1984 Turkey witnessed an ever-escalating war between the army and the Kurdish guerrilla movement. By the mid-1990s, the army had gradually gained the upper hand and the capture in 1998 of the PKK's charismatic leader, Abdullah Öcalan, dealt the Kurdish struggle a near-fatal blow. At the same time, the Islamist Welfare Party (*Refah Partisi*), heir to Islamist parties with close connections to the Nakşibendi dervish order, which had been active in Turkish politics since the beginning of the 1970s, emerged as the country's largest and most powerful political party in the municipal elections of March 1994 and the national elections of December 1995. In 1996 its veteran leader, Professor Necmettin Erbakan, managed to put together a coalition which brought him to power as prime minister.

The army was not slow to react to this challenge. In April 1997 'fundamentalism' (*irtica*) was officially declared Turkey's number one security concern by the General Staff, and a special military department, the Working Group West was set up to monitor the activities of Islamist organizations. With the support of the opposition parties, the president and the large majority of the business community and the media, the army increased the pressure on the ruling coalition to such an extent that it managed to bring it down in June 1997. Throughout the campaign against the Erbakan-led cabinet, the army kept on calling for measures against 'fundamentalists'. This went on even after the cabinet had been brought down and a coalition had been formed under Mesut Yılmaz, which promised to carry out the army's wishes. The Working Group West continued its monitoring of the situation against the express wishes of the new prime minister. Even in September 1997, the newspaper *Hürriyet* reported that the Chief of the General Staff had called for implementation of 'the methods employed by Atatürk to suppress Islamic reactionary movements in the 1930s'.

Again we have to ask ourselves: what is this 'fundamentalism', from which the army purported to save the country ? To get an answer, we have to look at the specific demands and actions of the military. The issues which caused confrontations between the military leadership and the cabinet in 1996–7 were:

- infiltration of the bureaucracy and the army by Islamic militants (*kadrolaşma*);
- attempts by Islamist businessmen (members of MÜSIAD) to take over parts of the armaments industry;
- attempts by members of the Welfare Party to negotiate the release of prisoners-of-war with the PKK;
- state visits by Prime Minister Erbakan to Iran, Libya and Nigeria;
- security cooperation between Turkey and Israel;
- participation of Welfare Party officials (including the mayor of Sincan) in Iran-sponsored 'Jerusalem Day' demonstrations; and, of course
- the introduction of eight years of compulsory primary-school education, with the attendant demise of *imam-hatip* schools.

What this shows is that, besides the issue of indivisibility of the national state, there are three areas which the Kemalist leadership considers sacrosanct: Turkey's Western orientation in foreign policy and defence; state control over religion and education (and thus: indoctrination); and immunity of the organs of state from infiltration by people with a non-Kemalist agenda. Groups and organizations which endanger one or all of these three basic points, be they from the left or the right, are still put beyond the pale. Their arguments are not considered part of a legitimate political, social or cultural debate. Hence the banning of the Kurdish HEP and DEP parties, and hence also the prosecution of the Welfare Party by the constitutional court.

In its efforts to maintain the Kemalist status quo, the army is ready to ally itself with those sections of society which feel threatened by the same enemy, even if their Kemalist credentials are doubtful. The 1960 military coup against the regime of Adnan Menderes brought about a coalition of officers and academics. In 1980–83, the army was ready to compromise over the issue of religion and to embrace state-controlled Islam in its struggle against the perceived dangers of communism and religious fundamentalism. In 1995–7 it was ready to ally itself with liberals and even social democrats in its effort to remove the Welfare Party from power.

Underlying both the actions of the military and the readiness of the Westernized elite to support them, there is still the old Kemalist concept of a Turkish nation 'united in language, culture and ideal' and the fierceness of the elite's reactions against the Islamic political movements can be better understood if one takes into account that in this view 'fundamentalism', contravening as it does the ideal which unifies the Turkish nation, constitutes high treason as much as does minority nationalism. Even after seventy-five years, the Kemalist political elite is still acutely aware of the fragility of the Turkish nation-state, which it sees as being threatened on all sides. Constantly, over these past seventy-five years its reaction has been to exclude those with a different vision from full citizenship, rather than to engage them in a political debate.

Notes

1 Erik-Jan Zürcher, 'Muslim Nationalism: The Missing Link in the Genesis of Modern Turkey', *Hamizrah Hehadash. The New East*, vol. 39 (1997–8), pp. 67–83; Zürcher, 'The Vocabulary of Muslim Nationalism', *International Journal of the Sociology of Language*, vol. 137 (1999), pp. 81–92.

2 İsmail Beşikçi, *Cumhuriyet Halk Fırkasının Tüzüğü (1927) ve Kürt Sorunu*, Istanbul, 1978, p. 83.

3 Sami N. Özerdim, *Atatürk Devrimi Kronolojisi*, Ankara: Halkevleri, 1974, p. 75.

4 Beşikçi, *Cumhuriyet*, p. 94.
5 *Tarih IV Türkiye Cumhuriyeti* (Istanbul: Devlet Matbaası, 1931), p. 182.
6 See, for example, Enver Ziya Karal, 'The Principles of Kemalism' in: Ali Kazancıgil and Ergun Özbudun, *Atatürk Founder of a Modern State* (London: Hurst, 1981), p. 18.
7 Cf. Bernard Lewis, *The Emergence of Modern Turkey* (London: Oxford University Press, 1961), p. 225–233.
8 Quoted in Paul Dumont, 'Origins of Kemalist ideology', in Jacob M. Landau, ed., *Atatürk and the Modernization of Turkey* (Boulder, CO: Westview Press, 1984), p. 29.
9 Tekin Alp, *Le Kémalisme* (Paris: 1937), pp. 251f.
10 See Uriel Heyd, *Foundations of Turkish Nationalism. The Life and Teachings of Zoya Gäkalp* (London, 1950), pp. 63f. Gökalp derived this part of his ideas from the German sociologist Ferdinand Tönnes.
11 Alp, *Le Kémalisme*, p. 264.
12 Erik-Jan Zürcher, *Political Opposition in the Early Turkish Republic: The Progressive Republican Party (1924–1925)* (Leiden: Brill, 1991), p. 177.
13 Robert Olson, *The Emergence of Kurdish Nationalism and the Sheikh Said Rebellion 1880–1925* (Austin, TX: University of Texas Press, 1989).
14 Sina Akşin, *31 Mart Olayı* [The 31 March Incident] (Ankara: Ankara Universitesi Siyasal Bilgiler Fakültesi, 1970).
15 *TBMM Zabit Ceridesi Cilt* 14 (Ankara: 1976), p. 308.
16 Şerif Mardin, *Religion and Social Change in Modern Turkey. The Case of Bediüzzaman Said Nursi* (Albany, NY: State University of New York Press, 1989.
17 *Hürriyet*, 12 September 1980, p. 1.

Conclusion: Opting Out of the Nation

Feroz Ahmad and Jacob M. Landau

The essays in this volume discuss, each in its own way, a theme central to politics in today's world: nationalism in nation-states. A potent factor in many states, nationalism urges the majority group to co-opt all elements of the population into the nation, while the counter-nationalism of discontented minority groups goads them, in numerous cases, to opt out of it and form their own national entities. Hence, frequent cases of conflict have arisen in many parts of the world in recent years. Although differing in detail, owing to history and local circumstances, these conflicts display remarkable common characteristics.

Very often, the majority group is challenged by the minorities' demands for autonomy, which the majority suspects contain intentions of ultimate political separatism. While the majority group may regard the emigration of some minorities with favour in certain circumstances, it is definitely reluctant to let them take their territories with them. It is most rare that any state willingly agrees to give up a part – any part – of its territories. But this is precisely what some minorities would like to happen, particularly when they are concentrated in one homogeneous area of the state.

The phenomenon of centrifugal and centripetal forces in conflict on the basis of rival nationalist conceptions is still known even in Western Europe. This is exemplified by the struggle for substantial autonomy or even separation by the Scots and Welsh in the United Kingdom, Bretons and Corsicans in France, or Basques and Catalans in Spain. The Middle East is a case in point, also, with the Kurds in Turkey and Iraq, the Cypriot Turks in Cyprus, or the Shi'ites in southern Iraq. However, it is in Eastern Europe and Central Asia that the struggle between competing nationalisms is strikingly evident, as the breakdown of the Soviet Union and Yugoslavia indicates. In both polities, carefully designed efforts extending over several decades at eradicating particularist nationalism in favour of communism failed and, indeed, may well have contributed to the breakdown of those states. The idea of nation and nationhood, with its emotional load, has persisted in both cases. So it has also among Magyars in Romania, Russians in Moldova, Abkhazians in Georgia, Armenians in Azerbaijan, some Tajik groups in Uzbekistan, some Uzbek groups in Tajikistan and Kyrgyzstan, some Azeri groups in Iran, not to speak of Aghanistan or, indeed, of the Russian Federation, where the Chechens are the best-known, but not sole, minority group voicing loud nationalist demands for political independence. Further instances are known in India and Pakistan, as well as in western China.

In the last decade of the twentieth century, the fissiparous character of the body politic, at least as perceived by some minority groups, encouraged them to promote their brands of nationalism, and opt out of the nation, while the majority seems, in many cases, to have attempted, no less vigorously, to keep them within the state by taking steps to discipline or persuade them to opt into the process of nation-building, and to weaken separatist tendencies among their discontented minorities. That the conflict has become more articulate, often more violent, is due not only to the high stakes involved – sometimes expressed, indeed, in terms of 'to be or not to be'. It also depends on the spread of education, the growth in the size of elites and their interest in politics, the electronic and written media, which facilitate propaganda, and other factors. The Caucasus and Central Asia are instructive examples of attempts to reject official state nationalism and opt out of the nation. The essays in this volume refer to this process in some detail.

Bert Fragner makes a view for understanding Soviet nationalism not so much as integrative but, rather, as manipulating the nationalism of minorities in the Soviet Union. This specific model of nationalism, perceived as a mass-mobilizing factor in the process of modernization, was primarily directed at preventing any autonomous type of nationalism and, even more so, any type directed towards political independence. Soviet nationalism, not a part of Marxist conceptions but parallel to them, aimed at dominating nationalist discourse throughout the Union with the objective of preventing any propaganda or attempt to opt out of the Union; this despite a variety of national republics and regions that had been set up organizationally within the Union. One might add that the fact of these geographical entities being multi-ethnic and multi-lingual assisted the central power in Moscow in controlling even more effectively any move towards autonomy and independence by the larger national groups in each separate republic. Although Soviet nationalism was the official ideology of nation-building over the entire area, in many of the ex-Soviet states patterns of nationalism and counter-nationalism have survived and continue almost unchanged, with the titular group inheriting the role of the defunct Soviet Union. Spokesmen of the majority cite history as a proof of their antiquity in the territory, while minorities produce their own testimonies – in both cases, true or invented. The Azeris and Armenians in Azerbaijan are an excellent example of this process. The political and intellectual circles of the majority in Uzbekistan and Tajikistan face an even more arduous task in striving to invent a territory, nation and language in each of these newly independent states. This is something which history cannot corroborate, since the earlier division of territories and people was radically different, as are regional perceptions in these states. Nor is language in the bilingual communities living there of definite relevance in determining identity.

The essay by Suha Bölükbaşı offers insights into nation-building in one of the former Soviet Muslim republics, Azerbaijan. The Soviet regime had contributed to the sense of nationhood there by identifying nationality with territory and by preserving national education and certain traditions, without political nationalism – all of this under Soviet control. Over time, however, many ethno-linguistic groups were consolidated into what resembled nations by mass education, exposure to the media, industrialization and urbanization. Bölükbaşı focuses on 1988–91, the three years before independence, when nationalist intellectuals – who had already worked painstakingly at reclaiming the Azeri past (or imagined past) – espoused nationalist objectives more vigorously than before. In Azerbaijan – as in some other cases – the Azeri nation-builders were challenged by a rival nationalism. The largest minority, the Armenians, demonstrated in 1988 and later, vociferously demanding the union of the mostly Armenian enclave of Nagorno-Karabakh with Armenia. Here one may perceive a clear expression of a determined desire to opt out, not via an autonomous solution, but via a separatist one of an irredentist character, as the Nagorno-Karabakh Armenians called for inclusion of their enclave in Armenia. Newspapers in Armenia, also, called for the 'return' of Nagorno-Karabakh to Armenia. Azeri historians, earlier and at this time, fruitlessly maintained that the inhabitants of Nagorno-Karabakh were not of Armenian stock but, rather, had early connections with the Azeris – a doomed attempt to include them in the Azeri nation. The conflict soon developed into a state of undeclared war, which turned into clashes and became unmanageable. Azeri leaders could hardly tolerate the call of Armenians in Nagorno-Karabakh to be united with Armenia. The two conflicting nationalisms were unmistakably on a collision course of what one might call two opposing irredentisms, particularly when one of them allowed open demands for the annexation of Iranian Azerbaijan, while the other was undisguisedly supported by a foreign state, Armenia. That Moscow was perceived as tilting towards Armenia hardened Azerbaijan attitudes and placed the nationalist discourse in the forefront, with the Nagorno-Karabakh issue at the centre of the discussion.

'The Iranian connection' is not only relevant to Azerbaijan, but highly interesting in itself. Touraj Atabaki's paper analyses the complex origins of Iranian nationalism that gradually took shape as a defensive discourse, to which both Persian and non-Persian loyalties contributed. This was necessary, for since the early twentieth century foreign powers, wishing to extend their influence, had been inciting the Azeris, Kurds, Assyrians and Armenians to break away from Iran and set up a state or states of their own. Of those powers, Atabaki singles out the Ottoman Empire. Before and during World War I, Ottomans imbued with Pan-Turkism aimed to extend their rule over Azerbaijan, among other areas. Azeris living in Istanbul and Baku were among the main agents of the call for a union of all Turks, writing and lecturing about the Turkish ethno-linguistic characteristics of Caucasian Azerbaijan. In October 1917, emissaries from Baku visited Tabriz and unsuccessfully attempted to induce local Azeris to separate from Iran and join with Baku in a large federation. This irredentist propaganda was countered in Baku itself by Iranians living there, organized in a Democratic party, who opposed what they considered a 'pan-Turkish plot' to have Azeris opt out of Iran and undermine the Iranian state. They and many Azeris in Iran promoted a sense of Iranian territorial state-patriotism which took precedence over their ethno-nationalist loyalties, thus rejecting pan-Turkism. Several months of Ottoman occupation in 1918 of Azeri-inhabited areas south and north of the Araxes failed to spread pan-Turkism there. Later, nationalists in multi-ethnic Iran rewrote history and reshaped language in order to reduce the danger of minorities opting out of the nation that those nationalists were striving to create. Negative stereotypes of non-Iranians were propagated, as the other face of the culture of a 'pure Iran'. Here were blueprints for Reza Shah's slogan of 'One country, one nation'. Pan-Turk irredentism had failed to bring about a break in the Iranian homeland. On the contrary, a group of Azeri intellectuals became convinced advocates of Iran's sovereignty and territorial integrity, distancing themselves from ethnic, linguistic and regional loyalties.

Although Asef Bayat's essay, too, deals with Iran, it focuses on a different issue, labour in that state and its stand on opting out of the nation. It questions the effectiveness of class awareness among workers when challenged by the cohesiveness of a nation, and explores class versus national consciousness in Iran after the 1979 Islamic Revolution. Its basic premise is that class and national identity are not necessarily contradictory there. The Islamic Republic promoted the notion of Islamic nationalism, bridging over ethnicity, class and ideology to cement the rifts in a bitterly divided community. Along these lines, the government propagated an Islamic ideology of work, in order to mobilize labour, emphasizing the dignity and piety of work, advocated as a religious duty, with Qur'anic and other traditional quotations in support. The concept of class was attacked as dangerously atheist. This ideological campaign was accompanied by harsh labour discipline against nonconformers. Strikes were banned and workers were forbidden to create independent unions, while various government agencies controlled worker activities, equating nonconformist workers with the imperialist enemy. Workers responded with labour unrest, sit-ins, industrial action and production decline – reflecting a growing sense of class, more marked than during the Shah's regime and, in the period discussed, employing Islamic terms to express their demands. Demands and strikes notwithstanding, Iranian workers in this period affirmed their patriotism by word and deed (donating money for the war with Iraq and enlisting in the army). Commitment to a revolutionary society partly explains this. Class awareness, although sometimes leading to struggles against employers and disruption in production, did not deconstruct the national myth, nor did it diminish the workers' feeling of belonging to the nation, which they did not try to opt out of.

The question of nationalism in South Asia, and specifically in Bengal/Bangladesh, has a character of its own. This is examined in detail in the essays by Tazeen M. Murshid and Willem van Schendel. If anything is omitted in these chapters, as in most others in this volume, it is the relationship between nationalism and class; only Asef Bayat tackles that question directly and then in relation to the working class in Iran rather than to the bourgeoisie. Yet the relationship between class and nationalism in South Asia (and elsewhere) is an intimate one. Nationalism, after all, was adopted by the emerging, Western-educated bourgeoisie in British India as an instrument to challenge the inequities of alien rule. When Indians found that there was no word in their vernacular languages to represent the idea of nationalism, they simply adopted the English word and called their organization, founded in 1885, the Indian National Congress. They then transliterated these words into such vernaculars as Urdu and Hindi. Later, in 1906, when Muslim notables founded their organization, they did the same and called it the Muslim League. One wonders what these names meant to the non-Westernized majority of their supporters. Very little, one would suspect, as the secular ideas of nationalism were too abstract and alien for the majority more familiar with religious identity and its symbols.

Politically Bengal was the most advanced province in British India. In the eighteenth century, the East India Company established its power base in Calcutta, which remained the capital until 1911. That is where the Western-educated 'Young Bengal' movement emerged after the founding of the Hindoo College. By and large the Muslims kept aloof from such activity. As a result there was an absence of a Muslim middle class and a lack of social and political awareness, and little Bengali Muslim participation in nationalist politics led by the Congress. Viceroy Curzon's intentions in partitioning Bengal in 1905 may have been purely administrative, but the Hindu elite, the so-called *bhadralok*, saw it as an attempt to undermine their power and the predominately Hindu nationalist sentiment in the province. The Partition was repeated in 1911 but not before the Muslim majority had tasted power. The British government exploited the Hindu–Muslim divide and institutionalized it by establishing separate electorates in the reforms of 1909.

Though Bengal was a Muslim-majority province, the student who thought up the acronym Pakistan did not include it within the imagined state's borders. PAK stood for Punjab, Afghania, and Kashmir while the ending ISTAN was said to include Sindh and Baluchistan. The idea of a separate Muslim state had come into existence, but scholars are questioning whether Mohammad Ali Jinnah, the leader of the Muslim League, really wanted a separate state or whether he was using the threat of separation to bargain with the Congress. Rather than separation, Jinnah wanted to share power with Congress, so that the Muslim League would form governments in such Muslim-majority provinces as Punjab and Bengal while Congress formed governments in the Hindu-majority provinces. Judging by the three-tier Cabinet Mission Plan of 1946, the British proposals met Jinnah's requirements without partitioning India. But the plan was sabotaged by Nehru, who had been elected president of Congress, paving the way to Partition. Stanley Wolpert, Nehru's biographer, writes: 'Nehru reflected that it was a mistake for him to have said what he did, with such arrogant self-assurance, at that press conference in early July 1946, when all India was still so calm and remarkably peaceful.'[1]

In August 1947 Pakistan, described by Jinnah as 'moth-eaten', came into being. The provinces – Bengal and Punjab – which had Muslim majorities were partitioned on the basis of religion. There were sound economic reasons for keeping Bengal united but the Hindu elite simply did not want to share power and the Muslims of Bengal had now to learn to become Pakistanis. Jinnah, however, had no intention of creating a theocracy modelled on 'the age of the rightly guided caliphs, the *Khulafa-i Rashidun*. He made that plain on 11 August 1947 when he informed the Constituent Assembly that the new state would be secular and democratic, not theocratic. His speech, now an embarrassment to the rulers of Pakistan, is worth quoting, even briefly. Jinnah said: 'You are free to go to your temples, you are free to go to your mosques or to any places of worship in this State of Pakistan. You may belong to any religion or caste or creed – that has nothing to do with the business of the State.... We are starting with this fundamental principle that we are all citizens and equal citizens of one State.... Now, I think we should keep that in front of us as our ideal and you will find in course of time Hindus would cease to be Hindus and Muslims would cease to be Muslims, not in the religious sense, because that is the personal faith of each individual, but in the political sense of citizens of the State.'[2]

Jinnah died on 11 September 1948. Had he lived longer he might have succeeded in creating institutions necessary to make the new state viable. Lesser men who succeeded him fell into the trap of attempting to centralize power and imposing Urdu as the national language. In neighbouring India, the Congress government attempted to impose Hindi, but backed down when faced with opposition from the non-Hindi-speaking states. In time India became a federation of linguistic states thanks to the maturity of India's bourgeoisie and the statesmanship of Nehru, who led the government until 1964. But for such flexibility, a number of Indian states might well have opted out of the Indian 'nation'.

In Pakistan there was neither a bourgeoisie nor a statesman capable of negotiating a new Pakistani identity. Though there was no bourgeoisie worthy of that description, there was a strong, urban petty bourgeoisie which fought for the spoils in the new state. This class became the backbone of the state for, without competition from the Hindu intelligentsia, it was able to fill the many openings in a state apparatus waiting to be created. In this process the Western wing was dominant and within it the majority Punjabi element. East Pakistan, that is to say, East Bengal, where the majority of Pakistan's population was located, was treated as a colony to be exploited for the benefit of the western wing. As in India the 'language issue [writes Murshid] galvanized Bengali opinion against the state'. The army, in power since 1958, responded with repression. Had the generals honoured the 1970 election victory of East Bengal's Awami League and permitted Mujibar Rahman to form the next government, the situation might have been saved and Pakistan given another opportunity to negotiate a new identity. Instead, the generals opted to crush the Bengali opposition by brute force, failed to achieve their goal and brought about the creation of Bangladesh in 1971.

At the time, there was much speculation about how Indian West Bengal would respond to the resurgence of Bengali nationalism. Would there be a move towards Bengali unity? There was no such initiative from either side, for the ruling classes of the two Bengals had too much to lose by reuniting into a single state. Instead, Bangladesh opted for independence and began to create a new identity, a process Willem van Schendel discusses in his essay. The task of creating an identity is not an easy one and is being contested by a variety of groups, Bengalis and non-Bengalis. By trying to impose the Bangladeshi identity with Bengali as the national language, the state elite seems to be making the same error with regard to the dissidents, especially the non-Bengalis, as the Punjabi elite did towards East Pakistan. Language, after all, defines a community and its culture. The rational answer seems to lie in a liberal approach to the problem which recognizes 'ethnicity, religion and sovereignty' in a system which provides for 'equity, democracy and citizens' rights'. Is the state elite capable of behaving rationally? So far it has not done so and the result has been political and socio-economic instability. This is doubly irrational in the age of globalization, which is already bringing about the demise of cultures (and languages) that are not rooted in the English language. The world's small languages are already disappearing quite rapidly and it is predicted that in this century 'half the world's currently spoken 6,000 languages will have died out'.[3] Perhaps that process will go some way to resolving the question of 'opting out of the nation'!

Afghanistan poses a different problem in terms of 'nation-building'. As Gabriele Rasuly-Paleczek shows, 'the formation of a uniform Afghan nation [has] been the primary [goal] of Afghanistan's rulers since the end of the nineteenth century ... [but] the envisaged aims could not be achieved'. In the predominantly tribal society there simply is no 'national' class which thinks in terms of an Afghan identity or is able to provide the vocabulary of nationalism or patriotism. The attempt by the Pashtuns to impose 'Pashtunism' has only prevented the development of a sentiment of national unity and caused the rejection of the state-sponsored model of Afghan nationhood by Afghanistan's citizens. The turmoil in the country in the 1970s and the 1980s has only made the problem worse. The collapse of the community regime and the civil war that followed led to greater polarization within Afghan society until the reunification brought about the Taleban regime in the early 1990s. During this period, 'Uzbek ethnicity became a driving force of politics'. The Uzbeks began to see themselves as a *qaum*, a term which has come to mean 'a people' and even 'nation' in some parts of the Muslim world. It remains to be seen whether the Uzbeks will be crushed, opt out of the Taleban 'state', or provide the focus of a totally different, secular Afghanistan.

Until the emergence of the Kurdish question, Turkey was considered a successful model of nation-building. Far from people wanting to opt out of the nation, Erik-Jan Zürcher argues that the Kemalists used 'fundamentalism (*irtica*) as an exclusionary device to keep out the Islamist alternative to the official ideology. It is true that the national struggle (1919–22) was fought on the basis of Muslim solidarity. But the statement that 'from 1923–4 onwards, the Kemalist leadership ... broke the bond of solidarity ... when it opted for far-reaching secularization and for Turkish (as opposed to Ottoman–Muslim) nationalism' is open to question. In fact the Kemalists opted for laicism – the state's control over religion – not secularism – the separation of religion and state and the state's abstention from religion. They had a reason for doing so: to permit religion to impinge on the political and social life of the new country would have threatened the radical reforms and the establishment of modernity, though not technological modernization.

There is an important distinction between modernity and modernization, although the two terms are often treated as synonymous. It is possible to modernize without achieving modernity, as the case of the late Ottoman Empire demonstrates so dramatically. Modernization may be accomplished by adopting the material benefits of the West (its technology, railways, radio, television and modern weapons) without coming close to modernity. There are numerous examples of such modernization in our world: Iran and the entire Middle East, India, Pakistan and China, and even Afghanistan under the Taleban. All of them can boast of using modern technology (some even have nuclear weapons and satellites) but they all lack some of the most fundamental elements of modernity.

Modernity implies a broader totality which includes political and cultural along with economic and technological dimensions. It implies the rejection of patriarchal society, and its ultimate goals are social justice, political democracy, human rights, an accountable state and the rule of law. Kemalist Turkey attempted to accomplish both modernization and modernity by radically reforming the tradition and patriarchal social structure it had inherited from its Ottoman–Muslim past. The Kemalist striving for modernity is illustrated by Hisham Sharabi's model for the Arab world which is equally applicable to pre-republican Turkey.[4]

Category	*Patriarchy*	*Modernity*
Knowledge	Myth/belief	Thought/reason
Truth	Religious/allegorical	Scientific/ironic
Language	Rhetorical	Analytical
Government	Neopatriarchal/sultanate	Democratic/socialist
Social relations	Vertical	Horizontal
Social stratification	Family/clan/sect	Class

If we examine the Kemalist record we find that in the categories of Knowledge, Truth, Language, Social relations, and Social stratification, Turkey moved away from traditionalism towards modernity.

Government was neither democratic nor socialist but it was no longer neopatriarchal/sultanate.

Islamists in Turkey today, especially the Nurcus, pay lip-service to almost all these elements of modernity. But gender equality is the acid test of modernity, and even a scholar sympathetic to the Nurcus, especially to their progressive faction led by Fethullah Gülen, admits that they have failed to establish equality between the sexes. He writes: 'as for gender equality, there is a gap between what Gülen teaches and how fast his community adapts and behaves. In his speeches, he advocates the integration of women into the work force without articulating equality for women. Gülen's community practises rigid segregation of the sexes and does not permit them to work in high positions. For example, there are no women in high positions in his vast networks or in his media empire'.[5]

The Kemalist record for gender equality is far from perfect but it is far better than those of most other Islamic societies and some non-Islamic ones as well. By the 1930s the urban middle class had acquired more political rights than women in some countries of Western Europe. OECD statistics reveal that there are more women in Turkey today working in the professions than in Europe. The new civil code before parliament promises even greater changes. Men will no longer be the sole authority in the family, and a woman will be able to keep her own last name instead of being forced to adopt her husband's. It is doubtful whether the Ottoman–Muslin alternative would have permitted women in Turkey, at least half the country's population, to make such progress.

In the 1920s, when the Kemalists spoke of 'Turk' and 'Turkish', both had yet to be created. As with other nationalisms, having created Turkey the Kemalists knew that they had to create 'the Turk' to replace 'the Ottoman'. The same was true for language; the Ottoman language had to be replaced with Turkish and changing the script from the Arabic to the Latin was part of that process. In doing so, virtually the entire literate population was made illiterate. The language was also 'purified' so that today few can understand Mustafa Kemal's speech of 1927 in its original form.

After crushing the Şeyh Sait rebellion and the opposition within the Kemalist movement, and having carried out a programme of radical reform, the Kemalists were convinced, rather naively as it turned out, that their revolution had taken root and won the support of the majority of the people. The popular support garnered by the recently founded Free Party and the violently reactionary incident in Menemen in December 1930 came as a shock. This incident, rather than the memory of the 31 March 1909 abortive counter-revolution, proved traumatic. In Menemen, the demand for the restoration of the caliphate and the *sharia* demonstrated that, even in the more advanced regions of Anatolia, people were still attached to the past, and tradition was stronger than innovation. This event forced the Kemalists to reconsider their programme and the result was the launching of their ideological offensive of the 'Six Arrows' and the determination to indoctrinate the people.

Despite the emphasis on creating a new nationalist culture, the Kemalists knew that it would be applicable to local traditions.[6] Throughout the 1930s the mosque was used to promote the national economy and ideology, and such slogans as 'Buy local goods', 'Long live the national pact', and 'Long live independence' appeared in *Mahya*, the Ramadan mosque illuminations.

We do not know what kind of Turkey would have emerged had the Kemalists not excluded the alternatives provided by Islamists, the socialist–communist left and the liberals of the Progressive Republican Party. We can be sure that the Islamist alternative would have allowed the new Turkey to be modernized but without achieving the level of modernity it did under Kemalism. Gender equality, affecting roughly half of Turkey's population, would have been sacrificed as a consequence.

The early Kemalist conception of identity was patriotic and inclusive rather than nationalist and exclusive. This is evident form Mustafa Kemal's early speeches, for example the ones he delivered on 8–9 July 1919 and 1 May 1920. The borders of the new state, he said, included Turks and Kurds, Circassians and Laz, as did the assembly. The Kemalists spoke of the 'state of Turkey' and the 'Republic of Turkey' (*Türkiye devleti* and *Türkiye Cumhuriyeti*) rather than 'the Turkish state' or 'The Turkish republic'. The term 'Türkeyli' was briefly used to describe all the peoples of Anatolia. All this changed around the time of the Şeyh Sait rebellion of 1925; thereafter the emphasis was on creating a monolithic identity.

What is surprising is that the attitude of the ruling class has not changed despite the dramatic and radical transformation that has taken place since the end of World War II. This has been the failure of the bourgeoisie which, although it has grown substantially, has failed to assume the responsibility to lead an emerging civil society. It has preferred to lean on the military–bureaucratic elite. That is why there has been no political solution to the Kurdish question and why the state has pursued contradictory steps towards political Islam. While there was a perceived threat from the left, Islam was used as the 'antidote to communism'; not surprisingly, therefore, the greatest expansion of religious education took place during the military regime after 1980. In the 1990s, with the collapse of communism, the generals, following Washington's lead, found the new enemy in 'fundamentalism', which they described as a greater threat then 'separatism'. Now that Turkey has been declared a candidate for the European Union, the role of the military–bureaucratic elite should decline and the bourgeoisie might take the lead and adopt inclusive policies with regard to both the Islamists and the Kurdish people.

Notes

1 Stanley Wolpert, *Nehru* (Oxford and New York: Oxford University Press, 1996), p. 371.

2 Jamiluddin Ahmad, ed., *Speeches and Writings of Jinnah*, vol. 2 (Lahore: Muhammad Ashraf, 1976, pp. 400–404, quoted in Ishtiaq Ahmed, *The Concept of an Islamic State* (London: Francis Pinter, 1987), pp. 78–9.

3 Will Hutton, 'English will be spoken but not as the British know it', *The Guardian Weekly* (London), 16–22 December 1999.

4 Hisham Sharabi, *Neopatriarchy* (Oxford and New York: Oxford University Press, 1988), p. 18.

5 Hakan Yavuz, 'Search for a New Social Contract in Turkey: Fethullah Gülen, the Virtue Party, and the Kurds', *SAIS Review*, vol. 19, no. 1 (winter–spring 1999), p. 125.

6 'Turkey's Islamic Swiss Civil Code: A Study in the Ottoman Foundations of Turkish Republican Civil Law'. This article is forthcoming in the *Journal of Islamic Studies* and for the moment the author remains anonymous.